PORK

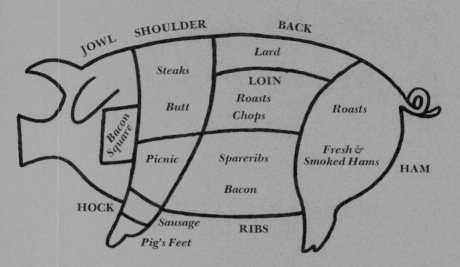

JOWL · SHOULDER · BACK

Lard

Steaks

LOIN

Roasts
Chops

Butt

Roasts

Bacon Square

Picnic

Spareribs

Fresh &
Smoked Hams

HAM

Bacon

HOCK

Sausage

Pig's Feet

RIBS

LAMB

NECK

Stews

RIBS · LOIN

LEG

SHOULDER

Stews

Chops

Roasts

Chops

Chops

Steaks

Stews

Roasts

SHANK

BREAST

THE
LEFTOVERS
COOKBOOK

THE LEFTOVERS COOKBOOK

by Loyta Wooding

DAVID WHITE

NEW YORK

David White, Inc., Publishers
60 East 55th Street, New York, New York 10022

For Ralph and Laurel
Ray and Judy

CONTENTS

FOREWORD

By definition, a good cook is a person who respects food. Consequently, the problem of what to do with leftovers has plagued cooks since cooking began. To throw away good food offends not only the sense of financial thrift but the feeling that something potentially delicious is not being used.

Naturally the problem is less serious in a large family, whose members are given to raiding the refrigerator for after school or bedtime snacks. I myself became increasingly aware of it as my own family diminished from a full house to two people and finally to only one. Old habits were so strong that for some time I continued to plan meals as I had previously done, unwilling to give up baked hams, succulent turkeys, juicy roasts, and other delights of large-scale cooking. As a result my refrigerator was constantly crowded with leftovers, many of which were eventually doomed to become garbage. Finding myself appalled by the waste of that aromatic stuffing, that cup of rice, those slices of fried eggplant, that half-bowl of waffle batter, I came to realize that with imagination and ingenuity I could use any and all leftovers in the concoction of new and delicious dishes.

My success has been proved by the number of times that I have had to confess to enthusiastic guests that the meal they were praising had been partly based on a leftover this or that. I began to be besieged with requests for suggestions on what could be done with "all that gravy, it's a shame to throw away" or that cup of "perfectly good mashed potatoes."

The next step, logically enough, was to start a file on these suggestions, and from that file, which rapidly assumed large proportions, came the genesis of this book.

Another logical development was the idea of planning several meals at the same time, all based on one large cut of meat as the basis of two or three main dishes with varied accompaniments,

thus converting leftovers into "planned-overs." This system avoids
the boring results of simply reheating and re-serving, which is
really what gives leftovers their bad name. Instead, the recipes
here defy any connoisseur to identify the leftover ingredients used.

The aim of the book is to provide menus which use food—
for the first, second, or even third time—to create imaginative and
nutritionally balanced meals. The unusual dishes in these menus
are marked by an asterik to indicate that the recipe is included;
these recipes either follow the particular menu or can be found
by consulting the index. Dishes not so marked are suggestions
for accompaniments, for which recipes can be found in any basic
cookbook. The cook who gets into the spirit of this novel method
will soon begin developing variations, often based on different
leftovers that turn up in her—or his—own refrigerator. In short,
what I hope to provide here is not so much a cookbook as a
technique.

Loyta Wooding

THE LEFTOVERS COOKBOOK

THE
PLANNED-OVERS

Even the most inexperienced food-shopper quickly learns that large cuts of meat are much less expensive per serving than the smaller cuts. What is less obvious but equally important is that by planning ahead to make several meals from the same large cut, much of the preparation can be done for the first meal, thus saving time and effort as well as money. Here your freezer or freezing compartment is invaluable, since meal-sized portions can be stored, and only the amount needed for each meal thawed.

For example, if you buy 6 or 7 pounds of economical chuck (a pot roast with a round bone, which has fine flavor and little waste), you can have delicious New England Beef the first day, a juicy meat pie a day or two later, and a hearty and nourishing soup for yet another day.

BEEF

CHUCK ROAST—ONE

Buy a 6- to 7-pound chuck roast of beef and plan three distinct meals, four servings each.

MEAL NO. 1

New England Beef with
Massachusetts Horseradish Sauce

Boiled Potatoes
Sautéed Cabbage   Mixed Green Salad
Baked Apples

MEAL NO. 2

Savoy House Beef Pie

Browned Parsnips   Cheese-stuffed Celery
Lettuce Wedges   Russian Dressing
Peach Melba

MEAL NO. 3

Old-Fashioned Hearty Soup

French Bread with Welsh Rarebit
Crisp Relishes
Sherbet   Cookies

New England Beef

6 to 7 pounds chuck roast
1 onion, halved
2 carrots, sliced
1 stalk celery, sliced
4 sprigs of parsley
1 green onion, sliced

1 bay leaf
1½ tablespoons salt
1 teaspoon peppercorns
Massachusetts Horseradish
Sauce

Place meat in a large, heavy kettle; add onion, carrots, celery, parsley, green onion, bay leaf, salt, and peppercorns. Add enough water just to cover meat; cover and bring to a boil. Reduce heat; simmer 2½ to 3 hours or until meat is fork tender. Remove meat to a heated platter; keep warm while making sauce. Strain broth; skim off fat. Measure 2 cups broth for sauce; refrigerate remainder for soup. Slice beef; serve with Massachusetts Horseradish Sauce. Makes 4 servings with meat left over.

Massachusetts Horseradish Sauce

3 tablespoons butter or
  margarine
⅓ cup flour
2 cups skimmed broth
½ teaspoon instant minced
  onion

¼ cup prepared horseradish
½ teaspoon salt
dash Worcestershire sauce

Melt butter in a small saucepan; stir in flour and blend well. Heat slowly, stirring constantly, until flour is browned. Remove from heat; stir in broth and onion. Cook for 1 minute, stirring constantly until sauce thickens and boils. Measure out 1 cup of sauce; refrigerate and reserve for Savoy House Beef Pie. Stir horseradish into remaining 1 cup. Season with salt and Worcestershire sauce. Serve hot. Makes about 1¼ cups.

Savoy House Beef Pie

3 cups cubed cooked beef
1 small onion
1 cup reserved brown sauce
　(See Mass. Horseradish
　Sauce)
½ teaspoon Worcestershire
　sauce

dash of Tabasco
1 package (2 envelopes)
　instant mashed potatoes
2 tablespoons chopped parsley
1 tablespoon minced celery

Heat oven to 350° F. Coarsely chop beef pieces and onion; stir into brown sauce. Add Worcestershire sauce and Tabasco; heat in large saucepan to boiling. Prepare instant mashed potatoes according to package directions; stir in parsley and celery. Spread half the potato mixture in a buttered, shallow 1½-quart baking dish; spoon hot meat mixture over. Top with remaining potatoes, swirling them in a circle. Bake 25 to 30 minutes or until pie is heated through and potatoes are lightly browned. Makes 4 servings.

Old-Fashioned Hearty Soup

6 cups skimmed, chilled
　broth
¾ cup finely diced carrots
¾ cup finely diced celery

¾ cup finely diced onions
1 small turnip, chopped
¾ teaspoon salt
⅛ teaspoon pepper

Combine broth and vegetables in a large saucepan; simmer 15 minutes or until vegetables are crisply tender. Season with salt and pepper. Serve hot. Makes 4 servings.

CHUCK ROAST—TWO

Have the butcher cut off about 2½ pounds from a 5- to 6-pound beef chuck roast, leaving the remaining piece intact. Then plan the following three meals.

MEAL NO. 1

Austrian Pot Roast

Mushroom Soufflé   Buttered Broccoli
French Fried Onion Rings
Orange Sherbet with Bourbon

MEAL NO. 2

Beef Salad Japonais

Hash Browned Potato Patties
Canned Tomato Aspic
Chocolate Angel Cake

MEAL NO. 3

Greek Beef with Chestnuts

Spinach with Pine Nuts
Anchovy Salad
Fresh Berry Tarts

Austrian Pot Roast

The Austrians are very proud of their coffee and they often include it in cooking for a piquant flavor.

3 to 3½ pounds chuck roast
  of beef
¼ teaspoon cumin
1 teaspoon black pepper
½ teaspoon Tabasco
2 tablespoons flour
2 tablespoons beef fat or
  shortening

1 cup consommé
¼ cup cold coffee
2 medium onions, sliced
1 teaspoon salt
¼ teaspoon pepper

Rub beef with mixture of cumin, black pepper, and Tabasco. Dust with flour. Melt beef fat in a Dutch oven; add meat and brown on all sides. Add remaining ingredients; cover and simmer 2 to 2½ hours, or until meat is tender. Makes 4 servings.

Beef Salad Japonais

A quick gourmet dish with an Oriental touch.

2 cups cooked Austrian pot
    roast, diced
½ cup water chestnuts, sliced
½ cup mayonnaise
1 teaspoon Dijon-type
    mustard

1 dill pickle, finely chopped
¾ cup chopped celery hearts
crisp lettuce leaves
2 hard-cooked eggs, sliced
few sprigs parsley

Combine meat with chestnuts, mayonnaise, mustard, pickle, and celery hearts. Pile lightly onto lettuce leaves. Garnish with egg slices and parsley. Makes 4 servings.

Greek Beef with Chestnuts

I have been served this dish in several restaurants in the lovely Peloponnesus area of Greece.

2½ pounds beef chuck, cut
    into 2-inch cubes
¾ teaspoon salt
⅛ teaspoon pepper
water
2 pounds chestnuts

1 medium onion, minced
1 cup hot consommé
1 tablespoon sugar
4 slices bread
2 tablespoons butter

Place meat in a heavy skillet; sprinkle with salt and pepper. Add water to cover. Cover skillet tightly; cook over medium heat 1 to 1½ hours, or until meat is tender. While meat is cooking, prepare chestnuts as follows. Heat oven to 400° F. Slash shells of chestnuts; place in a baking pan, and bake 15 minutes. Cool, then peel off shells and skins, being careful not to break the chestnuts. Set aside.

     Remove meat and liquid from skillet and reserve. Skim 2 tablespoons fat from reserved liquid and return to skillet. Add onion and sauté until limp. Add meat and chestnuts. Add consommé and remaining liquid. In a small pan caramelize the sugar with 1 teaspoon hot water. When it is a rich brown color, add to meat. Cover and cook 35 minutes. To make croutons, cut bread into cubes, discarding crusts; brown in butter. Turn meat onto a platter and surround with chestnuts and croutons. Makes 4 servings.

TOP ROUND STEAK—ONE

A 4- to 5-pound top round of beef can yield a substantial Sunday dinner and two delicious leftover meals for the family.

MEAL NO. 1

Beefsteak Parisienne

Green Beans Amandine
Corn Soufflé
Cucumber Salad Bowl
Orange Ring Cake

MEAL NO. 2

Stroganoff Burgers

French Fried Potatoes
Lettuce Wedges   Herb Mayonnaise
Celery Stalks
Jellied Fruit
Cookies

MEAL NO. 3

Beef Astoria

Stewed Tomatoes   Green Beans
Bibb Lettuce Salad
Plantation Pie

Beefsteak Parisienne

One of the many adopted American dishes served in Parisian restaurants.

4 to 5 pounds top round of
  beef
½ teaspoon pepper
½ teaspoon oregano
¾ teaspoon salt
2 tablespoons olive oil
1 clove garlic, minced
2 large green peppers, thinly
  sliced

1 red pepper, thinly sliced
¼ cup butter
1½ cups chopped celery
3 sprigs parsley
½ cup large stuffed green
  olives, halved
2 tablespoons capers
3 cups whole canned
  tomatoes, drained

Heat oven to 400° F. Lightly score the meat and rub in mixture of pepper, oregano, and salt. Pour olive oil into a shallow roasting pan. Add minced garlic and meat. Roast 35 minutes. Reduce heat to 350° F. and roast 1½ hours or until meat is tender. Sauté the green and red peppers in the butter; stir in the celery, parsley, and olives. Add sautéed mixture to roast with the capers and tomatoes; continue roasting 25 minutes. Serve meat on a heated platter with the vegetable sauce poured over it. Makes 6 servings.

Stroganoff Burgers

Here is an interesting variation of this ever-popular dish.

4 slices bacon, diced
½ cup chopped onion
1½ tablespoons flour
¼ teaspoon paprika
¾ teaspoon salt
⅛ teaspoon pepper
1 can (10½ ounces)
  condensed cream of
  mushroom soup

1½ cups cooked roast beef,
  ground
1 cup commercial sour cream
1 tablespoon chopped parsley
4 hamburger buns, split

Sauté bacon and onion in a medium skillet over moderate heat until lightly browned. Blend in flour, paprika, salt, and pepper.

Stir in mushroom soup; add meat. Cook over low heat, stirring frequently until thickened. Fold in sour cream and parsley; heat, stirring gently. Spoon mixture over buns. Makes 4 servings.

Beef Astoria

4 tablespoons butter
3 medium potatoes, pared, finely diced
½ teaspoon salt
⅛ teaspoon pepper
1 small onion, chopped
1 tablespoon chopped green pepper

2 tablespoons tomato sauce
¾ cup leftover gravy
3 tablespoons dry red wine
1 tablespoon chopped parsley
⅛ teaspoon basil
2 cups coarsely chopped cooked beef
½ teaspoon paprika

Heat 3 tablespoons of the butter in a large, heavy skillet; add the potatoes and sauté, stirring frequently, until well browned. Season with salt and pepper. In another skillet melt remaining tablespoon of butter; add onion and green pepper and sauté lightly. Stir in tomato sauce, gravy, wine, parsley, basil, and beef. Bring mixture to a boil. Stir in half the browned potatoes. Turn onto a heated serving platter. Top with remaining potatoes; sprinkle with paprika and serve. Makes 4 servings.

TOP ROUND STEAK—TWO

Have your butcher divide a 4½-pound piece of top round steak as follows: Cut 1½ pounds into ½-inch cubes. Grind up 1 pound. Reserve the remaining 2-pound piece for Beefsteak in Foil.

MEAL NO. 1

Donon Beefsteak and Kidney Pie

Potatoes au Gratin
Crisp Green Salad with
Bacon Bits
Blueberry Pudding

MEAL NO. 2

Baked Stuffed Eggplant Isis

Garlic Whipped Potatoes
Buttered Carrots
Tomato and Cucumber Salad
Apple Turnovers

MEAL NO. 3

Beefsteak in Foil

Buttered Lima Beans
Glazed Beets in Orange Sauce
Tossed Salad
Almond Torte

Donon Beefsteak and Kidney Pie

1½ pounds beef kidneys
1½ pounds round steak, cut
  in ½-inch cubes
¼ cup flour
½ teaspoon salt
½ cup shortening
1½ cups boiling water
1 thin slice lemon
1½ cups canned small white
  onions
1½ cups canned whole baby
  carrots

⅛ teaspoon thyme
⅛ teaspoon basil
¼ cup sherry
2 tablespoons flour
1 tablespoon Worcestershire
  sauce
dash Tabasco
⅛ teaspoon dry mustard
1 package pie crust mix

Wash kidneys; split, remove fat and large tubes. Soak in salted
water 1 hour. Drain kidneys. Cut crosswise into ½-inch slices.
Roll meats in flour mixed with salt; brown in shortening in a
heavy skillet. Remove to a heavy saucepan; add boiling water and
lemon. Simmer 1 hour. Add onions, carrots, and spices. Combine
sherry with flour, Worcestershire sauce, Tabasco, and mustard;
blend well. Add to mixture. Stir and cook until thickened. Heat
oven to 425° F. Divide mixture among 4 large individual heat-

proof casseroles. Prepare pie crust mix according to package directions. Roll out to ⅛ inch thickness. Cut into 4 portions and cover casseroles. Flute edges, prick tops, and bake casseroles 25 minutes. Makes 4 servings.

Baked Stuffed Eggplant Isis

As a child I was introduced to this delicate dish in Egypt, and it became one of my family's and my own favorites.

4 small eggplants (about 5 inches long)	1 teaspoon chopped parsley
2 tablespoons vegetable oil	¼ teaspoon sage
1 onion, chopped	½ cup water
1 pound ground round steak	1 egg
½ cup dry wine	½ cup grated Parmesan cheese
1½ teaspoons salt	¼ cup light cream
⅛ teaspoon pepper	¼ cup milk
⅛ teaspoon paprika	¼ teaspoon onion salt

Cut eggplants in half lengthwise; scoop out centers and reserve for filling. Place eggplant shells in heavily salted water; let stand 30 minutes. Rinse in cold water; dry with absorbent paper. Heat oil in a medium skillet. Add onion and meat; brown well. Chop eggplant centers and add to mixture. Add the wine, salt, pepper, and paprika. Add parsley and sage and stir until well blended. Heat oven to 350° F. Stuff eggplant shells with mixture; place in shallow baking pan. Pour water around, and bake 40 minutes. Beat egg lightly and add remaining ingredients; pour mixture over stuffed eggplant and brown under broiler. Makes 4 servings.

Beefsteak in Foil

2 pounds round steak, cut into 4 equal-sized pieces	4 green onions, chopped
1½ teaspoons salt	1 cup canned tomatoes
½ teaspoon pepper	4 tablespoons dry wine
½ teaspoon celery salt	½ teaspoon dill seed
3 tablespoons lemon juice	2 tablespoons olive oil
4 tablespoons butter	4 slices processed American cheese
2 large onions, chopped	

Rub meat with ½ the salt, the pepper and celery salt. Place in a shallow baking dish, add lemon juice and let stand 1 hour, turning frequently. Melt butter in a skillet; add onions and green onions and sauté until lightly browned. Add tomatoes, wine, and dill seed. Cover; simmer 15 minutes or until sauce is thick. Remove from heat; cool. In another skillet, brown meat on both sides in olive oil. Cut 4 12-inch squares of aluminum foil. Place 1 portion of meat in the center of each square and divide sauce equally over each. Place 1 slice of cheese on each. Fold securely and seal. Place on baking sheet. Bake 2 hours at 325° F. Makes 4 servings.

BEEF TENDERLOIN

The beef tenderloin is the aristocrat of meats. For company plan to serve Tenderloin Kobe Style. Order a 10-pound piece, cut off 1 three-pound and 1 one-pound piece for subsequent meals.

MEAL NO. 1

Tenderloin Kobe Style

Buttered Peas   Wild Rice
Bean Sprout and Pimiento Salad
Nesselrode Pie

MEAL NO. 2

Fillet of Beef Chateâu

Fluffy Rice   Stewed Tomatoes
Tossed Salad
Cherry Pie

MEAL NO. 3

Beef Tenderloin Josephine

Shoestring Potatoes　　Glazed Carrots
Avocado on Bibb Lettuce
with French Dressing
Peach Melba

Tenderloin Kobe Style

Japan is famous for its Kobe beef. The chef of the Okura Hotel gave me this recipe on a recent visit to Tokyo.

6 pounds beef tenderloin
2 tablespoons olive oil
1 teaspoon coarse salt
1 teaspoon thyme

½ teaspoon sage
2 cloves garlic, unpeeled
½ cup dry white wine

Heat oven to 375° F. Rub meat with olive oil. Sprinkle with salt and herbs. Place meat in a shallow baking pan and add garlic. Bake 35 minutes. Meat will be rare. Remove garlic and discard. Pour wine into pan; heat thoroughly and serve with meat. Makes 8 servings.

Fillet of Beef Chateâu

3 pounds beef tenderloin
½ cup olive oil
1 teaspoon pickling spices
1 large bay leaf

½ cup Madeira
1 onion, sliced
16 large mushrooms

Remove fat from beef; cut beef into 1½-inch cubes. Combine oil, pickling spices, bay leaf, wine, and onion slices separated in rings. Place meat in a shallow dish; pour marinade over it. Refrigerate overnight. To prepare fillet, remove stems from mushrooms, parboil mushrooms in lightly salted water 2 minutes, then drain and dry. Skewer meat and mushrooms alternately on 8-inch skewers. Broil 3 to 4 inches from source of heat 7 to 10 minutes, depending upon desired doneness. Serve immediately. Makes 6 servings.

Beef Tenderloin Josephine

1 pound beef
  tenderloin, sliced
  paper-thin
½ cup dry red wine
¼ cup tarragon vinegar
¼ cup lemon juice
1 tablespoon minced onion

1 teaspoon salt
⅛ teaspoon pepper
1 jar (2 ounces) red caviar
1 tablespoon minced chives
½ cup commercial sour cream
1 teaspoon finely chopped
  fresh dill

Place meat slices in a broiler-proof glass casserole. Combine wine, vinegar, and lemon juice, pour over meat, and toss lightly. Sprinkle with onion, salt and pepper. Refrigerate 3 hours. When ready to serve, drain meat and flatten slices with a spatula. Broil 3 inches from source of heat 1 minute on each side. Place all meat slices on a large, heated platter. Divide caviar among the slices, placing a dollop in each center. Sprinkle with chives, top with sour cream, sprinkle with dill. Serve immediately. Makes 4 servings.

RUMP ROAST

Buy a 6-pound rump roast of beef and cook it according to the following recipe, Sauerbraten American Style. Now, you may get either one or two additional meals from the leftovers, depending on your appetite and the size of your family. I suggest that you read the second two recipes, note the amounts of leftover Sauerbraten called for in each—and then make your decision.

MEAL NO. 1

Sauerbraten American Style with Noodles

Slivered Carrots and Celery
Shredded Lettuce Salad
Apple Pie

MEAL NO. 2

*Spiced Beef Slices with
Dumplings*

Buttered Lima Beans   Cauliflower Salad
Raisin Bread Pudding

MEAL NO. 3

Devon Hashburgers

French Fried Potatoes   Assorted Relishes
Lettuce Wedges with French Dressing
Butterscotch Brownies

Sauerbraten American Style
with Noodles

The German favorite with an American accent!

6-pound rump roast of beef
1 tablespoon salt
½ teaspoon pepper
2 tablespoons dry mustard
6 tablespoons butter
1 cup minced onions
1 teaspoon oregano
1 bay leaf, crushed
¼ teaspoon ground sage
¼ teaspoon thyme
¾ cup tarragon vinegar

2 cans (6 ounces each)
   tomato paste
2 cups meat stock
3 carrots, finely chopped
½ cup celery leaves
¼ cup dry red wine
1 tablespoon cornstarch
2 tablespoons cold water
1 package (8 ounces) wide
   noodles, cooked

Wipe meat with damp cloth. Rub entire surface with mixture of
salt, pepper, and dry mustard. Melt butter in a 5-quart Dutch
oven or heavy skillet; add onions and sauté until lightly browned.
Add meat; brown on all sides. Remove meat from Dutch oven.
Add oregano, bay leaf, sage, thyme, tarragon vinegar, tomato
paste, meat stock, carrots, and celery leaves. Bring to a boil.

Place meat on a rack in Dutch oven. Cover tightly; simmer gently about 3½ hours or until meat is fork tender, turning meat 3 or 4 times. Add wine during last 30 minutes of cooking.

When meat is done, remove from pan and keep warm. Thicken sauce with cornstarch mixed with cold water. Cook sauce, stirring constantly, 5 minutes. Turn cooked noodles onto a heated platter. Slice meat and arrange attractively in center of platter. Pour some sauce over all. Serve remaining sauce separately. Makes 6 servings, with meat left over.

Spiced Beef Slices with Dumplings

I discovered this recipe in Bavaria and adapted it to American tastes.

½ cup vinegar	6 slices sauerbraten
2 cups water	2 packages (4 envelopes)
10 cloves	instant mashed potatoes
3 bay leaves	¼ cup flour
8 gingersnaps	2 eggs, well beaten
1 tablespoon sugar	½ teaspoon salt
½ teaspoon salt	⅛ teaspoon white pepper
½ teaspoon Worcestershire	¾ cup buttered crumbs
sauce	

Combine the vinegar, water, cloves, bay leaves, gingersnaps, sugar, salt, and Worcestershire sauce in a large saucepan; bring to a boil, stirring until smooth. Add beef slices; heat gently 4 minutes. Set aside. To make the dumplings, prepare instant mashed potatoes according to package directions, but use ½ the liquid called for. Beat in the flour and eggs. Season with salt and white pepper. Shape into 6 dumplings. Drop into boiling water and cook until dumplings rise, about 8 to 10 minutes. Sprinkle dumplings with buttered crumbs and serve with hot beef slices. Makes 6 servings.

Devon Hashburgers

The original English countryside dish was served with buttered noodles, generously sprinkled with English Cheddar.

2 cups leftover sauerbraten,
  chopped
⅓ cup chili sauce
⅓ cup sliced stuffed olives
4 English muffins

4 slices processed American
  cheese
4 black olives, pitted
1 tablespoon chopped parsley
¼ teaspoon paprika

Preheat broiler 10 minutes. Combine chopped meat, chili sauce and stuffed olives. Split English muffins; toast split sides lightly. Spread with hash mixture; place under broiler just long enough to heat hash slightly. Top each muffin with a slice of cheese, quartering each slice to fit on muffin. Broil until cheese melts. Press a black olive into cheese on each muffin; sprinkle with paprika. Serve at once. Makes 4 servings.

RUMP OR CHUCK ROAST

A good rump or chuck roast of beef is always a welcome first meal. Here we offer an unusually flavored Flemish roast, a delightful Greek beef and onion dish, and to complete the international flavor, French Salmis of Beef. Buy a 7-pound roast and have the butcher cut off a 2-pound piece.

MEAL NO. 1

Flemish Roast

Potato Puffs   Creamed Cauliflower
Romaine Salad
Lord Baltimore Cake

MEAL NO. 2

Greek Stiffado

Whipped Potatoes   Julienne Carrots
Tossed Green Salad
Pistachio Ice Cream

MEAL NO. 3

French Salmis of Beef

Potatoes au Gratin   Buttered String Beans
Watercress Salad
Chocolate Pots de Crème

Flemish Roast

5-pound rump or chuck roast
  of beef
1 teaspoon ground coriander
1 teaspoon pepper
½ teaspoon red hot sauce
1½ tablespoons flour
2 tablespoons margarine
1½ cups beer
4 large onions, thinly sliced

2 cloves garlic, minced
1 tablespoon minced parsley
2 tablespoons butter
2 tablespoons vegetable oil
1½ teaspoons sugar
¾ teaspoon salt
½ teaspoon thyme
½ teaspoon sage
2 tablespoons chopped parsley

Rub roast with mixture of coriander, pepper, and hot sauce. Dust generously with flour. Melt margarine in a deep, heavy pan; brown meat on all sides. Add beer, bring to a boil; reduce heat, cover, and simmer 1½ hours. Sauté onions, garlic, and parsley in mixture of butter and oil. Add sugar and continue cooking until onions are light brown. Season with salt. Add onion mixture to meat, and sprinkle with thyme and sage. Cover, cook 1½ hours longer, or until meat is tender. Remove to a heated platter. Skim fat off sauce in pan. Spoon sauce over meat. Sprinkle with parsley. Makes 6 servings with leftovers.

Greek Stiffado

A traditional dish served throughout Greece and Turkey.

2 pounds rump or chuck
   roast
½ teaspoon salt
⅛ teaspoon pepper
1 tablespoon olive oil
1 onion, chopped
2 cloves garlic, finely
   chopped
4 tablespoons dry red wine
4 cups boiling water
1 tablespoon whole mixed
   spices

20 small white onions, peeled
1 tablespoon flour
¼ cup water
1 cup canned tomatoes
½ cup tomato sauce
1 teaspoon salt
¼ teaspoon pepper
4 bay leaves
⅓ cup wine vinegar
½ cup dry red wine

Cut meat into serving-size pieces; sprinkle with salt and pepper and set aside. Heat oil in a heavy skillet. Add chopped onion and garlic and sauté until golden brown. Add meat and brown on all sides. Add wine and boiling water. Tie spices in cheesecloth; add to meat. Cover; simmer 2 hours. Steam onions in water until just cooked. In a medium saucepan combine flour with water; gradually add remaining ingredients, stirring constantly until smooth. Cook 10 minutes, stirring. Skim fat from skillet. Add onions. Pour sauce over all gently. Cover; cook 25 minutes. Remove spice bag and serve. Makes 6 servings.

French Salmis of Beef

A party mixer so elegant to serve and so easy to make.

6 slices leftover Flemish
   Roast
2 tablespoons butter
2 tablespoons flour
¾ cup consommé

1 teaspoon lemon juice
½ cup dry red wine
1 teaspoon Worcestershire
   sauce

Trim meat slices. Melt butter in a large, heavy skillet, blend in flour, and cook 1 minute. Stir in consommé. Add lemon juice, wine, and Worcestershire sauce; stir until well blended and smooth. Add slices of meat. Spoon sauce over meat; cover, heat thoroughly over medium heat but do not boil. Makes 6 servings.

RIB ROAST

Entertaining? There's nothing more elegant than a handsome rib roast large enough for eight servings. Have the butcher cut off the short ribs and reserve them for an unusual family meal.

MEAL NO. 1

Peppered Rib Roast Americana

Twice-baked Potatoes
Broccoli Spears with Hollandaise
Cabbage—Carrot Slaw
Dutch Apple Pie

MEAL NO. 2

Fruited Short Ribs Italiano

Stewed Dried Lima Beans
Brussels Sprouts
Black Olive and Onion Salad
Date Bars

MEAL NO. 3

Western-style Beef

Mashed Potatoes   Glazed Carrots
Tossed Green Salad
Pickles
Sliced Pears and Oranges

Peppered Rib Roast Americana

3- or 4-rib roast of beef, about 8 pounds
2 teaspoons pepper
1½ teaspoons salt

½ cup consommé
1½ tablespoons flour
3 tablespoons water

Heat oven to 400° F. Rub pepper and salt over top of roast. Set in a roasting pan; bake 45 minutes or until top has crusted lightly. Reduce heat to 350° F; bake 2 hours longer or to desired doneness, adding consommé during last hour and basting frequently with pan drippings. When done, remove to a heated platter. Skim off fat from pan drippings; make paste with flour and water, add to pan drippings, and stir until well-blended. Heat thoroughly and serve. Makes 6 servings.

Fruited Short Ribs Italiano

½ package (8-ounce size) mixed dried fruit
1½ cups boiling water
1¼ teaspoons paprika
1 teaspoon salt
¼ teaspoon pepper

short ribs cut from rib roast
4 medium potatoes, pared, cut in wedges
8 small onions, peeled
2 carrots, chopped
1 tablespoon chopped parsley

Place fruit in a bowl; pour boiling water over and let stand. Combine paprika, salt, and pepper. Rub mixture into short ribs. Brown ribs in a heated, heavy skillet. Add ½ cup water from fruit, cover, and simmer 1½ hours. Add potatoes, onions, and carrots and simmer 30 minutes. Drain fruit, reserving liquid. Add fruit to meat mixture; simmer 15 minutes, or until meat is tender, adding more fruit, if necessary. Sprinkle with parsley. Makes 4 servings.

Western-style Beef

8 thin slices leftover roast
  beef
2 tablespoons butter
1 cup chopped onions
¼ cup chopped celery
1 tablespoon flour
1 cup consommé

¼ cup leftover roast beef
  gravy
½ cup tomato sauce
¾ teaspoon salt
¼ teaspoon pepper
¼ cup dry bread crumbs
1 tablespoon margarine

Heat oven to 450° F. Lay slices of meat in a heatproof dish, over-lapping them slightly. Melt butter in a skillet. Add onions and celery and sauté until just light brown, stirring frequently. Blend in flour and stir until smooth. Add consommé and gravy; stir. Add tomato sauce, stirring constantly until thickened. Season with salt and pepper. Pour sauce over meat. Sprinkle with bread crumbs; dot with margarine. Bake 10 to 15 minutes. Makes 4 servings.

CHOPPED BEEF

Who can resist a "special" on chopped meat? But you don't have to serve hamburgers. Three pounds of chopped beef will give you three gourmet dishes from three different countries. Try them all and see!

MEAL NO. 1

Mexican Chilis Rellenos

Whipped Potatoes
Cucumber and Tomato Salad
Fruit Cocktail

MEAL NO. 2

Danish Meat Balls

French Fried Potatoes
Buttered Peas
Apple, Orange, and Onion Salad
Sour Cream Cake

MEAL NO. 3

Arabian Hamburger Kebabs

Herbed Rice
Grapefruit and Avocado Salad
Caramel Custard

Mexican Chilis Rellenos

In Mexico they serve these green peppers on feast days.

5 medium green peppers
¼ cup olive oil
1 pound ground beef
¼ cup canned tomato paste
2 cloves garlic, minced
3 teaspoons chili powder
1 teaspoon salt

1 teaspoon oregano
¼ cup finely chopped peanuts
2 teaspoons flour
½ cup vegetable oil
1 can (1 pound, 1 ounce)
   red beans, heated
2 tomatoes, cut in wedges

Cut around stem of each green pepper. Gently pull out seeds and pulp with fingers and discard. Put peppers in a saucepan, add enough salted boiling water to cover, and cook 5 minutes. Drain and let cool 5 minutes. Heat olive oil in a skillet and add beef, tomato paste, garlic, chili powder, salt, oregano, and peanuts. Sauté mixture over low heat, stirring constantly, for 6 minutes. Cool slightly. Stuff peppers with mixture and lightly sprinkle with flour. Heat vegetable oil in a skillet. Fry peppers in oil, turning them once, until browned on all sides. Cover; cook 15 minutes. Put peppers in a ring on a serving platter, with heated red beans in the center. Garnish with tomato wedges. Serve hot. Makes 4 servings.

Danish Meat Balls

The most elegant of hot hors d'oeuvre.

1½ pounds ground beef
1 egg
1 teaspoon salt
2 tablespoons minced onion
1 cup finely ground cracker
  crumbs

¼ teaspoon pepper
½ cup commercial sour cream
2 tablespoons butter

Mix beef with all ingredients, except the butter. Blend well. Form into 24 small balls. Chill 4 hours. Fry in butter. Serve hot. Makes 6 to 8 servings.

Arabian Hamburger Kebabs

1 pound ground beef
½ teaspoon oregano
vegetable oil

1 small green pepper, cut
  into 8 pieces
4 thick slices sweet pickle
8 mushroom caps

Mix beef with oregano and shape into 8 balls. Fry in oil for 5 minutes or until lightly browned. Put on skewers with pieces of green pepper, sweet pickle and mushroom caps. Brush with oil. Broil 10 to 15 minutes depending on desired doneness. Turn skewers over to cook kebabs evenly. Makes 4 servings.

TONGUE

From Switzerland comes a delightful tongue recipe to serve eight generously and have enough left over for two other meals.

MEAL NO. 1

Berneplatte

Sauerkraut with Caraway Seeds
Green Salad
Black Bread   Sweet Butter
Chocolate Parfait

MEAL NO. 2

Petits Tongue Rolls

Creamed Potatoes and Peas
Avocado and Grapefruit Salad on Bibb Lettuce
Tapioca Pudding with Fruit Sauce

MEAL NO. 3

Allah Stuffed Eggplant

Potato Pancakes   Tomato and Cucumber Salad
Heated Hard Rolls
Almond Cookies

Berneplatte

Whenever I visit a German rathskeller, I hope to find this tasty
dish on the menu.

1 smoked beef tongue, about
  6 pounds
4 bay leaves
2 teaspoons dried dill
12 peppercorns
10 whole allspice
1 medium onion, diced
4 stalks celery, chopped

2 sprigs parsley
8 lean short ribs of beef
1 pound ham hock
½ pound smoked sausage, cut
  in 1-inch pieces
2 pounds sauerkraut
1 teaspoon caraway seed
¼ teaspoon fennel seed

Cover tongue with cold water; bring to a boil, skimming the top occasionally. Boil vigorously 15 minutes. Discard water. Cover tongue with fresh boiling water. Add bay leaves, dill, peppercorns, allspice, onion, celery, and parsley. Simmer, uncovered, 1 hour, adding water as needed to keep tongue completely immersed in water. Remove tongue; strain stock and reserve. Cool tongue under running cold water, and strip off skin. Cut in half, reserving one half for other meals. Return one half to reserved stock in pot with short ribs, ham hock, and cut-up sausage. Cook 1½ hours or until all meats are tender. Drain sauerkraut and mix with caraway and fennel seeds; place in baking dish and bake at 325° F. 45 minutes or until thoroughly heated. Turn onto a heated platter; surround sauerkraut with slices of tongue, short ribs, cut-up ham hock, and sausage. Makes 8 servings.

Petits Tongue Rolls

Austrians serve leftover tongue in this gracious way.

12 small slices cooked tongue, sliced very thin	½ teaspoon tarragon
½ teaspoon chervil	1 teaspoon capers
1 teaspoon minced parsley	½ teaspoon chopped gherkins
2 tablespoons minced green onions	6 anchovies, mashed
	4 slices crisp bacon, crumbled
	1 tablespoon butter

Cut slices of cooked tongue on a slant; set aside. Heat oven to 450° F. Combine remaining ingredients, mashing them to a paste. Cut 12 6-inch squares of aluminum foil; grease lightly on one side. Lay tongue slices on foil. Spread mixture over them. Roll up each slice firmly, then roll foil around it, folding in ends and wrapping securely. Lay rolls close together, seam side down, in a 1-quart casserole. Bake 15 minutes. Unwrap on heated serving platter. Makes 4 servings.

Allah Stuffed Eggplant

A Near Eastern delicacy substituting tongue for the original goat's meat.

1 large eggplant
2 tablespoons olive oil
½ cup chopped celery
1 tablespoon minced parsley
3 mushrooms, chopped
¼ cup minced onion
1 cup lightly buttered bread
  crumbs

½ teaspoon chervil
¼ teaspoon marjoram
¼ teaspoon sage
1½ cups diced cooked tongue
½ teaspoon salt
⅛ teaspoon pepper
½ teaspoon paprika

Heat oven to 350° F. Cut the stem from the eggplant, trimming it carefully. Cut eggplant in half lengthwise. Parboil in boiling salted water 15 minutes, turning halves occasionally to cook evenly. Drain well. Scoop out pulp leaving ⅜-inch wall all around. Chop pulp coarsely; set aside. Heat oil in a skillet; add celery, parsley, mushrooms, and onion and sauté until lightly browned. Add eggplant pulp; sauté 3 minutes. Remove from heat. Stir in half the bread crumbs, the chervil, marjoram, sage, tongue, salt, and pepper; blend well. Heap mixture onto eggplant shells. Top with remaining bread crumbs. Place in a greased, shallow baking dish. Add 1½ tablespoons water and bake 30 minutes. To serve, cut with sharp knife lengthwise and serve shell and stuffing. Makes 4 servings.

LAMB

CROWN ROAST OF LAMB

A crown roast of lamb will make a spectacular entrée for company and give you two more meals which will make you happy there are leftovers. Have the butcher put together enough racks of lamb to make a crown weighing 8 to 10 pounds. He should also remove the chine, cut the ribs, tie the crown, and furnish you with paper frills for the bone ends. Be sure to give him a few days advance notice to prepare this.

MEAL NO. 1

Crown Roast of Lamb Niçoise

Potatoes Anna   Curried Broccoli
Raw Mushroom and Bibb Lettuce Salad
Chocolate Eclairs

MEAL NO. 2

Deviled Roast Lamb Bones

French Fried Potatoes
Watercress and Tomato Salad
Spumoni   Almond Cookies

MEAL NO. 3

Lamb Custard

Minted Peas   Boiled Carrots
Lettuce Wedges with Herb Mayonnaise
Lincoln Logs

Crown Roast of Lamb Niçoise

When I visited France I found out that this recipe called for a whole hothouse lamb. This is a young, unweaned sheep which has never grazed.

crown roast of lamb, 8 to
   10 pounds
1½ teaspoons salt
¼ teaspoon pepper
1 teaspoon thyme
4 large carrots, diced
2 medium onions, diced

3 stalks of celery, diced
2 cloves garlic, minced
½ teaspoon sage
2 bay leaves
½ teaspoon rosemary
1 cup white wine
1½ cups consommé

Heat oven to 300° F. Wipe roast with damp cloth. Rub with salt, pepper, and thyme. Place in a shallow roasting pan; bake 2 hours. Add vegetables and herbs to pan; bake 45 minutes. [Total roasting time should be 30 minutes per pound.] Remove meat from pan to a heated platter. Skim fat off pan drippings, leaving vegetables in pan. Add wine and consommé. Boil vigorously 15 minutes. Strain, pressing vegetables through the strainer. Serve sauce with meat. Makes 8 servings.

Deviled Roast Lamb Bones

leftover lamb bones from
   cooked crown roast of lamb
2 teaspoons dry English
   mustard
½ cup water

½ cup bread crumbs
½ cup sherry
¼ cup prepared Dijon
   mustard
1½ cups lamb gravy

Leave a generous amount of meat on bones, cutting off remaining meat to make 1 cup for Lamb Custard. Combine English mustard with water; dip lamb bones into mixture. Coat bones with bread crumbs; place in a shallow baking pan. Broil 3 inches from source of heat, turning occasionally, until bones are brown, about 7 minutes. Place on a serving dish and keep hot. Heat wine over moderate heat and cook 1 minute. Add Dijon mustard and simmer 5 minutes. Add lamb gravy and heat thoroughly. Spoon sauce over bones and serve. Makes 4 servings.

Lamb Custard

Here's an instant gourmet meal which will delightfully surprise your friends.

1 cup cooked macaroni	½ teaspoon Angostura bitters
1 cup finely chopped cooked lamb	1 teaspoon minced onion
½ teaspoon salt	1 cup milk
⅛ teaspoon celery salt	½ cup light cream
⅛ teaspoon garlic salt	2 eggs, lightly beaten
½ teaspoon minced parsley	¼ cup grated Romano cheese

Heat oven to 350° F. Spread macaroni in a well-greased 1½-quart baking dish. Combine lamb with seasonings and onion. Arrange in a layer over macaroni. Combine milk, cream, and eggs and pour over meat. Bake 25 minutes. Sprinkle with cheese. Bake 5 minutes longer or until firm. Makes 4 servings.

SHOULDER OF LAMB—ONE

There are so many variations for a shoulder of lamb that you will soon make it a habit of having planned-over or leftover meats which will not only save you money, but also produce imaginative meals.

Have the butcher bone a 4- to 4½-pound shoulder of lamb. Save the bones for stock. Have 1½ pounds of meat ground.

MEAL NO. 1

Savory Stuffed Shoulder of Lamb

Creamed Onions   Succotash
Raw Spinach and Egg Salad
Spiced Pineapple Chunks
Vanilla Cookies

MEAL NO. 2

Lundi Lamb Casserole

Rice with Garbanzos   Sautéed Parsnips
Assorted Condiments
Cherry Pie

MEAL NO. 3

Mainland Meat Pie

Mashed Potatoes with Sesame Seeds
Creamed Cauliflower
Carrot Slaw
Fruit Cocktail

Savory Stuffed Shoulder of Lamb

3-pound boned shoulder of lamb
½ pound ground lamb
1 egg, well beaten
3 cups soft bread crumbs
2 tablespoons dry bread crumbs
2 tablespoons chopped onions
2 tablespoons chopped parsley
2 tablespoons fresh chopped mint leaves
3 tablespoons butter, melted
½ teaspoon salt
¼ teaspoon pepper
¼ teaspoon paprika
2 tablespoons tomato paste
1 teaspoon water

Heat oven to 350° F. Wipe meat with a damp cloth. Combine ground lamb, egg, all the bread crumbs, onions, parsley, and mint leaves to make the stuffing. Mix well. Spread mixture on shoulder of lamb. Roll and tie lamb securely with string. Brush with butter; season with salt, pepper, and paprika. Pour tomato paste diluted with water over meat. Place in a roasting pan; bake 1½ hours, basting occasionally, or until tender. Remove lamb from pan; cut strings and slice. Place slices on a heated platter, pour gravy over, and serve. Makes 6 servings.

Lundi Lamb Casserole

The blend of spices and tangy apples give this all-in-one meal its unusual flavor.

2 cups diced cooked lamb	1 tablespoon lemon juice
¾ cup cooked stuffing	1 teaspoon sugar
2 tablespoons butter	½ teaspoon salt
2 medium onions, coarsely chopped	¼ teaspoon pepper
	1 cup consommé
2 small green apples, pared, cored, sliced	¼ cup milk
	1 tablespoon flour
1 tablespoon curry powder	1 tablespoon water
½ teaspoon coriander	

Heat oven to 350° F. Combine lamb and stuffing in a 1-quart baking dish. Heat butter in a medium, heavy skillet. Add onions and sauté until transparent. Add apples, curry powder, coriander, lemon juice, sugar, seasonings, consommé, and milk. Mix well. Turn into the baking dish. Cover; bake 35 minutes. Combine flour and water to make a paste. Stir into the sauce; bake 5 minutes. Makes 6 servings.

Mainland Meat Pie

1 tablespoon butter	2 cups lamb broth
½ cup finely chopped onion	4 slices dry toast
1 pound ground lamb	2 cups milk
½ teaspoon salt	4 eggs, well beaten
⅛ teaspoon pepper	½ cup grated Parmesan cheese
⅛ teaspoon paprika	
½ teaspoon parsley	1 package pie crust mix
1 teaspoon cinnamon	melted butter
2 tablespoons tomato sauce	

Melt the 1 tablespoon butter in a large, heavy skillet. Add onion and sauté until limp. Add ground meat and brown well. Drain off fat. Add seasonings, parsley, cinnamon, tomato sauce, and lamb broth. Cover and simmer 45 minutes. Soak toast in milk to soften. Mash to a soft paste; add to meat sauce, blending well. Combine eggs with cheese. Prepare pie crust mix according to package directions. Heat oven to 350° F. Line bottom of an 8×8×2-inch baking dish with half the pie crust; spread meat sauce over pastry. Cover with egg and cheese mixture. Cover with remaining pie crust. Brush crust with melted butter. Cut slits on top of pie crust. Bake 45 minutes. Remove pie from oven; let stand 12 minutes before cutting. Makes 6 servings.

SHOULDER OF LAMB—TWO

A lamb shoulder can yield many tempting meals. Plan on a 7- to 8-pound shoulder. Have the butcher bone it, and save the bones; then cut the meat into 2-inch cubes. Divide into three portions. Wrap separately and freeze, if desired, until needed.

MEAL NO. 1

Lamb de Provence

Buttered Noodles   Peas and Onions
Apple, Banana, and Date Salad
Coffee Ice Cream

MEAL NO. 2

Lamb Italiano

Fluffy Rice   Buttered Asparagus
Onion and Celery Salad
Prune Whip with Custard Sauce

MEAL NO. 3

Greek Lamb with Avgolemono Sauce

Artichoke Hearts   Baked Potatoes
Tossed Green Salad
Marble Pound Cake

Lamb de Provence

White vermouth and herbs add piquancy to this Continental dish.

2½ to 3 pounds boned
    shoulder of lamb, cut into
    2-inch cubes
3 tablespoons vegetable oil
lamb bones
2 cups minced onions
3 cloves garlic, minced
1 tablespoon minced celery
6 tablespoons tomato paste

¼ teaspoon thyme
¼ teaspoon sage
2 bay leaves
2 cups dry white vermouth
3 cups beef bouillon
¾ cup water
¾ teaspoon salt
¼ teaspoon pepper

Brown lamb cubes in hot vegetable oil in a large, heavy skillet. Remove lamb cubes. Add bones and brown well; remove bones, add onions and brown lightly. Drain fat from skillet. Add meat and bones. Add garlic, celery, tomato paste, thyme, sage, bay leaves, vermouth, bouillon, and water; blend well. Bring to a boil: reduce heat, season with salt and pepper, cover, and simmer 1½ hours. Discard bones and bay leaves, skim off fat, and serve. Makes 6 servings.

Lamb Italiano

A quick and easy leftover meal with lots of flavor.

2 to 2½ pounds boned
    shoulder of lamb, cut into
    2-inch cubes
1 pound Mozzarella cheese
1½ pounds tomatoes, sliced

2 tablespoons butter, melted
¾ teaspoon salt
⅛ teaspoon pepper
⅛ teaspoon paprika
⅛ teaspoon oregano

Heat oven to 350° F. Place lamb in a 1½-quart baking dish. Cut cheese in small chunks and place on top of meat. Cover with tomatoes. Sprinkle with butter, salt, pepper, paprika, and oregano. Bake 1½ hours or until meat is tender. Makes 6 servings.

Greek Lamb with Avgolemono Sauce

The famous Greek lemon sauce gives the lamb its special flavor.

about 3 pounds boned
   shoulder of lamb, cut into
   2-inch cubes
2 tablespoons butter
1 chopped onion
½ cup white wine
4 cups boiling water
¾ teaspoon salt

½ teaspoon onion salt
¼ teaspoon white pepper
1 tablespoon flour
¼ cup cold water
2 cups hot stock
3 eggs
juice of 3 lemons

In a large, heavy skillet brown meat on all sides in butter; remove meat to platter. Add onion and sauté until tender but not browned. Drain off all fat. Add wine, cover, and simmer 5 minutes. Add meat and simmer 10 minutes longer. Add boiling water, salts, and white pepper. Cover and simmer 1½ to 2 hours or until meat is tender. Skim off fat. Make a paste of flour and cold water: add to hot stock and cook 5 minutes. Beat eggs 5 minutes or until thick. Continue beating vigorously while adding, alternately in very small quantities, the thickened hot stock and lemon juice. Drain meat; pour lemon sauce over meat and serve immediately. *Do not cover and do not reheat as sauce will curdle.* Makes 6 servings.

Note: To make stock, boil lamb bones with 1 onion, 1 small potato, 1 carrot and a sprig of parsley in water to cover for 1 hour. Strain; continue boiling until stock is reduced to 2 cups.

SHOULDER OF LAMB—THREE

A 5- to 6-pound boned and rolled lamb shoulder will serve you nicely with a roast, a chafing-dish lamb curry, and elegant lamb rolls good enough for an unexpected company meal.

MEAL NO. 1

Lamb alla Veneziana

Potato Puffs   Creamed Zucchini
Green Salad
Cream Puffs

MEAL NO. 2

Lamb a l'Indienne

Fluffy Rice   Exotic Condiments
Avocado and Grape Salad
Vanilla Pudding   Caramel Sauce

MEAL NO. 3

Lamb Rolls Waldorf

Macaroni au Gratin
Green Beans Amandine
Jellied Tomato Salad
Orange Sherbet

Lamb alla Veneziana

5- to 6-pound boned, rolled shoulder of lamb
1 teaspoon salt

¼ teaspoon pepper
2 tablespoons butter
2½ to 3 cups dry red wine

Wipe meat roll with a damp cloth. Sprinkle with salt and pepper. In a heavy, deep kettle melt butter; add lamb and brown well on all sides. Add 1 cup of the wine; cover tightly and simmer 1 hour. Skim off fat. Heat another 1 cup wine, add to meat, and cook 1 hour longer. Skim off fat again. Heat and add remaining wine; cook 25 minutes longer. Test for doneness. If meat is not tender, add ½ cup more heated wine and continue cooking until tender. Makes 6 servings with leftovers.

Lamb a l'Indienne

Coconut, curry powder, and cloves are uniquely combined in this popular Indian dish.

2 cups diced cooked lamb
2 medium cooking apples,
   cored, pared, sliced
1 green pepper, chopped
2 medium onions, sliced
1 clove garlic, minced
2 tablespoons olive oil
2 tablespoons flour
1½ tablespoons curry powder
½ teaspoon salt
⅛ teaspoon marjoram

pinch thyme
1 cup consommé
½ cup dry red wine
juice and grated rind of 1
   lemon
½ cup seedless raisins
2 whole cloves
¼ cup shredded coconut
2 tablespoons chopped
   pistachio nuts

Sauté lamb, apples, green pepper, onions, and garlic in olive oil in a large, heavy skillet until onions are soft and transparent. Remove meat; set aside. Blend into the skillet a mixture of flour, curry powder, salt, and herbs. Cook 5 minutes over low heat. Stir in consommé, wine, lemon juice and rind, raisins, and cloves. Cover and simmer over very low heat 20 to 25 minutes, stirring occasionally. Add sautéed meat, coconut, and pistachio nuts. Heat thoroughly, about 5 minutes. Makes 6 servings.

Lamb Rolls Waldorf

6 large, very thin slices
  cooked lamb
½ cup seasoned bread stuffing
½ cup leftover gravy
2 tablespoons butter

2 tablespoons currant jelly
¾ teaspoon salt
¼ teaspoon pepper
1 tablespoon capers

Heat oven to 400° F. Lamb slices should be thin enough to roll up. Place slices on a flat surface. Place a spoonful of stuffing on each; roll up, tie with string, or fasten with wooden picks. Place in a shallow, greased 1-quart baking dish. Heat gravy in a saucepan with butter and jelly; when jelly is dissolved, pour mixture over rolls. Season with salt and pepper. Sprinkle capers over rolls. Bake 15 minutes, basting several times. Makes 6 servings.

LEG OF LAMB—ONE

Lamb is one of the most versatile meats and the imaginative cook, when she clears the roast from the table, is already visualizing the other meals it will produce. For three generous meals buy a 10-pound leg of lamb. Have it cut in half. Bone one half of the leg, and do take the bones and clippings home for broth and to make gravy.

MEAL NO. 1

Roast Leg of Lamb

Pan-browned Potatoes   Green Beans Amandine
Mint Gelatin Salad
Strawberry Shortcake

MEAL NO. 2

Lamb Shishkebab

French Fried Potatoes
Relishes   Greek Salad
Apricots in Brandy

MEAL NO. 3

Lamb Frikadeller

Broccoli and Red Onion Salad
Red Cabbage
Bread Pudding with Cinnamon Cream

Roast Leg of Lamb

4- to 5-pound leg of lamb
2 cloves garlic, halved
1 teaspoon salt
¼ teaspoon pepper
3 tablespoons butter, melted
2 tablespoons lemon juice
1 onion, finely chopped

1 cup dry white wine
½ cup water
½ cup vegetable oil
18 small white potatoes,
  pared
sprigs of fresh mint

Heat oven to 325° F. Wipe lamb with damp cloth. Slit in four places and insert pieces of garlic. Season with salt and pepper. Combine butter with lemon juice; lightly brush over lamb. Place lamb in a roasting pan, add chopped onion, wine, and water. Cover and bake 2 hours. Uncover, increase heat to 375° F. and continue baking 1 hour, basting every 15 minutes. Transfer to a heated platter; cover and keep warm. In a medium skillet heat oil to sizzling. Add potatoes and fry until golden brown. Skim fat from baking pan; add potatoes to meat drippings. Bake; uncovered, 30 minutes or until tender. Arrange potatoes around lamb. Decorate with mint. Makes 6 servings.

Lamb Shishkebab

24 1½- to 2-inch lamb cubes
1 medium onion, diced
1 teaspoon salt
¼ teaspoon pepper
2 cloves garlic, minced
1 teaspoon oregano
1 teaspoon paprika
½ teaspoon dry mustard
½ cup olive oil

¾ cup red wine
12 white onions, peeled,
   parboiled 10 minutes
2 medium green peppers, cut
   in 1-inch cubes, parboiled
   10 minutes
24 small mushrooms
12 cubes Canadian bacon

Place lamb cubes in an earthenware bowl. Combine diced onion, salt, pepper, garlic, oregano, paprika, dry mustard, olive oil, and red wine; blend well. Pour marinade over meat; toss cubes until well coated. Refrigerate at least 24 hours in marinade. Fill 6 12-inch skewers, arranging on each equal portions of lamb, vegetables, and Canadian bacon. Broil 3 to 4 inches from source of heat for 15 minutes, turning two or three times during cooking. Serve hot. Makes 6 servings.

Lamb Frikadeller

A quick Dutch treat of lamb patties.

2 cups chopped cooked lamb
½ pound sausage meat
1 large onion, chopped
6 double saltine crackers,
   crushed

1 egg, well beaten
½ teaspoon salt
6 spiced crab apples
watercress

Combine lamb, sausage meat, and onion: mix well. Soak saltines in a cup with water to cover for 2 minutes; drain well. Combine with meat. Mix in egg and salt. Shape into 6 patties and brown slowly in a greased skillet 30 minutes, turning occasionally. Serve with crab apples and watercress. Makes 6 servings.

LEG OF LAMB—TWO

Here is another three-meal version of a leg of lamb using a 7- to 9-pound whole leg. Cut chops from the top of the leg for four servings, roast the remainder of the leg in paper, Continental Style, and serve Lamb Scallopini from the leftovers.

MEAL NO. 1

Lamb Breezoles

Rice Pilaf cooked in Lamb Broth
Parslied Carrots
Green Salad with Bleu Cheese Dressing
Apple Pie

MEAL NO. 2

Leg of Lamb Continental Style

Pan Fried Potatoes
Peas and Olives   Mint Jelly
Tossed Salad
Marble Cake with Ice Cream

MEAL NO. 3

Lamb Scallopini

Buttered Noodles
Okra with Tomatoes
Avocado and Onion Salad
Raspberry Gelatin

Lamb Breezoles

The Athenians like lemon juice generously squeezed over the lamb chops.

4 lamb chops, ¼ to ½ inch
   thick, cut from leg of lamb
¼ cup butter, melted
2 tablespoons lemon juice

1 teaspoon salt
¼ teaspoon pepper
½ teaspoon oregano
½ teaspoon thyme

Broil lamb chops 3 to 4 inches from source of heat. Combine remaining ingredients. When chops begin to sizzle brush generously with butter mixture. Turn, brush other side and broil. Continue brushing and turning until done. Medium-done requires 12 minutes for both sides. Makes 4 servings.

Leg of Lamb Continental Style

leg of lamb with chops
   removed
3 cloves garlic, sliced
½ lemon

1 teaspoon salt
½ teaspoon pepper
½ cup grated Romano cheese
butter

Heat oven to 325° F. Wipe lamb with damp cloth. Cut slits into lamb and insert garlic slices. Rub lamb with lemon; sprinkle with salt, pepper, and cheese. Wrap leg of lamb in heavy cooking paper, closing both ends of paper together. Smear paper with butter. Place lamb in a roasting pan. Bake 1½ hours. Remove pan from oven; carefully remove paper and return lamb to pan. Increase oven heat to 375° F.; bake 35 minutes or until done. Makes 4 servings with leftovers.

Lamb Scallopini

2 cups cooked lamb, cut in
1½-inch cubes
2 tablespoons butter
2 medium onions, sliced
1 small clove garlic, minced
2 small green peppers, sliced
¼ cup chopped celery

1 cup leftover lamb gravy
¼ cup red wine
½ teaspoon salt
¼ teaspoon pepper
2 tablespoons sherry
1 tablespoon minced parsley

Remove fat from lamb cubes. Heat butter in a medium skillet to sizzling; add onion, garlic, green peppers, and celery and lightly brown, stirring constantly. Blend in gravy and red wine. Season with salt and pepper. Add lamb cubes; stir gently, cover, and heat almost to boiling over low heat. Add sherry and stir. Sprinkle with parsley and serve. Makes 4 servings.

LEG OF LAMB—THREE

Buy a 7- to 9-pound leg of lamb. Have the butcher cut 2 lamb steaks about 1 inch thick from the center. Use thicker half for Roast Half Leg of Lamb. Reserve remaining meat uncooked for a third meal. Cook bones and reserve stock for gravy.

MEAL NO. 1

Roast Half Leg of Lamb

Roast Potatoes
Buttered Carrots with Mint
Grapefruit and Avocado Salad
Floating Island Custard

MEAL NO. 2

English Lamb Steaks

*Ginger Rice   Buttered Asparagus
Tossed Salad with Pistachio Nuts
Cheese Cake

MEAL NO. 3

Lamb à la Polsk

Mashed Potatoes   Minted Peas
Raw Spinach Salad
Sliced Peaches   Sponge Cake

Roast Half Leg of Lamb

½ leg of lamb (3 to 3½ pounds)	salt
garlic powder	1 small onion, sliced
	½ cup water

Heat oven to 350° F. Pierce lamb in about 6 places with skewers; fill holes with garlic powder. Rub salt over meat; place meat in a roasting pan. Add onion and water around lamb. Cover; roast until done to taste, 30 minutes per pound for well done. Remove cover; roast 15 minutes longer, or until browned. Makes 4 servings.

English Lamb Steaks

2 lamb steaks, about 1 inch thick, cut from half a leg of lamb	½ teaspoon ginger
	½ teaspoon curry powder
¾ cup canned pineapple juice	seeds from 1 cardamom pod, crushed
	Ginger Rice (*see below*)

Place steaks in a single layer in a shallow pan. Mix pineapple juice, ginger, curry powder, and crushed cardamon and pour over steaks. Cover; place in refrigerator for at least 12 hours, turning once. Drain; save marinade. Broil steaks, 4 inches from heat, 6 minutes on each side. Serve with Ginger Rice. Makes 4 servings.

Ginger Rice

pineapple-spice liquid	1 teaspoon salt
marinade	1 cup rice
water	

Measure pineapple-spice marinade from marinated lamb steaks and add enough water to make 2 cups liquid. Heat to boiling in a medium saucepan; stir in salt. Add rice; cover. Simmer 30 minutes or until rice is tender and liquid is absorbed. Makes 4 servings.

Lamb à la Polsk

This Polish recipe calls for a lamb shoulder with lots of sour cream, served with red cabbage.

2 cups leftover uncooked lamb	1 cup water
1¼ cups diced celery	1 cup commercial sour cream
3 medium carrots, scraped, thinly sliced	¼ cup chopped parsley
1 medium onion, chopped	2 tablespoons flour
1 small tomato, chopped	¾ teaspoon caraway seeds
1 teaspoon salt	1 cup biscuit mix
	6 tablespoons light cream

Heat oven to 375° F. Trim fat from lamb; cut lamb into cubes. Combine lamb with celery, carrots, onion, tomato, salt, and water in a 1½-quart pan. Cover tightly. Bake 1 hour or until meat is tender. Mix sour cream with parsley, flour, and caraway seeds in a small bowl. Combine biscuit mix and cream in a second bowl. Remove pan from oven; stir in sour-cream mixture. Drop biscuit dough from a teaspoon to make 8 mounds around edge of pan. Bake, uncovered, 15 to 20 minutes longer, or until biscuits are lightly browned. Makes 4 servings.

PORK AND HAM

FRESH HAM

A 5-pound fresh ham, shank end, is the inspiration for three unusual meals. Have the butcher cut off 2 pounds of meat, and cut it into 1½-inch cubes; have 1 pound of meat ground finely along with ⅓ pound of pork fat for the unusual homemade sausage cakes. The 2-pound piece is for Roast Fresh Ham.

MEAL NO. 1

Roast Fresh Ham with Apple Rings

Parslied Whipped Potatoes
Cabbage with Caraway Seeds
Butterscotch Pudding

MEAL NO. 2

Sweet Pork Ariadne

Buttered Broccoli Spears
Cherry Tomatoes and Hearts of Celery
Pineapple Pudding with Melba Sauce

MEAL NO. 3

Homemade Sausage Cakes Alexandra

Mashed Potatoes
String Beans with Almonds
Romaine Salad with Italian Dressing
Apple Pie

Roast Fresh Ham with Apple Rings

shank end of fresh ham
  (2 pounds)
¾ teaspoon celery salt
⅛ teaspoon pepper

1 teaspoon sage
2 large apples, unpeeled,
  cored
3 tablespoons shortening

Heat oven to 350° F. Rub ham with combined celery salt, pepper, and sage. Place in a roasting pan; roast, covered, 1½ hours. Uncover, continue roasting 30 minutes. Cut apples into rings and fry in shortening 2 minutes. Add apple rings to roasting pan; continue baking 25 minutes longer. Makes 4 servings.

Sweet Pork Ariadne

This is an adaptation of the Viennese favorite.

1½ cups boiling water
½ package (8 ounces) dried
  apricots
2 pounds boneless pork, cut
  in 1½-inch cubes
1 tablespoon butter
2½ tablespoons soy sauce

dash Tabasco
⅛ teaspoon pepper
6 green onions, cut in 2-inch
  pieces
2 cups fluffy, cooked rice
1 tablespoon chopped parsley

Pour boiling water over apricots and let stand. Brown meat in butter in a medium, heavy skillet until well browned on all sides. Add soy sauce, Tabasco, pepper, and half the apricot liquid. Cover and simmer 45 minutes. Add onions, apricots, and more apricot liquid if necessary. Simmer 10 minutes longer, or until meat and apricots are tender. Serve over rice; sprinkle with parsley. Makes 6 servings.

Homemade Sausage Cakes Alexandra

This is a luxurious hors d'oeuvre.

2 cups ground pork
⅔ cup ground pork fat
1½ teaspoons salt
½ teaspoon celery salt
⅛ teaspoon pepper
dash allspice

dash mace
⅛ teaspoon crumbled bay
　leaf
1 small clove garlic, minced
¼ cup cognac

Combine all ingredients in a large mixing bowl. Beat mixture vigorously until well blended. Form into cakes 2 inches in diameter and ½ inch thick. Brown cakes lightly on both sides in a heavy skillet and cook until well done. Drain on absorbent towels. Makes 6 servings.

PORK LOIN

Buy a 5-pound, 12-chop pork loin. Have the butcher cut 6 thick chops from the rib end. Trim the remaining shoulder pieces from the bones. Cube meat and freeze, if desired, until needed for your second meal. Freeze the bones, or prepare soup and freeze it until needed.

MEAL NO. 1

Pork Fruitadella

Spinach Soufflé　　Parslied Carrots
Tomato and Cucumber Salad
Pears with Lemon Velvet Sauce

MEAL NO. 2

Pork Mexicano

Succotash Amandine
Spicy Cole Slaw
Ice Cream Cake

MEAL NO. 3

Minnesota Pea Soup

Glazed Canadian Bacon
Sesame Toast
Double Chocolate Cake

Pork Fruitadella

6 thick pork chops from rib
    end of pork roast
½ teaspoon salt
¼ teaspoon pepper
dash of mace
2 large oranges

2 tablespoons brown sugar
⅛ teaspoon nutmeg
5 slices white bread, diced
½ cup whole-cranberry sauce
¼ teaspoon onion salt

Heat oven to 350° F. Trim excess fat from chops and place it in a large, heavy skillet. Heat until a small amount of liquid fat coats skillet; discard trimmings. Sprinkle chops with salt, pepper, and mace and brown them in the skillet. Remove chops and arrange in a single layer in a shallow baking dish.

Cut 6 even-size slices from middle of oranges and set aside. Squeeze juice from remaining pieces and add water, if necessary, to make ½ cup liquid. Stir in brown sugar and nutmeg and blend. Pour mixture over chops. Bake 45 minutes, basting occasionally. Mix diced bread, cranberry sauce, and onion salt in a small bowl; divide mixture evenly into mounds on the 6 orange slices and set on top of chops. Spoon juices from pan over all. Bake chops 15 minutes longer. Makes 6 servings.

Pork Mexicano

2 to 2½ pounds uncooked
  shoulder-end pork roast
1 large onion, sliced
1 can (1 pound) tomatoes
1 can (8 ounces) tomato
  sauce
¼ cup diced celery
¼ cup chopped parsley
1 teaspoon salt
1 teaspoon sugar
½ teaspoon chili powder
⅛ teaspoon pepper
⅛ teaspoon paprika
½ cup sliced stuffed green
  olives
1 package (8 ounces)
  noodles, cooked, drained,
  seasoned

Cut meat from bones and save bones for soup. Trim off fat and cube meat. Sauté meat and onion in a heavy, dry skillet until meat is lightly browned. Stir in tomatoes, tomato sauce, celery, parsley, salt, sugar, chili powder, pepper, and paprika. Heat mixture to boiling. Cover skillet, reduce heat, and simmer 1 hour or until meat is tender. Stir in olives and cook 5 minutes longer. Serve with hot noodles. Makes 6 servings.

Minnesota Pea Soup

A hearty soup for those cold winters, simmered to a perfect blend of flavors.

1 package (1 pound) split
  green peas
leftover uncooked pork bones
½ cup diced celery
¼ cup diced onion
½ cup diced carrots
¼ cup chopped green onions
1 bay leaf
1 tablespoon salt
¼ teaspoon pepper
5 cups water
4 cups canned mixed
  vegetable juice

Combine peas, pork bones, celery, onion, carrots, green onions, bay leaf, salt, pepper, water, and 2 cups of the vegetable juice in a large, heavy kettle; bring to a boil. Reduce heat and simmer, stirring occasionally, for 2 hours or until peas are mushy. Remove pork bones and bay leaf. Cut off any lean meat from bones and return it to soup. Stir in remaining 2 cups vegetable juice. Heat just to boiling and serve. Makes 8 to 10 cups.

SMOKED PORK SHOULDER

A simmered smoked pork shoulder is hearty family fare. It cooks ever so tender and is truly a no-fuss meal. For the planned second and third meals we feature a golden soufflé and a sherried casserole which are elegant enough for company fare.

MEAL NO. 1

Simmered Smoked Pork Shoulder

Boiled Potatoes
Harvard Beets
Cole Slaw
Baked Apples with Honey

MEAL NO. 2

Golden Pork Soufflé

Creamy Mashed Potatoes
Cranberried Carrot Slivers
Crisp Spinach and Radishes
Eclairs

MEAL NO. 3

Sherried Pork Casserole

Buttered Noodles
Broccoli with French Dressing
Mixed Green Salad
Coconut Cream Pie

Simmered Smoked Pork Shoulder

5- to 6-pound smoked pork   3 whole cloves
  shoulder   1 tablespoon brown sugar
1 large onion   1 celery stalk, cut up

Place meat in a large, heavy saucepan. Add water to cover; add
onion stuck with cloves, brown sugar, and celery. Bring to a boil,
reduce heat, and simmer 1½ hours or until meat is tender. When
done, remove meat to a heated platter. Discard onion with cloves
and celery. Reduce liquid to half by boiling; use as is, or thicken
with flour paste for a sauce. Makes 6 servings.

Golden Pork Soufflé

The substantial smoked pork is a surprise ingredient in this delicate dish.

½ cup butter   1 cup cooked, chopped,
6 eggs, separated   smoked pork
2 cups grated Parmesan   1 tablespoon finely chopped
  cheese   parsley
2 tablespoons finely chopped
  chives

Heat oven to 350° F. Cream butter until soft; add egg yolks,
one at a time, beating constantly, until mixture is light and fluffy.
Add cheese, chives, pork, and parsley. Beat egg whites until stiff
and fold into mixture. Pour into well-greased 1-quart baking dish.
Bake 30 to 35 minutes or until knife inserted near the center comes
out clean. Makes 6 servings.

Sherried Pork Casserole

2 eggs, well beaten
½ cup heavy cream
1 teaspoon Worcestershire
  sauce
dash Tabasco
½ cup sherry
4 cups leftover smoked pork,
  ground

2 tablespoons diced green
  pepper
2 cups cooked rice
2 medium tomatoes, peeled,
  chopped
1 tablespoon grated onion
1 teaspoon prepared mustard
⅛ teaspoon thyme

Heat oven to 350° F. Combine eggs with cream, Worcestershire sauce, Tabasco, and wine; blend well. Combine all remaining ingredients except thyme. Add to egg mixture, blending well. Turn into a well-greased 1½-quart baking dish. Bake 45 minutes. Sprinkle thyme over the top during last 15 minutes of baking. Makes 6 servings.

READY-TO-EAT HAM—ONE

Bake a big ham and the good eating has just begun, for there are so many ways to turn second-day servings into second-day bests.

MEAL NO. 1

Ham with Pineapple Glaze

Tomato Rice   Squash with Almonds
Mustard Sauce
Spring Salad
Orange Cake

MEAL NO. 2

Pineapple Upside-Down Delight

Mashed Sweet Potatoes
Red Cabbage
Crisp Green Salad
Chocolate Brownies

MEAL NO. 3

Ham Mousse Bordeaux

Fried Potato Puffs with Fennel
Caesar Salad
Cheese Cake

Ham with Pineapple Glaze

8- to 8½-pound ready-to-eat   1 cup brown sugar
  half ham   2 tablespoons honey
½ cup pineapple juice   ⅛ teaspoon nutmeg

Heat oven to 325° F. Score top of ham with diagonal cuts, making
diamonds. Place ham in a shallow baking dish; bake 1¼ hours.
Combine remaining ingredients and spread mixture over ham. Increase oven heat to 400° F. Bake 30 minutes longer, or until ham is
well glazed. Makes 6 to 8 servings with leftovers.

Pineapple Upside-Down Delight

An old recipe of the Midwest known also as Cinderella's Meal.

1 small onion, chopped
2 tablespoons butter
2 cups ground cooked ham
2 eggs, well beaten
½ cup bread crumbs
1 tablespoon ketchup
1 tablespoon chili sauce
1½ teaspoons Worcestershire
sauce

½ teaspoon Tabasco
¼ teaspoon prepared mustard
¼ teaspoon salt
⅛ teaspoon pepper
1½ tablespoons margarine
2 tablespoons brown sugar
3 slices canned pineapple
3 maraschino cherries

Heat oven to 350° F. Brown onion lightly in butter in a medium skillet. Combine with ham, eggs, bread crumbs, ketchup, chili sauce, Worcestershire sauce, Tabasco, prepared mustard, salt, and pepper. Melt margarine and sugar together and pour into a 9-inch square pan. Lay in the pineapple slices; place a cherry in center of each slice. Pile ham mixture on top. Bake 40 minutes. To serve, invert on a platter. Makes 6 servings.

Ham Mousse Bordeaux

A Cordon Bleu dish, streamlined for busy housewives.

1 tablespoon butter
1 tablespoon flour
1 cup milk
½ teaspoon salt
1 small onion, minced
2 tablespoons margarine
1 teaspoon paprika
1 teaspoon soy sauce

1½ tablespoons unflavored
gelatin
½ cup water
2 cups cooked ham, cut in
julienne strips
1 cup heavy cream, whipped
watercress
parsley

Combine butter, flour, milk, and salt in a small saucepan and cook, stirring constantly, until thickened. Cool. Cook onion in margarine in a medium saucepan until tender. Add cream sauce, paprika, and soy sauce; blend. Soak gelatin in water and dissolve over hot water. Stir into mixture. Stir in ham. Fold in whipped cream. Pour mixture into a 3-cup mold. Chill until firm. Unmold on a bed of watercress and parsley on a chilled platter. Makes 6 servings.

CANNED HAM

A canned cooked ham is an excellent buy as there is no waste. Plan the first meal as a culinary treat for your family or friends and let the planned-over second and third meals supply time-honored and delicious dinners.

MEAL NO. 1

Baked Ham Lieges

Baked Potatoes with Sour Cream
Lima Bean Salad
Lime Sherbert

MEAL NO. 2

Ham Holiday Mold

French Fried Potatoes
Cauliflower and Anchovy Salad
Orange Sherbet with Bourbon

MEAL NO. 3

Ham In Port Wine Elias

*Pimiento Waffles
Crisp Green Salad
Date Nut Bars á la Mode

Baked Ham Lieges

1½ cups raisins
1½ cups boiling water
1 can (4 to 5 pounds)
  boneless cooked ham
2 tablespoons prepared
  mustard

1 teaspoon dry mustard
¼ teaspoon cumin
1 package (10 ounces)
  frozen Brussels sprouts
1 cup slightly cooked carrot
  slices

Place raisins in a bowl; pour water over them and let stand. Heat oven to 350° F. Place ham in a shallow baking pan; brush top and sides of ham with prepared mustard. Sprinkle with combined dry mustard and cumin. Arrange vegetables around ham. Add raisins and raisin liquid. Bake 45 to 55 minutes, basting frequently, adding more water if necessary. Makes 4 to 6 servings.

Ham Holiday Mold

The distinctive flavor comes from all the ingredients but mostly from the cider and horseradish.

1 cup seedless raisins
1 quart sweet cider
4 whole cloves
¼ cup brown sugar
2 envelopes unflavored
  gelatin
3 tablespoons water
1 tablespoon lemon juice
½ teaspoon salt
dash cayenne

pinch nutmeg
2¼ cups cooked ham, cut in
  julienne strips
2 cups mixed cooked
  vegetables
¼ cup mayonnaise
1 teaspoon prepared
  horseradish
1 tablespoon chopped parsley

Soak raisins in cider 30 minutes. Add cloves and brown sugar; heat mixture slowly to boiling. Remove from heat. Soak gelatin in combined water and lemon juice for 3 minutes. Add cider mixture and stir until gelatin is dissolved. Add salt, cayenne, and nutmeg. Chill until mixture begins to thicken. Stir in ham. Pour mixture into a 4-cup ring mold and chill until firm. Unmold on a chilled platter. Combine cooked vegetables with mayonnaise and horseradish and spoon into center of mold. Sprinkle with parsley. Makes 6 servings.

Ham in Port Wine Elias

Elias, the amiable maître d'hôtel of the Minos Hotel in Crete, shared this recipe with me.

3 tablespoons butter
2 cups cooked ham, cut in
  2-inch cubes
½ cup port wine
1 dash Angostura bitters

dash Worcestershire sauce
1½ cups heavy cream
pinch ground cloves
pinch nutmeg
Pimiento Waffles (*see below*)

Heat butter to almost sizzling point in a heavy skillet. Add ham and lightly sauté. Add wine, bitters, and Worcestershire sauce and simmer until half the liquid remains. Stir in cream, cloves, and nutmeg. Increase heat slightly and cook, stirring constantly, until sauce is thickened. Serve on Pimiento Waffles. Makes 4 to 6 servings.

Pimiento Waffles

2 cups sifted cake flour
2 teaspoons baking powder
½ teaspoon salt
2 egg yolks
1¼ cups milk

6 tablespoons vegetable oil
3 egg whites
3 tablespoons chopped
  pimiento

Preheat waffle iron. Combine flour, baking powder, and salt; set aside. In a medium bowl beat egg yolks, milk, and vegetable oil until well blended. Gradually add flour mixture, a little at a time, beating after each addition; beat only until smooth. In a small bowl, beat egg whites until stiff peaks form when beater is raised. Gently fold egg whites into batter just until combined. Stir in pimiento. For each waffle, pour batter into center of preheated waffle iron until it spreads to 1 inch from edge, about ½ cup. Cook to desired doneness, 4 to 5 minutes. Serve hot. Makes 4 to 6 waffles, depending on size of waffle iron.

READY-TO-EAT HAM—TWO

It has been argued that leftover meats can be used to make meals that have more excitement and savor than the original roasts. And many homemakers plan-over their extra meals not merely as a necessary economy but as real table luxuries. Half a ham can give generous servings for six to eight with at least three meals planned around the original roast.

MEAL NO. 1

Baked Ham à la Gregory

Scalloped Potatoes   Caraway Cabbage
Orange and Apple Salad
Sour Cream Cake

MEAL NO. 2

New Orleans Gumbo

Sesame French Bread Chunks
Chick Peas and Tossed Greens Salad
Blueberry Turnovers

MEAL NO. 3

Chinese Pork Curry

Hot Fluffy Rice   Applesauce with Mint
Fried Squash
Almond Cookies

Baked Ham à la Gregory

8- to 9-pound ready-to-eat
  half ham, shank end
1 can (1 pound 14 ounces)
  pitted Bing cherries
¼ cup honey
2 tablespoons cornstarch
¼ teaspoon cinnamon

⅛ teaspoon cloves
⅛ teaspoon mace
½ teaspoon dry mustard
½ teaspoon salt
2 tablespoons sugar
¼ cup sherry

Have butcher bone ham; save bones for another meal. Remove skin from top of ham. Stuff ham pocket formed by removing bones with drained cherries, reserving liquid and remaining cherries for sauce. Tie string around ham. Score top with diagonal cuts, making diamonds. Heat oven to 325° F. Place ham in a shallow baking dish and bake 1½ hours. Increase oven heat to 400° F. Drizzle honey over ham; bake ½ hour longer or until ham is glazed. Prepare sauce by stirring cornstarch, cinnamon, cloves, mace, mustard, salt, sugar, and wine into reserved cherry juice. Heat almost to boiling, add remaining cherries, and simmer 1 minute. Makes 6 to 8 servings with leftovers.

New Orleans Gumbo

In the elegant old-quarter restaurants, gumbos are varied but all are traditionally served with rice.

4 bacon strips
½ cup chopped green onions
1 clove garlic, minced
5 tablespoons flour
5 cups water
2½ teaspoons salt
½ teaspoon thyme
¼ teaspoon pepper
2 cans (1 pound each)
  whole tomatoes, drained
2 bay leaves

1½ cups cooked ham, cut
  into ¾-inch cubes
1 package (10 ounces)
  frozen okra
2 pounds uncooked medium
  shrimp, peeled, deveined,
  split lengthwise
1 package (6 ounces) frozen
  Alaska king crab meat
1¼ cups cooked hot rice

In a large, heavy skillet sauté bacon until crisp. Remove, chop coarsely and set aside. In bacon drippings, sauté green onions and garlic until tender. Sprinkle in flour and stir until blended. Gradually add water, stirring until smooth. Add salt, thyme, pepper, tomatoes, bay leaves, and ham. Cover and simmer 30 minutes, stirring occasionally. Cut okra in half and add. Cook 14 minutes. Add shrimp and crab meat and simmer, uncovered, 10 minutes or until shrimp are tender. Remove bay leaves. Sprinkle bacon bits over mixture. Serve in soup bowls, first spooning rice into each. Makes 8 servings.

Chinese Pork Curry

A mix of Oriental cuisines makes this a happy Hong Kong concoction.

¼ cup butter
1 large Bermuda onion, finely
   chopped
¼ teaspoon salt
½ teaspoon celery salt
⅛ teaspoon ground cloves
⅛ teaspoon nutmeg
¼ teaspoon pepper

⅛ teaspoon thyme
2 tablespoons curry powder
2 cups chicken consommé
¾ cup heavy cream
1½ tablespoons flour
3 cups diced cooked lean
   pork

Melt butter in a heavy skillet; cook onion in butter until it begins to turn yellow. Add salts, cloves, nutmeg, pepper, thyme, and curry powder and simmer 15 minutes. Add consommé and simmer 10 minutes. Strain through a fine sieve into a large saucepan. Bring to a boil and gradually stir in cream. Stir in flour until smooth. Add meat. Cook slowly 15 to 20 minutes until thoroughly heated. Makes 8 servings.

FRESH HAM

A fresh ham is a welcome change in the winter. Have the butcher cut off two slices, each about ½ inch thick, for one meal and plan to serve the remainder with a succulent stuffing. The butcher will bone the ham for you and make a pocket for the stuffing.

MEAL NO. 1

Stuffed Fresh Ham Supreme

Mashed Potatoes   Brussels Sprouts
Lettuce Hearts with Roquefort Dressing
Fresh Berry Tarts

MEAL NO. 2

Mock Goose Trianon

Sweet Potato Pie   Eggplant Parmigiana
Grapefruit and Avocado Salad
Coffee Ice Cream

MEAL NO. 3

Pork and Stuffing Loaf

Noodles Romanoff   Fried Apple Rings
Endive and Watercress Salad
Pecan Pie

Stuffed Fresh Ham Supreme

A Mediterranean version with plump raisins in the stuffing.

5- to 6-pound fresh ham,
  boned
1 cup packaged savory
  stuffing
3 cups stale bread crumbs
1½ cups chopped onion
½ cup chopped celery
¼ cup butter, melted

¼ cup light cream
1 cup seedless raisins
1 teaspoon dried sage leaves
¾ teaspoon salt
⅛ teaspoon pepper
2 tablespoons flour
2 tablespoons water

Have butcher bone a fresh ham to make a pocket for stuffing. Heat
oven to 350° F. Combine remaining ingredients, except flour and
water; mix well. Stuff pocket of meat loosely with stuffing. Bake,

covered, 1½ hours. Uncover, continue baking 1 hour longer or until meat is tender. Skim fat off drippings. Keep ham warm on a heated platter. Make gravy with a paste of flour and water. Makes 6 servings with leftovers.

Mock Goose Trianon

The original time-consuming recipe was a Trianon favorite—our version is quick, easy and tasty.

2 slices fresh ham, ½ inch thick
½ teaspoon salt
¼ teaspoon pepper
1 cup dried apple rings, soaked in water
4 maraschino cherries

2 tablespoons butter
1 jar (1 pound) sweet-sour red cabbage
1 tablespoon light brown sugar
1 teaspoon caraway seed

Pound meat slices thin and halve them lengthwise. Season with salt and pepper. Place 1 apple ring and 1 cherry on each, roll up, and secure with a wooden pick. Brown butter in a heavy skillet; add meat rolls and brown evenly on all sides. Mix cabbage, sugar, and caraway seed. Remove meat rolls from skillet. Arrange cabbage mixture in bottom of skillet. Top with meat rolls. Cover, bring to a boil, reduce heat and simmer 1 hour or until tender. Add water, if necessary. Remove wooden picks before serving. Makes 4 servings.

Pork and Stuffing Loaf

Intriguing enough for company. Especially good for informal buffet service.

4 cups coarsely ground cooked pork
1 cup packaged savory stuffing
¾ cup pork gravy
2 eggs, well beaten
1 can (5⅓ ounces) evaporated milk
½ cup chopped celery

¼ cup chopped green pepper
¼ cup chopped red pepper
1 small onion, minced
4 tablespoons butter, melted
¾ teaspoon salt
¼ teaspoon pepper
¼ cup dry bread crumbs
3 pimiento strips
1 tablespoon chopped parsley

Heat oven to 400° F. Combine pork, stuffing, gravy, eggs, evaporated milk, celery, green and red peppers, onion, 2 tablespoons of the butter, salt, and pepper. Pat into a greased 1½-quart loaf pan. Sprinkle with bread crumbs and remaining 2 tablespoons butter. Bake 45 minutes. Unmold on a heated platter. Garnish with pimiento strips and parsley. Makes 6 servings.

LOIN OF PORK

What remains of the roast can be the beginning of some excellent dishes. Many of the world's great traditional dishes were developed by cooks who found the cupboard not bare but full of leftovers. Inventively combining ingredients and improvising, they came up with new culinary triumphs.

Take a loin of pork, for instance, and have the butcher cut off 4 large pork chops from the lean end; plan the Roast Loin of Pork Island Style as your main meal, the Pork Chops Marseilles for a tasty supper, and any leftover cooked pork, cut in thin strips, will give you the exotic Chinatown Chop Suey.

MEAL NO. 1

Roast Loin of Pork Island Style

Potatoes au Gratin
Waldorf Salad   Cucumber Sticks
Fudge Cake

MEAL NO. 2

Pork Chops Marseilles

Rissole Potatoes   Fresh Asparagus
Chicory Salad
Angel Food Cake

MEAL NO. 3

Chinatown Chop Suey

Fried Egg Noodles
Tossed Greens
Ice Cream   Fortune Cookies

Roast Loin of Pork Island Style

1½ teaspoons salt
1 teaspoon whole allspice
½ teaspoon nutmeg
1 teaspoon ground cloves
½ teaspoon black pepper
½ teaspoon marjoram
½ teaspoon sage
½ teaspoon thyme
1 crumbled bay leaf
1 tablespoon grated lemon
   rind
2 tablespoons lemon juice

2½ cups consommé
2¼ cups water
6- to 6½-pound pork loin
   roast
3 cups cubed cooked carrots
12 small white onions, cooked
3 medium tomatoes
1 tablespoon chopped parsley
1 teaspoon celery salt
½ teaspoon paprika
½ teaspoon oregano

To make marinade, combine the first thirteen ingredients in a medium saucepan and bring to a boil. Cover, reduce heat and simmer 10 minutes. Cool. Place pork roast in a roasting pan and add marinade. Refrigerate one day, turning meat several times. Pour marinade into a bowl and reserve. Heat oven to 325° F. Roast pork uncovered, 2 hours. Add carrots and onions; pour marinade over all. Continue baking 45 minutes longer. Halve tomatoes, add to roasting pan, and sprinkle remaining 4 ingredients over them. Bake 15 minutes longer. Turn pork onto a heated platter. Arrange vegetables around meat, pour drippings over, and serve. Makes 6 servings.

Pork Chops Marseilles

The port of a thousand nationalities yielded this hearty dish.

1 cup dried apricots	1 teaspoon salt
¼ cup raisins	⅛ teaspoon pepper
boiling water	2 tablespoons butter
4 large pork chops	½ cup consommé
3 tablespoons flour	¼ cup brown sugar

Place apricots and raisins in a bowl; add boiling water to cover and let stand overnight. Force mixture through a sieve or purée in an electric blender. Coat pork chops with combined flour, salt, and pepper. Place in a shallow 2-quart baking pan; top with fruit purée. Pour consommé over all and bake 45 minutes, covered. Uncover; sprinkle with brown sugar. Bake, uncovered, 20 minutes longer or until chops are tender. Makes 4 servings.

Chinatown Chop Suey

½ cup water	¼ cup sliced water chestnuts
1 package frozen green beans, French style	1 large onion, sliced
1 cup frozen peas	1 cup bouillon
1 cup diced celery	3 tablespoons soy sauce
¼ cup frozen lima beans	1 can (1 pound) bean sprouts, drained
3 cups cooked pork, cut in thin strips	2 tablespoons cornstarch
¼ cup diced green pepper	2 tablespoons water
¼ cup diced red pepper	2 cups fried rice
	6 strips candied ginger

Bring ½ cup water to a boil in a large saucepan. Add green beans, peas, celery, and lima beans; cook 5 minutes. Add meat, green and red pepper, water chestnuts, onion, cup of bouillon, soy sauce, and bean sprouts and cook until liquid comes to a boil. Blend cornstarch with water and stir into mixture. Cook until thickened. Serve with fried rice and ginger. Makes 6 servings.

VEAL

BREAST OF VEAL—ONE

Order an 8½-pound breast of veal and have butcher cut it into 3-pound, 3½-pound and 2-pound pieces. Have the first two pieces prepared for stuffing by cutting in a pocket. Have the 2-pound piece cut into 3-inch cubes.

MEAL NO. 1

Veal Del Mar

Green Beans with Almonds
Parslied New Potatoes
Sliced Tomatoes
Cherry Jubilee Meringue

MEAL NO. 2

Pennsylvania Dutch Veal

Creamed Carrots   Fried Potato Balls
Mixed Greens with Chiffonade Dressing
Apple Cobbler

MEAL NO. 3

Blanquette De Veau

Tiny Peas with Pearl Onions
Mashed Potatoes
Bibb Lettuce with French Dressing
Chocolate Mousse

Veal Del Mar

Because veal is a bit bland it is ideal to team with unusual ingredients, in this case, oysters.

3 pounds breast of veal
½ pint oysters with liquid
2 cups seasoned dry bread
  stuffing
¼ teaspoon salt

¼ teaspoon celery salt
⅛ teaspoon pepper
dash paprika
⅛ teaspoon basil

Heat oven to 350° F. Have the butcher prepare veal for stuffing, making a wide pocket. Drain oysters; reserve liquid. Chop oysters; combine with bread stuffing, oyster liquid, salts, pepper, paprika, and basil. Stuff pocket with mixture. Fasten opening with skewers. Place meat in a baking pan. Bake 1 hour or until tender. Makes 4 servings.

Pennsylvania Dutch Veal

3½ pounds breast of veal
2 tablespoons butter, softened
¾ teaspoon salt
¼ teaspoon celery salt
⅛ teaspoon pepper
¼ pound bulk pork sausage
¼ cup chopped onion
1 teaspoon grated orange rind

½ teaspoon lemon juice
⅛ teaspoon basil
⅛ teaspoon tarragon
6 tablespoons boiling water
1 cup seasoned dry bread
  stuffing
1 egg, slightly beaten
¾ cup chicken broth

Heat oven to 350° F. Have the butcher prepare veal for stuffing, making a wide pocket. Rub meat with butter, salts, and pepper. Sauté sausage; remove from skillet and drain. Sauté onion in sausage drippings until just tender. Combine orange rind, lemon juice, basil, tarragon, and boiling water; mix well. Pour mixture over bread stuffing. Add sausage, onion, and egg. Mix well and stuff pocket in the veal. Place in a baking pan and roast, uncovered, 1¼ hours or until tender. During last half hour of cooking, baste with broth. Serve meat with pan liquid, thickened if desired. Makes 4 servings.

Blanquette De Veau

There are many versions of this dish which are laborious and time-consuming—here's our shortcut version.

2 pounds breast of veal, cut into 3-inch cubes	¾ teaspoon salt
	pinch thyme
12 small onions, peeled	1 tablespoon flour
2 cloves	1 tablespoon water
1 carrot, diced	2 egg yolks
sprig of celery	2 tablespoons lemon juice
4 sprigs of parsley	¼ teaspoon grated lemon rind

Put meat in a large kettle; add water to cover. Bring to a boil; reduce heat to simmer and skim. Add 2 of the onions stuck with cloves, carrot, celery, 1 sprig of the parsley, salt, and thyme. Simmer ¾ hour or until tender. Ten minutes before cooking time ends, add remaining onions. Strain broth. Put veal and onions on a heated platter. Make a paste of flour and water and stir into the broth until smooth. Add meat and onions. Beat egg yolks slightly with a little gravy; return to pan. Add lemon juice and lemon rind; stir. Heat 4 minutes. Do not boil. Garnish with remaining parsley and serve. Makes 4 servings.

BREAST OF VEAL—TWO

An unusual main dish with an interesting leftover bonus can be made from a breast of veal, which also yields a third dish to round out meals for three days. Have the butcher cut 1 pound of boned meat from a 6- to 7-pound breast of veal and have it ground. Ask him to cut a deep pocket in the breast for stuffing and to crack the bones in several places.

MEAL NO. 1

German Breast of Veal
with
Potato Stuffing

Buttered Brussels Sprouts
Mixed Raw Vegetable Salad with
Lemon and Oil Dressing
Apple Strudel

MEAL NO. 2

Ricardo's Veal and Kidney Beans

Buttered Zucchini
*Double Cornbread
Marinated Sliced Tomatoes
Spanish Flan

MEAL NO. 3

Creamed Veal Delon
with Noodles

Raw Spinach Salad
Honey Spice Cake

German Breast of Veal

The potato stuffing is a favorite with the Germans.

6-pound breast of veal	2 eggs
1 clove garlic, sliced	½ cup flour
3 teaspoons flour	1 teaspoon onion salt
½ teaspoon salt	⅛ teaspoon pepper
6 medium potatoes, pared	1 tablespoon minced parsley
1 onion, peeled	½ cup shortening, melted

Rub veal with garlic. Sprinkle with mixture of the 3 teaspoons flour and salt. Grate potatoes in a deep bowl; squeeze out excess moisture. Grate onion in the same bowl. Add eggs, the ½ cup flour, onion salt, pepper, and parsley. Mix well. Pour shortening over all and stir until well blended. Let stand 10 minutes. Heat oven to 325° F. Fill pocket of veal with this stuffing; fasten opening securely with skewers. Place meat in a baking pan; bake 3 to 3½ hours or until done. Makes 6 servings.

Ricardo's Veal and Kidney Beans

2 cups kidney beans
10 cups water
4 teaspoons salt
3 teaspoons chili powder
2 cups sliced onion
½ cup chopped parsley

1 clove garlic, minced
1 pound ground veal
2 tablespoons shortening
3 cups canned tomatoes, drained

Soak kidney beans in 6 cups of the water overnight. Drain; place in pan with remaining 4 cups of water, 2 teaspoons of the salt and 1½ teaspoons of the chili powder. Cover; bring to a boil. Reduce heat; simmer 3 hours. Drain; cool and store in refrigerator. Mix onion, parsley, and garlic; set aside. Brown meat in shortening in a large, heavy skillet. Add onion mixture and sauté 5 minutes. Add tomatoes and remaining salt and chili powder. Stir in the beans. Cover; simmer 20 to 25 minutes. Makes 6 servings.

Double Cornbread

1 cup flour
1 cup yellow cornmeal
4 teaspoons baking powder
1 teaspoon salt
¼ cup sugar

2 eggs, slightly beaten
1 cup milk
3 tablespoons butter, melted
1 can (8¾ ounces) cream-style corn

Heat oven to 425° F. Grease a 9-inch square pan. Combine flour, cornmeal, baking powder, salt, and sugar; set aside. In a medium bowl, combine eggs, milk, butter, and corn. Add flour mixture, stirring only until flour mixture is moistened. Spoon batter into the prepared pan. Bake 25 to 30 minutes or until a knife inserted in the center comes out clean and top is golden brown. Cut into squares; serve hot. Makes 9 squares.

Creamed Veal Delon

4 tablespoons butter
¼ cup flour
1½ cups milk
½ cup heavy cream
1 teaspoon salt
⅛ teaspoon white pepper
2 cups diced cooked veal

1 cup diced cooked celery
1 cup cooked peas
2 tablespoons margarine
⅛ teaspoon thyme
¼ cup minced parsley
4 cups hot cooked noodles
4 sprigs parsley

Melt butter in a medium saucepan; blend in flour, stirring constantly. Gradually add milk and cook over low heat, stirring constantly, until sauce is thickened. Add cream and blend it in. Add salt and pepper. Cook 5 minutes, stirring frequently. Add veal, celery, and peas. Combine margarine, thyme and minced parsley. Add to hot noodles; mix well. Press noodles into an oiled 6-cup ring mold. Unmold on a hot serving plate; fill center with veal mixture. Garnish with parsley. Makes 6 servings.

LEG OF VEAL—ONE

A leg of veal can serve many a festive occasion and, if carefully planned from the beginning, it can yield a variety of delectable dishes. Order an 8-pound leg of veal; have butcher bone it and divide it into a 4-pound piece for roasting, a 2½-pound piece for the unusual veal-and-tuna dish, and a ¼ inch thick slice from the center part of the leg.

MEAL NO. 1

Roast Leg of Veal Mandarin

Baked Potatoes   Peas Amandine
Mixed Green Salad with Water Chestnuts and Capers
Orange Chiffon Pie

MEAL NO. 2

Vitello Tonnato

French Fried Potatoes
Julienne Carrots
Wilted Lettuce
Marble Cake with Chocolate Ice Cream

MEAL NO. 3

Wiener Schnitzel

Twice-baked potatoes   Buttered Zucchini
Cucumber and Tomato Salad
Linzer Torte

MEAL NO. 4

Veal Salad Flammarion

Potato Chips   Crisp Cauliflower
Mocha Cake

Roast Leg of Veal Mandarin

Soy sauce lends a piquancy to veal and bacon adds extra flavor in this adaption of an oriental delicacy.

4-pound leg of veal, boned
2 cloves garlic, cut in half
1 teaspoon salt
¼ teaspoon pepper

2 tablespoons soy sauce
6 slices bacon
½ teaspoon paprika

Heat oven to 325° F. Wipe meat with damp cloth. Rub it all over with cut garlic. Season with salt and pepper. Brush with soy sauce. Arrange bacon slices to cover top. Place veal in a baking pan. Sprinkle with paprika. Bake 2 to 2½ hours. Makes 8 servings.

Vitello Tonnato

A very popular Italian dish combining two unlikely ingredients—
veal and tuna fish.

2½ pound piece of leg of   ⅔ cup olive oil
   veal, boned   2 teaspoons capers
1 small onion   8 chopped anchovies
2 cloves   ⅛ teaspoon white pepper
1 small bay leaf   ½ cup lemon juice
2 sprigs parsley   (approximately)
1 small stalk celery   water cress
⅛ teaspoon pepper
2 cans (6 ounces each) tuna
   fish

Place meat in a heavy kettle with water to cover. Add onion stuck
with the cloves, bay leaf, parsley, celery, and pepper. Cover; simmer 1 hour or until tender. Remove meat. Cool and place on
serving platter; slice. Combine tuna fish, olive oil, capers, anchovies, pepper, and enough lemon juice to taste. Work mixture until
smooth using blender or mortar and pestle. Serve sauce with meat.
Makes 6 servings.

Wiener Schnitzel

1½ pounds veal cut into 4   ¾ cup flour
   slices ¼ inch thick   ¾ cup fine bread crumbs
1 teaspoon salt   ½ cup butter
¼ teaspoon pepper   4 lemon slices
1 egg, slightly beaten   2 hard-cooked eggs, halved

Sprinkle veal slices with salt and pepper. Dip in egg, then in mixture
of flour and bread crumbs. Let stand 25 minutes. Sauté slices in
butter until tender and well browned on both sides. Serve with
lemon slices and eggs. Makes 4 servings.

Veal Salad Flammarion

2 cups diced cooked veal
¼ cup chopped onion
¼ cup chopped celery
½ cup toasted blanched
    almonds
1 cup mayonnaise

1 teaspoon tarragon
1 tablespoon lemon juice
lettuce leaves
8 cherry tomatoes
8 ripe olives

Combine veal with onion, celery, and almonds. Mix mayonnaise with tarragon and lemon juice; blend well. Add enough mayonnaise mixture to veal mixture to bind it. Heap onto lettuce leaves. Garnish with tomatoes and olives and serve with extra mayonnaise mixture. Makes 4 servings.

LEG OF VEAL—TWO

A leg of veal will yield many interesting meals. Order an 8- to 9-pound leg and have butcher cut a 2-pound slice from the top of the leg. Have him pound this to ¼-inch thickness. Or place veal on a wooden board, remove the round center bone and pound meat with wooden mallet until thin enough to roll.

MEAL NO. 1

Lord Essex's Roast Leg of Veal

Wild and White Rice   French Artichokes
Romaine Salad with Lorenzo Dressing
Coffee Chiffon Pie

MEAL NO. 2

Veal and Ham Roll Beatrice

Baked Sweet Potatoes   Buttered Asparagus
Coleslaw
Cheesecake

MEAL NO. 3

Veal Braziliano

Scalloped Potatoes   Succotash
Mandarin Orange Salad
Spanish Cream   Macaroons

Lord Essex's Roast Leg of Veal

6- to 7-pound leg of veal,
  boned, rolled
4 veal kidneys, cleaned,
  rolled inside roast
½ cup butter
2 teaspoons salt
½ teaspoon pepper
¼ teaspoon thyme
¼ teaspoon sage
¼ teaspoon mace
¼ teaspoon rosemary
½ teaspoon basil

4 tender stalks celery, cut in
  half
3 medium carrots, sliced
1 medium onion, sliced
2 shallots, chopped
½ cup white wine
1 cup beef bouillon
½ cup chicken bouillon
½ cup heavy cream
2 teaspoons tarragon
water cress

Heat oven to 350° F. Wipe meat with damp cloth. Combine half the butter with salt, pepper, and herbs. Spread mixture over meat. Melt remaining butter and pour into a baking pan, covering entire surface. Place meat in pan. Arrange vegetables around meat. Pour wine over all. Bake 2½ to 3 hours, basting frequently, or until tender. Remove meat to heated platter. Add bouillon to pan drippings, simmer 5 minutes. Strain into saucepan. Spoon off fat. Stir in cream and tarragon; heat through but do not boil. Serve in slices garnished with water cress. Makes 6 servings with leftovers.

Veal and Ham Roll Beatrice

2-pound slice of veal cut
   from top of leg
1 clove garlic, minced
2 teaspoons salt
1 medium onion, chopped
1 tablespoon butter
3 slices day old white bread,
   trimmed
1 pound ground lean raw
   ham

1 egg
¼ teaspoon pepper
½ teaspoon paprika
¼ teaspoon celery salt
⅛ teaspoon cayenne
2 tablespoons flour
2 tablespoons margarine,
   melted
¼ cup chopped green onions
1 cup water

Spread meat evenly with mixture of garlic and salt; set aside. Sauté onion in butter. Soak bread in cold water; squeeze dry. Mix with ham; add to onion. Combine egg, pepper, paprika, and celery salt. Beat slightly; knead into onion mixture; shape filling into an oblong roll. Place lengthwise in the center of the meat. Roll veal around filling; tie securely with string and secure with skewers. Heat oven to 325° F. Place veal roll in a baking pan. Combine cayenne and flour and sprinkle over meat. Pour melted margarine into pan; brown meat on all sides. Add green onions and blend in water. Place pan in oven; bake 1 to 1½ hours or until tender, basting frequently. When done, remove meat to heated platter; remove string and skewers, slice and serve with natural pan juices. Makes 6 servings.

Veal Braziliano

Olives, garlic, and chili powder combine to make this a zippy dish.

¾ cup butter
½ cup flour
2 cups veal stock
2 cups chicken broth
4 cups diced cooked veal
2 medium onions, minced
1 green pepper, chopped
¼ cup chopped pitted ripe
   olives

3 green stuffed olives,
   chopped
½ clove garlic, minced
2 hard-cooked eggs, coarsely
   chopped
1¼ teaspoons chili powder
½ teaspoon salt
¼ teaspoon pepper
1½ cups soft bread crumbs

Heat oven to 350° F. Melt ½ cup of the butter in a medium skillet; blend in flour. Cook over low heat, stirring constantly, until mixture browns. Slowly add veal stock and chicken broth, stirring constantly until thickened. Add remaining ingredients, except bread crumbs. Pour mixture into a 2½-quart baking pan. Melt remaining ¼ cup butter; toss with bread crumbs. Top veal mixture with crumbs. Bake 30 to 35 minutes. Makes 4 servings.

RUMP OF VEAL—ONE

Order a 9-pound rump of veal and have the butcher bone it, reserving the bones. Have two pounds cut into very thin 2-inch strips. Have 1½ pounds cut into 6 pieces about ½ inch thick.

MEAL NO. 1

Poached Veal à la Vert

Creamed Carrots
Baked Potatoes
Tomatoes Vinaigrette
Apple Pie à la Mode

MEAL NO. 2

Finnish Hunter's Steak

Wild Rice with Toasted Almonds
Buttered Zucchini
Caesar Salad
Napoleons

MEAL NO. 3

Veal à la Française

French-Fried Potatoes
Buttered Green Beans
Molded Salad
Toffee Cake

Poached Veal à la Vert

A Parisian dish with a green sauce that's heavenly.

4 pounds rump of veal,
  boned
veal bones
2 teaspoons salt
1 teaspoon pepper
1 large clove garlic, minced
5 tablespoons finely chopped
  chives
5 tablespoons finely chopped
  green pepper

3 tablespoons finely chopped
  dill pickle
¼ cup capers, drained
5 tablespoons lemon juice
1 small clove garlic, minced
¼ cup vegetable oil
⅛ teaspoon sugar
2 dashes hot pepper sauce
1 dash Tabasco

Place meat and bones in a medium kettle; cover with water. Add salt, pepper, and large clove garlic. Bring to boiling, reduce heat, cover, and simmer 2 to 2½ hours or until meat is fork tender, turning meat occasionally. Combine chives, green pepper, pickle, capers, lemon juice, small clove garlic, vegetable oil, sugar, hot pepper sauce and Tabasco in a small saucepan. Add 1 cup of the veal broth. Heat slowly to boiling point, stirring occasionally. Turn meat onto a hot platter; slice. Spoon over some of the sauce and serve the rest in a separate bowl. Makes 6 servings.

Finnish Hunter's Steak

2 pounds veal cut into very
  thin 2-inch strips
4 tablespoons flour
¾ teaspoon salt
¼ teaspoon pepper
⅛ teaspoon paprika
6 tablespoons butter

½ pound fresh mushrooms,
  sliced
1 medium onion, sliced
½ teaspoon onion salt
⅛ teaspoon white pepper
1½ cups milk
½ cup light cream

Roll meat in a mixture of 2 tablespoons of the flour, salt, pepper and paprika. Melt 2 tablespoons of the butter in a large, heavy skillet; add meat and brown all over. Remove meat from pan; keep hot. Add remaining butter to skillet. Add mushrooms and onion.

Cook, stirring, 5 minutes. Stir in remaining flour, onion salt, and white pepper. Blend in milk and cream, stirring constantly over medium heat until smooth and thickened. Pour sauce over veal on a hot platter and serve. Makes 6 servings.

Veal à la Française

1½ pounds veal, cut into 6 pieces	1 tablespoon chopped parsley
6 tablespoons flour	1 clove garlic, minced
¾ teaspoon salt	1 cup consommé
¼ teaspoon pepper	½ cup chicken broth
½ cup bacon drippings	2 cups canned tomatoes, drained, sliced
1 small onion, chopped	1 cup canned mushrooms

Heat oven to 350° F. Dredge veal in a mixture of 2 tablespoons of the flour, salt, and pepper. Heat bacon drippings in a large, heavy skillet; add onion, parsley, and garlic; cook until golden brown. Remove from fat. Brown meat in the skillet; remove to a platter. Add remaining flour to skillet. Stir until browned. Add consommé and chicken broth. Cook, stirring constantly, until smooth. Arrange tomatoes in a 1½-quart baking dish. Place meat on top. Pour sauce over it. Cover; bake 45 to 50 minutes. During last 15 minutes of cooking add mushrooms and continue baking uncovered. Makes 6 servings.

RUMP OF VEAL—TWO

A 7-pound veal rump makes delicious meals in many ways. Veal is the main meat of Germany, Switzerland and Italy and, being white meat, it should be cooked slowly and thoroughly. Have a rump of veal boned and cut into a 4-pound and a 3-pound piece. Save the bones.

MEAL NO. 1

Veal with Anchovy Paste Marceline

Asparagus with Hollandaise Sauce
Whipped Potatoes
Tomato Aspic with Artichoke Hearts
Fruit with Assorted Cheeses

MEAL NO. 2

Veal Anastasia

Stuffed Potatoes   Harvard Beets
Cold Green Beans with French Dressing
Ice Cream and Florentines

MEAL NO. 3

Party Jellied Veal Loaf

Corn Soufflé   Pink Potato Salad
Avocado on the Half Shell
Cream-Frosted Chocolate Mousse

Veal with Anchovy Paste Marceline

In Brussels I had a taste of this extraordinary concoction and
cornered the chef for the recipe.

veal bones
1 quart water
½ teaspoon salt
2 peppercorns
¼ teaspoon dry mustard
1½ tablespoons anchovy paste
1½ teaspoons lemon juice

1½ cloves garlic, minced
¼ teaspoon pepper
2 teaspoons grated lemon rind
3 to 4 pounds veal rump,
boned
5 slices bacon
1 tablespoon flour

Put bones, water, salt, and peppercorns in a large, heavy kettle; cover and simmer 4 hours. Strain and reserve stock. Cool and then remove fat. Combine mustard with anchovy paste, lemon juice, garlic, pepper, and lemon rind; mix well. Spread ⅓ of paste inside meat. Roll up tight and secure with string. Spread remaining paste all over outside of veal. Cover lightly with foil; let stand at room temperature 1½ hours.

Heat oven to 350° F. Place meat in a baking pan; cover top with bacon slices. Bake, uncovered, 2 to 2½ hours. Remove bacon 15 minutes before end of baking time. Turn meat onto a heated platter. Remove fat from liquid in baking pan. Add 1½ cups reserved veal stock. Stir well. Heat to simmering. Thicken slightly with flour. Cook, stirring, until smooth. Makes 6 servings.

Veal Anastasia

3 pounds veal rump, boned
1 teaspoon salt
½ pound fresh mushrooms, halved
½ cup chopped celery
½ cup chopped onion
¼ cup butter

2 tablespoons flour
2 tablespoons water
¾ teaspoon salt
⅛ teaspoon pepper
¾ cup commercial sour cream
6 bacon slices, crisply cooked, crumbled

Place meat in a deep, heavy kettle; cover with cold water. Add salt. Cover; simmer 2 hours or until tender. Remove meat; cool slightly. Reserve stock. Cut meat into 1½-inch cubes. Sauté mushrooms, celery, and onion in butter until lightly browned. Heat oven to 375° F. Make a smooth paste of flour and water; add to 2 cups of veal stock. Season with salt and pepper. Cook, stirring constantly, until thickened. Place meat and vegetables in a 1½-quart baking dish. Pour gravy over all. Bake 15 minutes. Cover top with sour cream. Sprinkle with crumbled bacon; serve immediately. Makes 6 servings.

Party Jellied Veal Loaf

An inexpensive but delicious way to serve a crowd.

3 cups ground cooked veal
2 tablespoons minced onion
¾ cup finely diced cucumber
¼ cup diced celery
2 tablespoons cold water

1 tablespoon (1 envelope)
  unflavored gelatin
1¾ cups medium white sauce,
  hot
1 cup chilled evaporated milk

Combine veal, onion, cucumber, and celery; set aside. Soak gelatin in water. Add to hot white sauce; stir until dissolved. Add veal mixture to sauce. Chill. When veal mixture begins to set, whip evaporated milk stiff and fold in quickly and thoroughly. Pour into an 8-cup mold. Refrigerate overnight or until set. Turn out on a serving platter and slice when ready to serve. Makes 12 servings.

SHOULDER OF VEAL—ONE

Have the butcher bone a 7-pound shoulder of veal, dividing it thus: one 3-pound piece cut open and laid flat; 2 pounds cut for stew; and 2 pounds cut into 1½-inch cubes. Save the bones.

MEAL NO. 1

Veal Roll Allemande

Scalloped Potatoes   Buttered Lima Beans
*Coleslaw with Grapes
Spiced Fruit Compote

MEAL NO. 2

Gettysburg Veal

Stewed Tomatoes with Croutons
Corn Soufflé
Mixed Green Salad
Lady Baltimore Cake

MEAL NO. 3

Veal à la Russe

Pilaf   Lemon-Glazed Carrots
Cucumber and Tomato Salad
Date Nut Torte

Veal Roll Allemande

A German hausfrau served me this while I was traveling through Germany one fall, and she kindly gave me the recipe.

1 medium onion, finely chopped
¾ cup finely chopped mushrooms
1 tablespoon butter
1 cup sauerkraut and liquid
1 cup dry bread crumbs
1 tablespoon chopped parsley
1 teaspoon chopped celery
½ teaspoon salt
⅛ teaspoon rosemary
⅛ teaspoon thyme

⅛ teaspoon oregano
⅛ teaspoon basil
⅛ teaspoon pepper
1 egg, slightly beaten
3 pounds shoulder of veal, boned
2 cans (10½ ounces each) consommé
1 tablespoon flour
½ cup water
⅛ teaspoon paprika

Heat oven to 325° F. Sauté onion and mushrooms in butter in a heavy skillet 10 minutes or until butter is absorbed, stirring constantly so that vegetables will not brown. Drain and reserve liquid from sauerkraut. Combine bread crumbs, sauerkraut, onion and mushroom mixture, parsley, celery, salt, herbs, pepper, and egg; mix well. Lay meat open and spread with stuffing, leaving ½ inch uncovered on all sides. Roll up jelly-roll fashion; tie with string and secure with skewers. Place in a baking pan. Combine sauerkraut juice with 1 can of the consommé; pour over veal. Bake, uncovered, 2½ to 3 hours or until fork tender, basting occasionally. Remove meat to a heated platter. Add remaining can of consommé and water to pan drippings. Bring to a boil. Thicken with a paste made of flour and water. Sprinkle with paprika. Cook and stir until well blended. Makes 4 servings.

Coleslaw with Grapes

4 cups shredded white cabbage	¾ cup Sour Cream Dressing 1 cup seedless green grapes

Mix cabbage and dressing thoroughly. Add grapes and toss carefully with a fork. Makes 4 servings.

Sour Cream Dressing

1 cup commercial sour cream 2 tablespoons sugar ½ teaspoon dry mustard ½ teaspoon paprika	1 teaspoon salt 3 tablespoons vinegar 1 egg

Combine all ingredients; heat in top of double boiler 3 minutes or until dressing thickens, stirring constantly. Cool to room temperature; store in refrigerator. Makes 1½ cups.

Gettysburg Veal

1 teaspoon salt	1¼ cups orange juice
¼ teaspoon celery salt	¼ cup lemon juice
⅛ teaspoon pepper	3 tablespoons grated orange rind
¼ teaspoon nutmeg	
¼ teaspoon mace	1 small clove garlic, crushed
¼ teaspoon dry mustard	1 tablespoon vinegar
¼ cup flour	2 cups water
2 pounds shoulder of veal, boned, cut for stew	¾ cup seedless raisins
	¼ cup chopped almonds
3 tablespoons shortening	

Combine salts, pepper, nutmeg, mace, dry mustard, and flour. Heat shortening in a medium skillet. Roll pieces of meat in seasoned flour; reserve remaining flour mixture to thicken gravy. Brown meat well. Add orange and lemon juices, orange rind, garlic, and vinegar; cover and simmer 45 minutes or until meat is tender. Add water and thicken with remaining seasoned flour. Add raisins and almonds; simmer 10 minutes. Makes 4 servings.

Veal à la Russe

2 pounds veal shoulder, boned, cut into 1½-inch cubes	¼ cup chopped parsley
veal bones	½ cup chopped onion
1½ teaspoons salt	2 tablespoons flour
½ pound mushrooms	dash cayenne
4 tablespoons butter	¾ cup commercial sour cream
¼ cup chopped celery	8 slices bacon, cooked crisp and crumbled

Place meat in a large, heavy skillet, with bones. Cover with cold water and 1 teaspoon of the salt. Cover; simmer 2 hours or until tender. Remove bones; skim off foam. Strain and reserve broth. Cut mushrooms in half; sauté in butter with celery, parsley, and onion until light brown. Set aside. Mix flour with a little water to make a paste. Add to 2 cups reserved veal broth; add remaining salt and cayenne. Cook, stirring, until thickened. Heat oven to 375° F. Place meat and vegetables in a 2-quart baking dish. Pour gravy over all. Bake 20 minutes. Add sour cream. Sprinkle with bacon and serve immediately. Makes 4 servings.

SHOULDER OF VEAL—TWO

Order a 7-pound shoulder of veal and have the butcher bone it. For the following three meals you will need a 3½-pound piece, rolled and tied, 2 pounds cut into 1½-inch cubes, and 1½ pounds ground. Save the bones.

MEAL NO. 1

Jaipur Veal Curry

Corn Fritters   Okra and Tomatoes
Citrus Fruit Salad with French Dressing
Lemon Chiffon Pie

MEAL NO. 2

Veal Di Brangata

*Fluffy Risotto   Buttered Asparagus
Hearts of Lettuce with Herbed Dressing
Pear Zabaglione

MEAL NO. 3

Veal Patties with Mushrooms

Julienne Potatoes
Wax Beans au Gratin
Tray of Crisped Greens
Fruit Compote   Cookies

Jaipur Veal Curry

¼ teaspoon marjoram
¼ teaspoon thyme
⅛ teaspoon sage
2 teaspoons curry powder
¾ teaspoon salt
¼ teaspoon onion salt
⅛ teaspoon pepper
⅛ teaspoon paprika
3½ pounds shoulder of veal,
  boned and rolled

3 tablespoons vegetable oil
3 tablespoons flour
1½ cups canned chicken broth
½ cup consommé
2 small cloves garlic, minced
2 medium onions, chopped
veal bones
1 large apple, with skin,
  cored, quartered
¼ cup currants

Combine marjoram, thyme, sage, curry powder, salts, pepper, and paprika; mix well. Brush meat over entire surface with 1 tablespoon vegetable oil. Rub in mixed seasonings. Dredge veal with 1½ tablespoons of the flour, rubbing it in well. Pour remaining vegetable oil into a large kettle; brown meat evenly on all sides. Pour in 1 cup of the chicken broth and the consommé. Add garlic, onions, veal bones, apple, and currants. Reduce heat; cover kettle tightly and simmer 1½ hours or until fork tender, turning meat frequently. Remove meat to a heated platter and keep warm. If tied, remove strings. Remove bones from liquid and pour off excess fat. Combine remaining flour and chicken broth, blending until smooth. Add to kettle and cook, stirring, until thickened. Strain gravy; serve separately. Makes six servings.

Veal Di Brangata

An Italian friend of mine and I developed this recipe.

2 pounds veal shoulder, cut
 into 1½-inch cubes
1½ tablespoons flour
¼ teaspoon pepper
3 tablespoons olive oil
1 clove garlic, crushed
1 large onion, thinly sliced
½ teaspoon rosemary
¼ teaspoon basil

¼ teaspoon celery seed
1 teaspoon salt
¼ cup tomato sauce
½ cup chicken broth
½ cup white wine
16 pitted ripe olives, sliced
½ cup minced parsley
1 tablespoon minced celery

Remove fat or gristle from veal cubes if there is any. Combine flour with pepper and dredge meat well. Pour olive oil in a large skillet; brown meat well. Add garlic and onion. Sauté until onion is transparent, about 5 minutes. Add rosemary, basil, celery seed, salt, tomato sauce, chicken broth, and wine. Cover; simmer 2 hours or until tender. If necessary, add a little boiling water. At the end of the first hour add olives. Add parsley and celery 20 minutes before meat is done. Serve hot. Makes six servings.

Fluffy Risotto

1 cup rice
¼ cup butter
4 cups chicken broth, hot
½ cup grated Cheddar cheese
⅛ teaspoon cayenne

¼ teaspoon paprika
⅛ teaspoon saffron
2 teaspoons salt
1 large clove garlic, minced

Sauté rice in butter in a medium skillet until straw-colored, stirring frequently. Pour hot broth over rice. Add cheese, cayenne, paprika, saffron, salt, and garlic; blend well. Transfer mixture to top of double boiler; steam over hot water 55 minutes. Makes six servings.

Veal Patties with Mushrooms

A many-flavored dish fit for a king and adapted to our tastes.

1½ pounds ground veal
⅓ cup finely chopped celery
¼ cup minced parsley
1 tablespoon finely chopped
    raw carrot
1 cup soft bread crumbs
⅓ cup milk
⅓ cup light cream
2 eggs, slightly beaten
¾ tablespoon grated onion
1½ teaspoons salt
⅛ teaspoon pepper

⅛ teaspoon paprika
pinch thyme
pinch marjoram
pinch basil
¼ cup shortening
⅔ cup water
1 can (10½ ounces) cream of
    mushroom soup
½ cup canned mushrooms,
    coarsely chopped
1 teaspoon Worcestershire
    sauce

Combine veal, celery, parsley, carrot, bread crumbs, milk, cream, eggs, onion, salt, pepper, paprika, thyme, marjoram, and basil. Mix all together thoroughly. Shape into 18 patties, handling them carefully as mixture will be soft. Brown patties, a few at a time, in shortening in a skillet. Heat oven to 350° F. Place patties in a shallow baking pan. Drain off excess fat and add water to drippings in skillet. Stir and cook 5 minutes over medium heat. Blend in mushroom soup and mushrooms. Stir in Worcestershire sauce. Pour over patties. Bake 30 mintues, basting patties occasionally. Makes six servings.

CHICKEN

ROAST CHICKEN—ONE

A delicately scented roast chicken for the main meal, an unusual Mexican Chicken Pie, and Haitian Chicken Turnovers are the rewards for careful planning.

MEAL NO. 1

Roast Chicken Oreganaki

Corn Soufflé   Buttered Artichoke Hearts
Cinnamon Pear Halves
Carrot and Celery Sticks
Orange Chiffon Pie

MEAL NO. 2

Mexican Chicken Pie

Buttered Garbanzos   Stewed Tomatoes
Green Salad
Honey Cake

MEAL NO. 3

Haitian Chicken Turnovers

Green Peas with Mushrooms
Buttered Beets
Lettuce Wedges with Caesar Dressing
Lemon Icebox Dessert

Roast Chicken Oreganaki

5- to 6-pound roasting
   chicken
½ cup butter
¼ cup lemon juice
¾ cup dry white wine
1 teaspoon salt

⅛ teaspoon pepper
1 teaspoon oregano
¼ teaspoon thyme
1 clove garlic
½ cup boiling water

Heat oven to 325° F. Wipe chicken with damp cloth. In a small saucepan, melt butter and add lemon juice, 2 tablespoons of the wine, salt, pepper, oregano, and thyme. Brush chicken with mixture inside and out. Place garlic inside chicken. Place chicken in a roasting pan; combine remaining butter sauce with remaining wine and boiling water and pour over chicken. Cover chicken with aluminum foil and bake 45 minutes. Remove foil, baste chicken, and cover again with foil. Baste in this manner every 25 minutes for 2½ hours or until chicken is tender. Skim fat from drippings. Serve sauce with chicken. Makes 4 servings with leftovers.

Mexican Chicken Pie

One-plate meal designed to be consumed quickly and with pleasure.

2 cups water
1½ teaspoons salt
½ cup corn meal
2 sweetbreads
3 tablespoons flour
2 cups coarsely diced cooked
   chicken
5 tablespoons butter
½ teaspoon chopped parsley

3 canned artichoke bottoms,
   drained and quartered
½ teaspoon chopped celery
1½ cups light cream
½ cup heavy cream
¼ cup sherry
½ teaspoon salt
¼ teaspoon pepper

Bring water to a rapid boil; add salt. Reduce heat; very slowly add corn meal in a thin stream, stirring constantly and rapidly as it thickens. Place in top of double boiler over hot water and cook, uncovered, 30 minutes. Spread on a well-greased pan to ½-inch thickness. Chill overnight.

Put sweetbreads in cold water; let stand 1 hour; drain. Cover with boiling water, adding 1 teaspoon salt and 2 tablespoons lemon juice. Simmer 20 minutes, drain, and plunge into cold water. When sweetbreads are cold, remove membranes and tubes; dice. Put flour in a paper bag and shake sweetbread pieces in it. Sprinkle remaining flour over chicken. Melt 3 tablespoons of the butter in a heavy skillet; add chicken and sweetbreads and lightly brown. Heat oven to 400° F. Turn chicken and sweetbreads into a 2-quart baking dish. Add artichoke bottoms. Sprinkle with parsley and celery. Pour creams in the skillet in which meats were browned; cook 5 minutes, stirring constantly. Add sherry; pour cream sauce over meats. Spread with cold corn meal mush and remaining butter. Bake 20 minutes. Makes 4 servings.

Haitian Chicken Turnovers

The island's contribution to Monday's leftover.

¼ pound unsalted butter	½ teaspoon salt
¼ pound mushrooms, thinly sliced	⅛ teaspoon pepper
2 cups diced cooked chicken	2 tablespoons flour
1½ cups heavy cream	2 tablespoons butter
½ cup light cream	2 cups hot cooked spaghettini
1 tablespoon sherry	3 tablespoons grated Parmesan cheese
2 tablespoons dry white wine	½ teaspoon basil

Heat oven to 375° F. Melt ¼ pound unsalted butter in a large, heavy skillet; add mushrooms and sauté 3 minutes. Add chicken, creams, wines, salt, and pepper; heat almost to boiling. Combine flour and the 2 tablespoons butter to make a smooth paste; stir into chicken mixture and continue cooking over low heat, stirring constantly until thickened. Spread spaghettini in bottom of a shallow, greased 1½-quart baking dish. Pour chicken mixture over it. Sprinkle with cheese and basil. Bake 20 minutes or until top is golden brown. Makes 4 servings.

ROAST CHICKEN—TWO

Poultry meals can be made exciting by varying the stuffings.
Even a 4-pound roasting chicken can yield two leftover meals for
the smaller family and here is our version.

MEAL NO. 1

Roast Chicken
with Pilgrim Bread Stuffing

Glazed Sweet Potaotes with Marshmallows
Creamed Onions   Buttered Peas
Bibb Lettuce with White French Dressing
Swiss Chocolate Cake

MEAL NO. 2

Chicken à la Russe

Creamed Corn   Baked Zucchini
Beet Salad
Butterscotch Pie

MEAL NO. 3

Golden Chicken Soufflé

Parslied Potatoes   Peas and Onions
Orange and Grapefruit Salad
Spumoni Ice Cream

Roast Chicken
with Pilgrim Bread Stuffing

4-pound ready-to-cook
  chicken
1 recipe Pilgrim Bread
  Stuffing (*see below*)

2 teaspoons butter, melted
1 teaspoon lemon juice

Stuff the chicken and truss it. Heat oven to 325° F. Place chicken on rack of roasting pan. Brush with a mixture of the butter and lemon juice. Bake 1½ to 2 hours or until done. Makes 4 servings with leftovers.

Pilgrim Bread Stuffing

Use 1 cup of stuffing for each pound of the ready-to-cook weight. The recipe below is for a 4-pound chicken.

⅓ cup butter
¼ cup finely minced onion
4 cups coarse, dry bread
  crumbs or bread cubes
¼ cup chopped celery
¼ cup chopped parsley
1 tablespoon chopped walnut
  meats

1 teaspoon salt
¼ teaspoon pepper
½ teaspoon dried sage
¼ teaspoon thyme
¼ teaspoon marjoram
poultry seasoning to taste
  (½ to 1 teaspoon)
hot chicken broth

Melt butter in a large, heavy skillet. Add onion and cook until yellow, stirring occasionally. Stir in 1 cup of the bread crumbs. Heat, stirring to prevent excessive browning. Turn into a deep bowl. Mix in remaining ingredients lightly. For dry stuffing, add little or no broth. For a moist stuffing, mix in lightly with a fork just enough hot broth to moisten the dry crumbs. Cool; place stuffing loosely in chicken when ready to bake. Makes 1 quart.

Chicken à la Russe

1 tablespoon butter
2 teaspoons flour
½ cup light cream
½ teaspoon salt
⅛ teaspoon pepper
1 cup chopped cooked
  chicken
¼ cup chopped almonds

¼ cup chopped, sautéed
  mushrooms
pancake batter (to make 8
  pancakes)
½ cup commercial sour cream
¼ cup grated Cheddar cheese
2 tablespoons butter

Heat oven to 375° F. Melt butter in a medium skillet; blend in flour. Cook 1 minute. Add cream gradually, stirring constantly, until sauce is smooth and thick. Season with salt and pepper; simmer over low heat 1 minute. Add chicken, almonds, and mushrooms; mix well. Use your favorite pancake batter. Make 8 large, thin pancakes. As each is done, top with a generous tablespoonful of chicken mixture, roll up, and arrange side by side in a greased, shallow 2-quart baking dish. Place 1 teaspoon sour cream on top of each roll. Sprinkle with cheese and dot with butter. Bake 20 minutes. Makes 4 servings.

Golden Chicken Soufflé

3 tablespoons butter
3 tablespoons flour
¼ cup milk
¼ cup light cream
½ cup condensed cream of
  mushroom soup
½ teaspoon salt

⅛ teaspoon pepper
1 cup coarsely chopped
  cooked chicken
1 teaspoon minced parsley
1 teaspoon finely cut chives
dash paprika
3 eggs, separated

Heat oven to 350° F. Melt butter in a medium skillet; stir in flour and cook 1 minute. Gradually add milk and cream, stirring constantly. Add soup; continue stirring until smooth and thick. Season with salt and pepper and simmer 3 to 4 minutes. Add chicken, parsley, chives, paprika, and well-beaten egg yolks, stirring constantly. Cool to lukewarm. Beat egg whites until stiff but not dry; fold in gently. Turn into a greased 1-quart casserole. Bake 35 to 45 minutes or until soufflé is firm. Makes 4 servings.

ROAST CHICKEN—THREE

Two 5-pound roasting chickens can give you four excellent meals, each one "gourmet" enough for company. Serve the roast chickens with Napoleon's Brandy Sauce for a gala occasion. Plan a luncheon for your bridge party and two more meals which no one will guess were made with leftovers.

MEAL NO. 1

Roast Chicken with Pecan Stuffing

*Napoleon's Brandy Sauce
Whipped Parslied Potatoes
Peas and Onions
Cheese   Apples
Irish Coffee

MEAL NO. 2

Japanese Chicken Mousse

Boiled Baby Carrots   Sesame Toast
Petits Fours

MEAL NO. 3

Southern Lady Casserole

Buttered Broccoli
Cranberry Jelly
Mocha Cake

MEAL NO. 4

Poulet en Crème

Hot Cornbread   Buttered Peas
Tossed Green Salad
Raspberry Turnovers

Roast Chicken with Pecan Stuffing

2 5-pound roasting chickens
6 tablespoons butter
3 medium onions, chopped
3 celery stalks, chopped
½ teaspoon basil
½ teaspoon thyme
½ teaspoon sage
1½ teaspoons salt

½ teaspoon paprika
7 cups soft white bread
  crumbs
1½ teaspoons minced parsley
½ cup chopped almonds
1 cup chopped pecans
Napoleon's Brandy Sauce
  (*see below*)

Wipe chickens with a damp cloth. To make the stuffing, melt butter in a large skillet. Add onions and celery and sauté until tender. Add seasonings and stir. Mix bread crumbs, parsley, and nuts in a large bowl. Add onion and celery mixture and blend well. Stuff chickens and truss them. Heat oven to 300° F. Place chickens in an open pan and roast 2 to 2½ hours until tender and brown. Transfer chickens to a serving platter. Reserve pan drippings.

Napoleon's Brandy Sauce

½ cup butter
½ cup flour
4 cups milk, scalded
¾ teaspoon salt

1 cup heavy cream
½ cup brandy
pan drippings from roast
  chicken

Melt butter in a saucepan; add flour and beat with a rotary beater over medium heat for 4 minutes. Add milk and salt. Stir and bring to a boil; reduce heat, simmer 1 minute. Add cream and brandy. Remove fat from roasting pan drippings. Add cream sauce to pan; blend well and heat through. Strain and serve piping hot in a gravy boat.

Japanese Chicken Mousse

A westernized Japanese delicacy for a special occasion.

3 egg yolks, slightly beaten
⅛ teaspoon onion salt
⅛ teaspoon salt
¼ teaspoon celery salt
¼ teaspoon paprika
1 cup hot chicken broth
1 envelope unflavored gelatin
¼ cup cold water

¾ cup minced cooked chicken
¼ cup chopped toasted
   almonds
¼ cup chopped filberts
½ cup seedless white grapes
½ teaspoon grated onion
1 cup heavy cream, whipped
4 tablespoons saké or sherry

Combine egg yolks, salts, and paprika in top of a double boiler. Gradually pour hot broth over mixture; cook over hot water until thickened, stirring constantly. Soften gelatin in water and add to mixture, stirring until dissolved. Remove from heat; add chicken, nuts, grapes, and onion. Cool to lukewarm; fold in whipped cream and wine. Pour into a 4-cup mold. Chill until firm. Unmold on a chilled platter. Serve with mayonnaise. Makes 6 servings.

Southern Lady Casserole

2 cups chicken broth
2 cups cooked rice
¼ cup butter
¼ cup flour
1½ cups milk
½ cup light cream
½ teaspoon salt
⅛ teaspoon pepper
1 tablespoon minced onion
⅛ teaspoon ground ginger
¼ teaspoon nutmeg

pinch mace
3 cups diced cooked chicken
1½ cups sliced mushrooms,
   sautéed slightly
½ cup chopped walnuts
¼ cup blanched almonds,
   toasted, chopped
2 cups fresh bread crumbs,
   buttered
½ teaspoon paprika

Heat oven to 300° F. Pour half the chicken broth over rice and stir well; set aside. Melt butter in a large, heavy skillet; blend in flour and cook 1 minute. Stir in remaining chicken broth, milk, and cream. Stir until smooth; simmer until thickened. Add seasonings, onion and spices. In a greased 2-quart baking dish arrange layers of rice, chicken, cream sauce, mushrooms, and nuts; repeat until all is used. Sprinkle crumbs on top; sprinkle with paprika. Bake 35 minutes or until browned. Makes 6 servings.

Poulet en Crème

So quick to prepare—perfect for busy days.

3 cups cooked chicken, diced	½ cup sherry, warmed
3 cups heavy cream, scalded	½ teaspoon salt
2 egg yolks, well beaten	dash white pepper

Add chicken to scalded cream. Add a little of this to beaten egg yolks, then stir yolks into cream mixture. Bring almost to a boil. Stir in wine; season with salt and pepper. Makes 6 servings.

FRYING CHICKENS

For a truly different planned-over array of meals, buy three frying chickens, 2½ to 3 pounds each. Have the butcher bone the breasts, leaving them whole; separate thighs from drumsticks and use remaining parts (wings, back, and bones) for broth and a light meal.

MEAL NO. 1

Deviled Drumsticks

Home-fried Potatoes   Wax Beans and Onion Rings
Creamy Cabbage Slaw
Pineapple Upside-down Cake

MEAL NO. 2

Chicken Breasts Eugénie

New Potatoes   Fresh Asparagus
Mixed Green Salad
Melon and Prosciutto

MEAL NO. 3

Chicken Almond and Eggs Blanchard

Canadian Bacon   Shoestring Potatoes
Orange and Avocado Salad
Pound Cake

MEAL NO. 4

Chicken Thighs with Walnut Sauce

Buttered Rice   Brussels Sprouts
Lima Bean Salad
Pecan Pie

Deviled Drumsticks

A Continental favorite served hot or cold.

6 chicken drumsticks
1 small carrot, diced
1 small onion, sliced
pinch marjoram
½ teaspoon salt

⅛ teaspoon pepper
½ cup prepared mustard
½ cup butter, melted
dash Tabasco

Cook drumsticks in water with carrot, onion, and marjoram 12
minutes or until just tender. Drain. Score skin lightly. Combine
remaining ingredients. Generously coat drumsticks with mixture.

Refrigerate overnight. Just before serving, broil drumsticks 3 inches from source of heat about 15 minutes, turning frequently and brushing with sauce. Remove to a heated platter. Heat remaining sauce, pour over drumsticks, and serve. Makes 4 servings.

Chicken Breasts Eugénie

Chicken and ham superbly complement one another in this haute cuisine company dish.

3 boned chicken breasts
3 tablespoons butter
4 slices cooked ham, ¼ inch thick
3 tablespoons flour
1 cup heavy cream
1 cup light cream
¾ teaspoon salt

¼ teaspoon white pepper
3 egg yolks
½ cup Madeira
8 large mushroom caps
2 tablespoons butter, melted
4 slices toast
4 sprigs parsley

Heat oven to 350° F. Sauté chicken in butter in a large, heavy skillet until golden. Remove from skillet and keep warm. Fry ham in same butter, turning over once, until browned; remove and keep warm. Stir in flour to make a paste. Slowly add creams, stirring constantly until well blended. Season with salt and pepper. Beat egg yolks and slowly add some of cream mixture; add yolks to cream sauce and stir until well blended. Strain. Clean skillet and return sauce to it. Add chicken and ham; simmer very gently 15 minutes, stirring occasionally. Do not boil. Add Madeira. Sauté mushrooms in melted butter in a small skillet. To serve place 1 slice of toast in each of 4 heatproof individual casseroles. Lay a slice of ham and a portion of chicken breast in each. Place two mushroom caps on top of each. Pour sauce over. Cover and bake 10 minutes or until heated. Serve at once. Garnish with parsley. Makes 4 servings.

Chicken Almond and Eggs Blanchard

I adapted the French Provençale dish by borrowing from a Chinese method of cooking chicken and thus combined East and West.

leftover chicken parts
4 tablespoons butter
½ cup blanched, toasted
  almonds, finely chopped
1 small onion, minced
dash Tabasco
dash Worcestershire sauce

¼ teaspoon chili powder
¼ teaspoon curry powder
½ cup light cream
¼ cup dry white wine
4 eggs, lightly beaten
½ teaspoon salt
⅛ teaspoon pepper

Barely cover chicken parts with lightly salted water and boil until meat falls from bones. Discard skin and bones and shred enough meat to make 1 cup finely chopped chicken. Boil broth down to ¼ cup; set aside. Melt butter in a heavy skillet; add almonds, onion, seasonings and chicken. Brown lightly, stirring frequently. Stir in cream, reserved broth, and wine. Cook until liquid has almost evaporated. Pour in eggs; season with salt and pepper. Stir gently until just set. Serve at once. Makes 4 servings.

Chicken Thighs with Walnut Sauce

6 chicken thighs
½ teaspoon salt
⅛ teaspoon pepper
¼ cup flour
¼ cup butter
1 small onion, finely chopped
⅓ cup dry white wine

1 cup boiling water
2 tablespoons cornstarch
½ cup milk
½ cup light cream
2 egg yolks
½ cup finely ground walnuts
2 tablespoons chopped parsley

Sprinkle chicken thighs with salt and pepper; dredge with flour. Melt butter in a heavy skillet. Add onion and chicken and brown on all sides. Add wine, cover, and simmer 10 minutes. Add boiling water, cover, and cook over low heat 45 minutes. Remove chicken to a pan; keep warm. Combine cornstarch, milk, and cream. Slowly add mixture to stock in skillet, stirring constantly. Beat egg yolks slightly. Add some of hot sauce to egg yolks, pour all into the skillet, stirring over low heat until thickened. Add walnuts and cook 5 minutes longer. Return chicken thighs to sauce; heat through for a few minutes. Makes 4 servings.

STEWING CHICKEN

Even a large stewing chicken can yield some very tempting second and third meals which look and taste as if they had been planned individually as gourmet treats.

MEAL NO. 1

Chicken Salad Romeo

Cream Cheese and Date Nut Bread Sandwiches
Shoestring Potatoes
Créme St. Honoré

MEAL NO. 2

Chicken Pickle Aspic Dryone

Open Face Danish Sandwiches
German Potato Salad
Sliced Peaches in White Wine
Cookies

MEAL NO. 3

Chicken Turnovers Alex

Tomato Soup
Buttered Asparagus   Pickled Beets
Apricot Whip with Madeira

Chicken Salad Romeo

7-pound stewing chicken
3 small onions
2 stalks celery
1 bay leaf
1 teaspoon salt
leftover veal stock or
  chicken bouillon
¼ cup heavy cream, whipped
¼ cup mayonnaise
1½ teaspoons ketchup

½ teaspoon Worcestershire
  sauce
½ teaspoon Tabasco
2 tablespoons lemon juice
¼ teaspoon cognac
1 large orange, peeled,
  sectioned
1 firm banana, sliced
1¼ cups seedless green
  grapes

Simmer chicken, onions, celery, bay leaf, and salt in veal stock or bouillon for 3 hours. Remove chicken. Pull off skin, bone, and return skin and bones to stock. Simmer 2 hours. Cool and refrigerate stock. Reserve for other recipe. Cool chicken meat. Cube half of it into 1½-inch cubes; refrigerate. Reserve remaining meat for other recipe. Combine whipped cream, mayonnaise, ketchup, Worcestershire sauce, Tabasco, lemon juice, and cognac until well blended. Add cold chicken cubes. Fold in remaining ingredients. Serve on lettuce leaves or water cress. Makes 4 servings.

Chicken Pickle Aspic Dryone

Here's a clever and tasty way to use leftover chicken stock.

2 tablespoons unflavored
  gelatin
1 cup cold chicken stock
5 cups hot chicken stock

2 cups chopped sweet pickle
6 strips pimiento
6 strips sweet pickle
6 black olives

Soften gelatin in cold chicken stock; dissolve in boiling stock, stirring well. Chill gelatin until slightly thickened and syrupy. Fold in chopped pickles; turn into a 1-quart mold. Chill overnight. Unmold on a platter and garnish with remaining ingredients. Makes 4 servings.

Chicken Turnovers Alex

An adaptation of the Russian turnovers with saffron as a new ingredient.

1 cup ground cooked chicken
6 slices white bread, crusts removed
1 egg yolk, slightly beaten
1 small clove garlic, minced
2 tablespoons chopped onion
1 tablespoon chopped parsley
1 tablespoon chopped celery
¼ cup chopped stuffed green olives

¼ teaspoon rosemary
⅛ teaspoon ginger
dash powdered saffron
1 tablespoon lemon juice
dash Tabasco
1 teaspoon salt
⅛ teaspoon pepper
1 package instant pie crust mix

Heat oven to 400° F. Chill chicken 10 minutes. Cover bread with water; let stand 1 minute. Squeeze out water. Mash bread and mix with chicken, egg yolk, garlic, onion, parsley, celery, olives, spices, and combined lemon juice and seasonings. Prepare pie crust mix according to directions on package. Roll pastry to ⅛ inch thick. Cut in 2-inch squares for canapés, or 6-inch squares for luncheon turnovers. Divide filling among squares, placing it in center of each. Fold squares into triangles. Brush edges with water, press together, and crimp edges with fork. Brush tops with milk or unbeaten egg white. Bake 8 to 10 minutes for small turnovers, 12 to 15 minutes for larger ones. Makes 18 small or 8 large turnovers.

TURKEY

ROAST TURKEY—ONE

Turkey is no longer reserved for Christmas or Thanksgiving. Plan to serve it often and prove to your family that some of the best meals are inspired by planning leftovers. Plan three gala meals for eight servings each with one turkey.

MEAL NO. 1

Roast Turkey with Sage Stuffing

Sweet Potato Casserole
Creamed Onions   Buttered Carrots
Green Goddess Salad
Pumpkin Pie
Mince Pie

MEAL NO. 2

Turkey à la King Beaujolais

Whipped Potatoes   Peas and Onions
Cranberry and Pineapple Relish
Tomato and Cucumber Salad
Apple Pie à la Mode

MEAL NO. 3

Aztec Turkey Molé

Saffron Rice   Buttered Broccoli
Sliced Tomatoes
Relishes
Fruit Cocktail

Roast Turkey with Sage Stuffing

turkey neck, wing tips, and
  giblets
1 onion
1 stalk celery
1 quart water
2 teaspoons salt
½ teaspoon pepper

10- to 12-pound turkey
2 tablespoons butter, melted
3 tablespoons lemon juice
Sage Stuffing (*see below*)
1 cup dry white wine
1 tablespoon flour

To make stock, wash neck, wing tips, and giblets and place in a large, heavy kettle with onion, celery, water, 1 teaspoon of the salt, and ¼ teaspoon of the pepper. Cover and cook until meat falls from neck bones, about 1½ hours. Strain and reserve stock. Reserve giblets to add to gravy, if desired.

While stock is cooking, wash turkey inside and out and dry well. Rub it with melted butter. Sprinkle with the remaining salt and pepper and the lemon juice. Prepare stuffing. Stuff and truss turkey and tie the legs together. Heat oven to 325° F. Place turkey on a rack in a roasting pan, cover with aluminum foil, and bake 1½ hours. Remove turkey from rack and return to pan. Pour wine over it, cover again, and continue roasting 2 hours. Pour 2 cups of the reserved stock into a saucepan. Combine flour and another ¼ cup stock and add flour mixture to stock in saucepan. Bring to a boil and simmer 5 minutes, stirring constantly.

Skim fat from roasting pan. Pour thickened stock over turkey. Increase oven temperature to 375° F. and continue baking, uncovered, another 30 minutes or until nicely browned. Baste frequently. Remove turkey to a serving platter. Serve the pan gravy in a gravy boat. Makes 8 servings with leftovers.

Sage Stuffing

1 cup butter
½ cup chopped onion
1 cup chopped celery
8 cups small bread cubes,
  toasted

¼ cup chopped parsley
1 teaspoon salt
½ teaspoon pepper
2 teaspoons ground sage
½ cup turkey stock

Melt butter in a heavy skillet. Add onion and celery and sauté until onion is golden. Combine bread cubes, parsley, salt, pepper, and sage in a large mixing bowl. Add sautéed mixture and toss stuffing lightly with two forks to mix well. Add turkey stock and toss again.

Turkey à la King Beaujolais

1 can (6 ounces) sliced mushrooms, drained
½ cup diced green pepper
½ cup margarine
7 tablespoons flour
¾ teaspoon salt
¼ teaspoon celery salt
⅛ teaspoon pepper

⅛ teapoon paprika
2 cups canned chicken broth
1½ cups light cream
½ cup heavy cream
2 cups cooked, cubed turkey
¼ cup chopped pimiento
2 tablespoons Beaujolais wine
8 baked patty shells

Sauté mushrooms and green pepper in margarine for 5 minutes. Remove from heat. Blend in flour, salts, pepper, and paprika. Cook over low heat, stirring constantly, until mixture is bubbly. Remove from heat. Slowly stir in broth and creams. Heat mixture to boiling, stirring constantly; boil 1 minute. Add turkey, pimiento, and wine; heat 4 minutes. Serve hot in patty shells. Makes 8 servngs.

Aztec Turkey Molé

2 green peppers, cut and seeded
2 small onions, peeled
2 cans (1 pound each) tomatoes
1 can (4 ounces) pimiento, drained
¼ cup blanched almonds
¼ cup pecans
¼ cup vegetable oil
1 tablespoon chili powder

1¼ teaspoons salt
¼ teaspoon Tabasco
¼ teaspoon Worcestershire sauce
⅛ teaspoon ground cinnamon
⅛ teaspoon ground cloves
2 chicken bouillon cubes
¼ cup fine dry bread crumbs
1 square (1 ounce) unsweetened chocolate
8 large slices cooked turkey

Heat oven to 350° F. Put peppers, onions, tomatoes, pimiento, almonds, and pecans in electric blender; blend until smooth. Heat oil in a large, heavy skillet. Add blended mixture, seasonings, and bouillon cubes. Bring to a boil. Reduce heat, cover, and simmer 30 minutes. Stir in bread crumbs and chocolate. Heat, stirring occasionally, until chocolate is melted. Make alternate layers of turkey slices and mixture in a 2½-quart casserole. Bake 20 minutes. Makes 8 servings.

ROAST TURKEY—TWO

In the Near East, turkey is stuffed with ground meat to make an unusually flavored stuffing. A 10-pound turkey or even a slightly smaller one will yield three delicious meals.

MEAL NO. 1

Oriental Stuffed Turkey

Pan-browned Potatoes   Stewed Celery
Glazed Carrots
Cranberry Sauce   Romaine Salad
Cherry Cobbler with Hard Sauce

MEAL NO. 2

Turkey Roll-Ups

Buttered Peas   Lima Beans and Bacon
Pineapple Salad
Stewed Pears with Marmalade

MEAL NO. 3

Turkey Bisque Madeleine

French-toasted Ham and Cheese Sandwiches
Raw Spinach Salad
Orange Relish
Applesauce Cake

Oriental Stuffed Turkey

The dining room of the Imperial Hotel in Yokohama served this superb meat-stuffed turkey when I was there recently.

turkey neck, wing tips, and giblets	9- to 10-pound turkey
1 onion	2 tablespoons butter, melted
1 stalk celery	2 tablespoons lemon juice
1 quart water	Oriental Ground Meat Stuffing (*see below*)
1¾ teaspoons salt	1 cup dry white wine
⅜ teaspoon pepper	1 tablespoon flour

Followed method of preparation of Roast Turkey with Sage Stuffing (page 107).

Oriental Ground Meat Stuffing

2 tablespoons butter	¾ pound chestnuts, roasted and chopped
1 small onion, grated	1 cup dry toasted crumbs
1 pound lean ground beef	3 tablespoons currants
½ cup dry white wine	2 tablespoons chopped parsley
1 tablespoon tomato sauce	½ teaspoon sage
1 teaspoon salt	¼ teaspoon basil
¼ teaspoon pepper	¼ teaspoon oregano
¼ cup pignolia nuts	

Melt butter in a heavy skillet; add onion and meat and sauté until lightly browned. Add wine, tomato sauce, salt, and pepper. Cover and simmer 15 minutes. Skim off any fat. Add remaining ingredients and mix well. Cool thoroughly before stuffing turkey.

Turkey Roll-Ups

A casserole with contrasting flavors, easily put together.

2 tablespoons chopped onion
½ cup butter or margarine
2½ cups cooked potatoes,
  diced
1½ cups cooked, drained
  spinach
dash of white pepper

12 large thin slices cooked
  turkey
½ cup slivered toasted
  almonds
2 teaspoons steak sauce
1 teaspoon Worcestershire
  sauce

Heat oven to 350° F. Sauté onion in 2 tablespoons of the butter until transparent. Remove from heat and add potatoes, spinach, and pepper. Toss together lightly. Spoon some of the mixture in the center of each turkey slice; fold ends over and secure with wooden pick. Place roll-ups in a 1½-quart casserole. Melt the remaining butter, stir in the almonds, steak sauce, and Worcestershire sauce. Pour over the roll-ups. Bake 25 minutes or until lightly browned. Makes 6 servings.

Turkey Bisque Madeleine

3 tablespoons butter or
  margarine
3 tablespoons flour
2½ cups turkey broth or
  canned chicken broth
½ cup sauterne
1 cup cooked ground turkey
1 cup light cream

1 tablespoon sherry
dash of nutmeg
dash of mace
½ teaspoon salt
⅛ teaspoon pepper
⅛ teaspoon paprika
1 tablespoon chopped parsley
1 teaspoon chopped chives

Melt butter in a skillet; stir in flour. Add broth, sauterne, and turkey; cook, stirring constantly, until mixture boils and thickens. Simmer 5 minutes. Add cream, sherry, nutmeg, mace, salt, pepper, and paprika. Heat until piping hot. Pour into heated soup bowls or cups; garnish each serving with a sprinkling of parsley and chives. Makes 4½ cups or 6 to 8 servings.

ROAST TURKEY—THREE

A 9- to 10-pound turkey can yield many interesting meals which need not just be heated up or eaten cold as leftovers. Use the cooked meat as an ingredient in a delicious main dish and it will take on new importance.

MEAL NO. 1

Pilgrim's Roast Turkey with Chestnut Stuffing

Whipped Parslied Potatoes
Green Peas and White Onions
Cranberry Sauce
Celery, Walnut, and Pimiento Salad
Orange Sherbet

MEAL NO. 2

Steamboat Turkey Balls

Fluffy Saffron Rice
Glazed Carrots   Waldorf Salad
Chocolate Eclairs

MEAL NO. 3

The Captain's Turkey Chowder

Cheese Soufflé
Tossed green Salad
Buttered French Bread Chunks
Coconut Cream Pie

MEAL NO. 4

Turkey Tetrazzini

Buttered Broccoli Spears
Spiced Apple Wedges
Chocolate Brownie à la Mode

Pilgrim's Roast Turkey with Chestnut Stuffing

9½-pound turkey
½ cup chopped onions
¼ cup chopped green onions
2 tablespoons butter
½ pound sausage meat
turkey liver, coarsely chopped
2¼ cups dry bread crumbs
¼ teaspoon thyme
¼ teaspoon marjoram
3 tablespoons finely chopped
  parsley

1 teaspoon finely chopped
  celery
2 teaspoons salt
¼ teaspoon pepper
¼ teaspoon paprika
1 teaspoon lemon juice
20 cooked chestnuts, peeled
¼ cup heavy cream
3 tablespoons margarine,
  softened

Wash turkey thoroughly and dry well inside and out. To make the stuffing, sauté onions in butter until lightly browned. Stir in sausage meat and turkey liver; cook 5 minutes. Stir in bread crumbs, thyme, marjoram, parsley, celery, seasonings, and lemon juice; mix lightly. Purée chestnuts in a sieve; add to mixture. Moisten with heavy cream. Heat oven to 350° F. Stuff turkey. Rub turkey with softened margarine; set on rack in roasting pan. Roast 4 to 4½ hours, basting frequently with pan drippings. When turkey is done, let stand 15 minutes before carving. Make gravy with drippings. Makes 6 servings with turkey left over.

Steamboat Turkey Balls

The old riverboat menus featured this dish quite often.

½ cup white wine
½ cup water
¼ teaspoon salt
12 oysters
1 cup finely chopped cooked turkey
1 tablespoon finely chopped green onions
2 tablespoons butter
4 egg yolks

1 teaspoon lemon juice
¼ cup heavy cream
¼ teaspoon salt
¼ teaspoon onion salt
½ teaspoon Tabasco
1 tablespoon finely chopped celery
½ cup dry bread crumbs
½ cup ground pecans
shortening for frying

Combine wine, water, and salt in a medium saucepan. Bring to a boil, then reduce heat to simmering. Add oysters and simmer for 2 minutes. Remove oysters; chop finely. Combine with turkey. Sauté green onions in butter until transparent; add to turkey mixture. Add 2 of the egg yolks, lemon juice, 2 tablespoons of the heavy cream, salts, Tabasco, and celery; mix well. Shape into ¾-inch balls; chill 1 hour. Combine remaining egg yolks with remaining cream. Combine bread crumbs with pecans. Dip balls in egg-yolk mixture; roll in crumbs and pecan mixture; chill 1 hour. Fry a few balls at a time in deep fat, at 375° F. Cook until delicately browned on all sides; drain on absorbent paper. Makes 6 servings.

The Captain's Turkey Chowder

A flavorful soup ideally suited for a midnight snack, served with chunks of French bread.

1 medium onion, chopped
¼ cup finely chopped celery
6 mushrooms, chopped
2 tablespoons butter
4 cups boiling water
¼ cup rice
1½ teaspoons salt

½ teaspoon pepper
turkey carcass, cut in pieces
2 cups milk
1 cup light cream
2 tablespoons finely chopped parsley

Sauté onion, celery, and mushrooms in butter 5 minutes or until onion is golden, in a large, heavy saucepan. Add boiling water, rice, seasonings, and turkey carcass. Cover saucepan. Heat to boiling; simmer 30 minutes or until rice is tender. Remove bones. Scrape off meat and return to soup. Add milk and cream; heat thoroughly but do not boil. Serve with a sprinkling of parsley. Makes 6 servings.

Turkey Tetrazzini

Another version of the ever-popular Italian dish.

½ cup turkey or chicken broth

1 can (10½ ounces) condensed cream of mushroom soup

1 tablespoon steak sauce

½ teaspoon Worcestershire sauce

1 cup shredded Cheddar cheese

1 can (2 ounces) mushroom stems and pieces, drained

¾ package (8 ounces) spaghetti, cooked according to package directions

2 cups diced cooked turkey

2 tablespoons slivered almonds

2 tablespoons chopped pecans

¼ cup grated Romano cheese

Heat oven to 350° F. Blend broth, mushroom soup, steak sauce and Worcestershire sauce; stir in remaining ingredients except Romano cheese. Pour into a 1½-quart baking dish; sprinkle with cheese. Bake 30 minutes. Makes 4 servings.

DUCK

ROAST DUCK

If your hunter comes home with ducks, try these different menus which will add a piquancy to each dish and make your husband happy that he brought his prizes home.

MEAL NO. 1

Duck Casserole Chasseur

Green Goddess Salad
French Bread with Garlic Butter
Lemon Chiffon Pie

MEAL NO. 2

Germain's Duck Soup

Grilled Ham and Swiss Cheese Sandwiches
Marinated Vegetable Salad
Fresh Fruit Wedges

MEAL NO. 3

Duck Del Sol

Creamed Spinach
Saffron Rice   Jellied Salad
Mint Parfait

Duck Casserole Chasseur

2 medium ducks, skinned and
   cut up
1 teaspoon salt
½ teaspoon pepper
⅛ teaspoon thyme
⅛ teaspoon sage
4 teaspoons ground ginger
4 tablespoons butter
2 green onions, chopped
1 pound fresh mushrooms

1½ cups rice
1 package (10 ounces)
   frozen peas
1½ cups claret wine
1½ cups chicken broth
1 teaspoon chervil
½ teaspoon marjoram
½ teaspoon rosemary
2 medium tomatoes, chopped
1 teaspoon onion salt

Heat oven to 325° F. Rub duck pieces with mixture of salt, pepper, thyme, sage, and ginger; brown in the butter in a heavy skillet over high heat. Remove duck to a heavy 5-quart casserole. Pour off excess fat and in the same skillet sauté onions and mushrooms 5 minutes. Add to duck pieces. Bake 1 hour. Remove duck to a heated platter. Pour off all accumulated fat from casserole. Place rice in bottom of casserole. Add duck, peas, wine, broth, seasonings, tomatoes, and onion salt. Cover. Increase oven heat to 350° F. and bake 45 minutes. Makes 6 servings.

Germain's Duck Soup

carcasses of ducks, cut in
   pieces
7 cups water
3 stalks celery, cut up
1 carrot, sliced

1 small turnip, sliced
1 teaspoon minced parsley
¾ teaspoon salt
¼ teaspoon pepper
2 cups cooked rice

Put duck carcasses in a large kettle with water, celery, carrot, turnip, and parsley. Heat to boiling; reduce heat and skim top. Cover and simmer 2 hours. Strain. Skim off excess fat. Add any bits of duck meat from bones. Season with salt and pepper, stir in rice, and reheat. Makes 8 servings.

Duck Del Sol

2 tablespoons sherry
1 cup ground cooked duck
  meat
¾ cup milk
1 cup soft bread crumbs
1 teaspoon minced shallot

1 teaspoon minced parsley
1 teaspoon minced celery
½ teaspoon salt
⅛ teaspoon pepper
½ teaspoon nutmeg
3 egg whites, stiffly beaten

Pour wine over meat and let stand. Heat oven to 375° F. Pour milk over bread crumbs in a medium saucepan; cook over low heat 5 minutes. Combine crumb mixture with duck meat, shallot, parsley, celery, and seasonings. Gently fold in egg whites. Turn into a well-buttered, 4-cup ring mold. Set in a pan of hot water. Bake 30 minutes or until top is firm to the touch. Let stand 1 minute. Unmold on a heated platter. Makes 6 servings.

GOOSE

ROAST GOOSE

Buy a 10- to 12-pound goose and plan to have two meals. Plan on
¾ pound per person to be served for the main meal.

MEAL NO. 1

Roast Goose Provençale

*Wild Rice Limores
Orange-Cranberry Relish
Gingered Carrots
Avocado and Pecan Salad
Top Plum Pudding

MEAL NO. 2

Taj Mahal Salad

French Fried Potatoes   Hot Garlic Rolls
Baba au Rhum

Roast Goose Provençale

The traditional paysanne goose served during the holidays.

10- to 12-pound goose
6 tablespoons butter
3 medium onions, chopped
3 celery stalks, chopped
½ teaspoon thyme
½ teaspoon sage
¼ teaspoon basil

¼ teaspoon oregano
2 teaspoons salt
7 cups soft white bread
  crumbs
1½ tablespoons minced parsley
2 medium apples, pared,
  cored, finely chopped

Wipe goose with a damp cloth; remove large layers of fat inside goose. Heat oven to 300° F. To make the stuffing, melt butter in a large, heavy skillet. Add onions and celery; sauté 5 minutes or until tender but not browned. Stir in seasonings. Combine bread crumbs, parsley, and apples. Pour seasoned mixture over crumb mixture and blend well. Stuff goose and truss it. Place on rack, breast down, in a roasting pan and bake 30 minutes to the pound. Add 1 cup water while it roasts. Remove fat from roasting pan and make gravy from pan drippings. Add chopped cooked giblets to gravy, if desired. Makes 6 servings.

Wild Rice Limores

heart, neck, gizzard, and liver
  of goose
1 onion, chopped
2 stalks celery, sliced
1 teaspoon salt

1 bay leaf
1 quart water
2 cups wild rice
1 teaspoon onion salt

Simmer together heart, neck, gizzard (add liver last 15 minutes of cooking), onion, celery, salt, and bay leaf in water for 2½ hours. Strain broth; discard bones and vegetables. Chop giblets and set aside for gravy. Wash rice until water is almost clear. Soak in cold water 1 hour. Drain. Measure 4 cups giblet broth in a medium saucepan; add wild rice and onion salt. Bring to boil. Cover; reduce heat and cook 30 minutes or until tender. Makes 6 servings.

Taj Mahal Salad

2 cups diced cooked goose
1 tablespoon tarragon vinegar
½ teaspoon minced onion
½ teaspoon dry mustard
¼ cup mayonnaise
¾ cup commercial sour cream
¼ cup chutney, coarsely
  chopped
½ teaspoon salt

⅛ teaspoon pepper
dash paprika
dash nutmeg
1 medium avocado, pared,
  diced
1 large orange, peeled, sliced,
  cut into bite-sized pieces
crisp lettuce leaves
6 lime slices

Remove all fat from goose meat. Blend vinegar, onion, and mustard into a smooth paste. Blend with mayonnaise, sour cream, and chutney. Add seasonings; let stand 1 hour. Add dressing to mixture of goose meat, avocado, and orange, tossing lightly. Chill 1 hour. Serve on crisp lettuce leaves. Garnish with lime slices. Makes 6 servings.

FISH

RED SNAPPER

A whole red snapper may tempt you to plan some fish meals as a change of pace. The unusual Delphi Mold may be served as a first course at a formal dinner.

MEAL NO. 1

Baked Fish au Vin

Twice-baked Potatoes
Sliced Eggs on Romaine
Nesselrode Pie

MEAL NO. 2

Delphi Mold

Beef Fillett Niçoise
Buttered Zucchini Circles
Grapefruit and Avocado Salad
Boston Cream Pie

MEAL NO. 3

Eastern Fish Chowder

Egg and Minced Ham Sandwiches
Salad with Creamy Italian Dressing
Apple Cupcakes

Baked Fish au Vin

6 tablespoons olive oil
6- to 7-pound red snapper
½ cup dry white wine
juice of 1 lemon
1½ teaspoons salt
¼ teaspoon pepper

½ pound fresh spinach
12 to 14 green onions,
  chopped
1 large onion, chopped
2 cups canned tomatoes
¼ cup dark currants

Heat oven to 350° F. Pour 1 tablespoon of the olive oil in bottom of a shallow baking dish large enough to accommodate fish. Arrange fish in pan. Pour wine over it. Sprinkle with lemon juice and season with salt and pepper. Bake 15 minutes. Wilt spinach in boiling water; drain. In a heavy skillet heat remaining olive oil; add green onions and onion; sauté until lightly browned. Add spinach; cook 3 minutes. Add tomatoes and currants; cook 12 minutes. Remove fish from oven; spread vegetables over it. Return to oven; bake 45 minutes longer. If sauce becomes watery, thicken with flour paste, cook 10 minutes more. Remove fish carefully onto a heated platter. Makes 6 servings.

Delphi Mold

An elegant cold party dish, ideal for buffet serving.

⅔ cup cream cheese, mashed
½ cup grated American
  Cheddar cheese, mashed
1 cup crumbled Roquefort
  cheese, mashed
2 tablespoons unflavored
  gelatin
juice of 1 lemon, strained
½ cup boiling water
½ teaspoon salt

2 cups heavy cream, whipped
½ cup minced chives
2 cups leftover cooked fish
1 cup celery, cut into 1-inch
  pieces
½ cup mayonnaise
¼ cup heavy cream
2 tablespoons chopped parsley
lettuce or water cress

Combine cheeses; set aside. Soak gelatin in lemon juice; dissolve in boiling water. Stir cheeses into gelatin. Add salt. Fold in whipped cream and chives. Turn into a 2-quart ring mold; chill overnight.

Combine remaining ingredients. Unmold cheese ring on a platter garnished with crisp lettuce leaves or water cress; fill center with fish mixture. Makes 6 servings.

Eastern Fish Chowder

2 cups cooked fish, coarsely flaked
5 strips crisp bacon, chopped
1 onion, chopped
2 cups potatoes, pared, diced
1 cup water
1 can (10½ ounces) condensed cream of celery soup

1 can (10½ ounces) condensed New England-style clam chowder
2 cups milk
1 cup light cream
1 teaspoon salt
¼ teaspoon pepper
3 tablespoons minced parsley

Keep fish refrigerated until needed. In bacon fat, cook the onion until tender but not browned. Add potatoes; fry 4 minutes. Add water, soups, milk, and cream; stir until well blended. Season with salt and pepper. Gently stir in fish and bacon bits. Stir in ½ the parsley. Heat until piping hot. Pour into a large soup tureen; sprinkle with remaining parsley and serve hot. Makes 6 servings.

FILLET OF SOLE

Frozen or fresh fish can be served in many tempting ways. Try these fillet of sole specialties next time you want something different.

MEAL NO. 1

Fillet of Sole à la Française

Fluffy Rice
Creamed Spinach
Cucumber and Chicory Salad
Strawberry Pie

MEAL NO. 2

Broiled Fish à la Grecque

*Lemon Sauce
Artichokes   Baby Carrots
Endive and Water Cress Salad
Cream Puffs

MEAL NO. 3

Fish Pie Devonshire

Buttered Lima Beans
Green Beans with Mushrooms
Orange Gelatin Salad
Cupcakes

Fillet of Sole à la Française

2 teaspoons butter
2 pounds fillet of sole
½ cup bottled clam juice
1 cup dry white wine
1 cup canned tomatoes,
    drained, mashed
4 tablespoons minced parsley
1 tablespoon minced celery

4 tablespoons minced shallots
2 tablespoons minced green
    onion tops
½ teaspoon thyme
¼ teaspoon rosemary
¼ teaspoon basil
6 tablespoons butter

Melt the 2 teaspoons butter in a large, heavy skillet. Roll each fillet into a ball and secure with wooden picks. Place fillets in skillet; pour in clam juice and wine. Simmer 2 minutes. Add tomatoes, parsley, celery, shallots, green onion tops, thyme, rosemary, and basil. Simmer 10 minutes longer. Remove fish to a heated serving platter. Remove wooden picks. Boil sauce in skillet 3 or 4 minutes. Stir in the 6 tablespoons butter and blend well. Pour over fish and serve. Makes 4 servings.

Broiled Fish à la Grecque

The Grecian way of serving fish with a lemon sauce.

4 pounds fillet of sole
1½ teaspoons salt
¼ teaspoon pepper

1 cup Lemon Sauce (*see below*), heated

Sprinkle fish with salt and pepper. Place on aluminum foil on broiler rack. Brush with hot Lemon Sauce. Broil 5 minutes on each side or until thoroughly cooked, basting fish frequently with Lemon Sauce. Place on a heated platter; pour balance of sauce over fish. Makes 8 servings.

Lemon Sauce

½ cup olive oil
½ cup lemon juice
1 teaspoon oregano

pinch of sage
½ teaspoon salt

Combine all ingredients in a covered jar; shake well. Makes 1 cup.

Fish Pie Devonshire

The English are famous for their pastries and pies; this fish pie is a sophisticated favorite of the Soho.

2½ tablespoons butter
2 medium onions, sliced
2 cups cooked fish
2 hard-cooked eggs, sliced
2 small tomatoes, peeled, sliced
1 teaspoon salt

¼ teaspoon pepper
1 egg, well beaten
2 cups mashed potatoes
1 tablespoon chopped parsley
2 tablespoons chopped almonds

Heat oven to 400° F. Heat 1 tablespoon of the butter in a skillet; add onions and sauté until lightly browned. Stir in fish; mix gently. Melt another ½ tablespoon butter in a 1-quart baking dish. Lay in slices of egg and tomato and top with fish mixture, repeating until all these ingredients are used. Season to taste. Mix ¾ the beaten egg with the mashed potatoes, parsley, and almonds. Spread over top of baking dish. Dot with remaining butter and brush with remaining egg. Bake 25 minutes or until top is well browned. Makes 4 servings.

HADDOCK

Sometimes fresh fish looks so tempting that you cannot resist buying more than you need for one meal. Here we show you how to use haddock in three deliciously different meals.

MEAL NO. 1

Fish of the Islands

Spinach Soufflé   Baked Potatoes
Caesar Salad
Banana Cream Pie

MEAL NO. 2

Harry's Haddock Hash

Broiled Tomatoes   Buttered Chick Peas
Romaine Salad
Marble Cake

MEAL NO. 3

New Way Fish Roll

Succotash   Creamed Peas
Cucumber Salad
Ice Cream Pie

Fish of the Islands

2 pounds boned, skinned
  haddock
1 teaspoon salt
1 cup lime juice
2 tablespoons grated fresh
  coconut

1 cup prepared French
  dressing
2 hard-cooked eggs, sliced
1 tablespoon chopped parsley

Cut fish into 1-inch squares. Place fish squares in a shallow heat-proof dish and sprinkle with salt and lime juice. Let stand 4 hours. Add coconut to French dressing. Drain fish and discard lime juice. Pour French dressing over fish. Simmer 10 minutes. Serve with garnish of egg slices and parsley. Makes 4 servings.

Harry's Haddock Hash

Harry was a San Francisco character who enjoyed cooking. The story goes that he improvised this fish hash because he never ate meat.

1 cup coarsely flaked cooked
  haddock
1 cup chopped boiled potatoes
1 teaspoon chopped parsley
1 teaspoon chopped green
  pepper

½ teaspoon salt
⅛ teaspoon pepper
dash cayenne
dash Tabasco
pinch nutmeg
1 tablespoon butter

Mix fish and potatoes lightly; add parsley, green pepper, and seasonings. Heat butter in a medium skillet. Add fish mixture; brown lightly over medium heat, stirring with a fork. Pat mixture lightly and continue cooking until well browned on bottom. Fold over and slide onto a heated platter. Makes 4 servings.

New Way Fish Roll

2 tablespoons butter
2 tablespoons chopped onion
2 tablespoons flour
¾ cup light cream
1 tablespoon minced parsley
1 tablespoon minced celery
¼ cup diced celery

1 cup cooked haddock
¾ teaspoon salt
⅛ teaspoon pepper
⅛ teaspoon paprika
1 recipe Herb Biscuits, page 143

Heat oven to 425° F. Melt butter in a skillet; add onion and sauté until slightly browned. Stir in flour and cook 1 minute. Gradually add cream, stirring constantly until thickened and smooth. Remove from heat. Add parsley, celery, haddock, and seasonings. Roll out biscuit dough on a floured surface into a rectangle ½ inch thick. Spread fish mixture over dough. Roll up like a jelly roll. With greased, sharp knife cut roll into 1-inch slices. Place on a greased cookie sheet. Bake 12 to 15 minutes or until well browned. Makes 4 servings.

FISH FILLETS

If you bought more fish than you planned to use, don't despair. Cook it all in a rich curry, serve as much as needed and plan to use the balance in other meals.

MEAL NO. 1

Fish Curry Hawaiian

Fluffy Rice   Creamed Spinach
Cabbage-Carrot Slaw
Spiced Bananas and Grapes
Cookies

MEAL NO. 2

Kedgeree

Brussels Sprouts
Apple, Banana, and Date Salad
Plantation Cake

MEAL NO. 3

Fish Coladone

French Fried Potatoes
Buttered Broccoli
Wilted Greens Salad
Chocolate Cake

Fish Curry Hawaiian

½ cup vegetable oil
4 medium onions, chopped
2 tablespoons curry powder
1 teaspoon paprika
1 teaspoon pepper

1½ teaspoons salt
1 cup tomato sauce
4 cups hot water
3 pounds fish fillets

Heat oil in a large, heavy saucepan; add onions, curry powder, paprika, pepper, and salt and brown lightly. Add tomato sauce. Cook over moderate heat, stirring constantly, 15 minutes or until almost dry. Stir in hot water. Simmer 20 minutes. Add fish and simmer 15 minutes or until tender. Serve at once. Makes 6 servings.

Kedgeree

The English colonials in nineteenth-century India had about a dozen ways of serving this delicious dish. Here is one of my favorites.

1 tablespoon butter
2 tablespoons minced onion
1 cup cooked rice
1 tablespoon minced parsley
1 teaspoon minced green
  pepper

1 teaspoon curry powder
½ teaspoon Worcestershire
  sauce
1 cup cooked fish curry fillet,
  flaked
2 tablespoons sherry

Melt butter in a medium skillet; add onion and sauté until tender. Stir in rice, parsley, green pepper, curry powder, and Worcestershire sauce. Blend well and cook 2 minutes. Remove from heat. Let stand 15 minutes. Heat oven to 400° F. Turn fish into a greased 1-quart baking dish. Pour sherry over it. Top with rice mixture. Bake 20 minutes or until bubbly hot. Makes 4 servings.

Fish Coladone

6 hard-cooked eggs
¼ cup leftover fish curry fillets
1 teaspoon prepared mustard
dash cayenne
¼ teaspoon curry powder
mayonnaise
2 tablespoons butter
2 tablespoons flour

½ cup light cream
½ cup milk
½ teaspoon salt
⅛ teaspoon pepper
¼ cup grated sharp Cheddar
  cheese
1 egg yolk, lightly beaten

Heat oven to 375° F. Slit eggs lengthwise; remove yolks to a mixing bowl and mash thoroughly. Add fish, prepared mustard, cayenne, and curry powder and mix well. Add enough mayonnaise to hold mixture together. Stuff egg whites with mixture. Place in a greased, shallow baking dish. Melt butter in a saucepan; stir in flour until smooth. Stir in cream and milk. Season with salt and pepper. Cook, stirring constantly, until thickened. Stir in cheese and egg yolk. Pour over stuffed eggs. Bake 15 minutes or until lightly browned. Makes 4 servings.

THE LEFTOVERS

BEEF

Beef Hong Kong

The original recipe called for beef tenderloin cubes, but the ingredients are so varied that cooked beef is a good substitute.

2 tablespoons butter
3 cups cooked roast beef, cut in 1-inch cubes
1 medium onion, sliced thin
½ teaspoon curry powder
¼ teaspoon ground ginger
⅛ teaspoon ground mace
½ teaspoon sugar
1½ teaspoons Worcestershire sauce
½ teaspoon lemon juice

½ teaspoon salt
¼ teaspoon pepper
¼ teaspoon paprika
½ cup consommé
½ cup red wine
1 cup sour cream
1 tablespoon prepared horseradish
1 teaspoon minced parsley
3 cups hot fluffy cooked rice

Heat oven to 300° F. Heat butter in a skillet to sizzling point; add beef and brown lightly. Transfer beef cubes to a 1½-quart casserole and arrange onion slices on top. Add to remaining butter in the skillet the curry powder, ginger, mace, sugar, Worcestershire sauce, lemon juice, salt, pepper, paprika, consommé, and red wine. Blend well; pour mixture into the casserole. Cover and heat in oven 30 to 35 minutes. Just before serving stir in sour cream and horse-radish. Sprinkle with parsley. Serve at once over rice. Makes 6 servings.

Avonshire Beef and Kidney Pie

1 beef kidney
2¾ cups hot water
½ cup diced celery
¼ cup chopped parsley
1½ teaspoons salt
¼ teaspoon pepper
½ cup cold water

2 tablespoons flour
2¼ cups cubed cooked roast beef
1 cup cooked whole onions
1 cup sliced cooked carrots
Bacon Pastry (*see below*)

Remove any outer membrane from the kidney; cut it in half with scissors and remove all fat and white veins. Cut kidney into ¼-inch slices, then into cubes. Cover with cold water; squeeze out blood. Drain and cover again with cold water; soak 2 hours. Drain well. Place cubed kidney in a medium saucepan. Add hot water; simmer 1½ hours. Add celery, parsley, salt, and pepper; simmer 30 minutes longer. Heat oven to 425° F. Blend cold water and flour. Stir into kidney mixture; cook over moderate heat until thickened. Add beef, onions, and carrots. Pour mixture into a 1½-quart casserole. Top with Bacon Pastry. Turn edges under to form a rim. Flute the edge. Bake 30 minutes or until pastry is browned. Makes 6 servings.

Bacon Pastry

1 cup flour
4½ tablespoons bacon drippings (at room temperature)

½ teaspoon salt
2 tablespoons cold water

Combine flour and salt in a bowl. Make a well in center of flour mixture. Pour in bacon drippings and water; stir vigorously with a fork until all flour particles are moistened and mixture forms a ball away from sides of bowl. Cover a pastry board with waxed paper. Flatten ball of dough on paper; cover with second piece of waxed paper. Roll to ⅛-inch thickness. Use as directed above.

Beef Salad Vinaigrette

4 cups cooked roast beef, cut
   in julienne strips
1 cup onion rings
2 tablespoons chopped parsley
1 tablespoon chopped celery
2 teaspoons chopped tarragon
2 teaspoons chopped chervil
2 teaspoons chopped chives

2 tablespoons capers
¼ cup vinegar
½ cup olive oil
¼ teaspoon dry mustard
dash Tabasco
dash Worcestershire sauce
romaine lettuce leaves

Combine all ingredients, except lettuce leaves, and blend well. Let
mixture stand in the refrigerator 3½ hours before serving, stirring
occasionally. Serve on lettuce leaves. Makes 6 servings.

Tijuana Tamale Pie

When I lived in Southern California I used to visit Mexico almost
every weekend. This dish was served to me quite often and was
easily adapted to leftover beef.

4 cups boiling water
1 cup white cornmeal
1½ teaspoons salt
¼ teaspoon pepper
¼ teaspoon paprika
¼ teaspoon Tabasco
¼ teaspoon Worcestershire
   sauce
½ cup chopped ripe olives
2 tablespoons butter

1 medium onion, minced
1 clove garlic, minced
1 tablespoon minced celery
2 cups finely chopped roast
   beef
1½ cups canned tomatoes
1 tablespoon chili powder
dash nutmeg
½ cup fine bread crumbs

Pour boiling water into top part of a double boiler; slowly stir in
cornmeal, keeping water boiling over direct medium heat. Add half
the salt, the pepper, paprika, Tabasco, Worcestershire sauce, and
olives. Heat oven to 375° F. Heat half the butter in a medium
skillet. Add onion, garlic, and celery, and lightly brown. Stir in meat
and cook 4 minutes. Add remaining salt, tomatoes, chili powder,
and nutmeg; mix well. Remove from heat. Grease a 2-quart casse-

role. Spread a thin layer of cornmeal mush on the bottom; add a layer of meat mixture, and continue alternating layers until ingredients are used, ending with cornmeal mush. Melt remaining butter, mix with crumbs and spread on top. Bake 25 to 30 minutes or until well browned. Makes 6 servings.

Elegant Baked Hash

¼ cup finely chopped onions
¼ teaspoon marjoram
¼ teaspoon thyme
¼ teaspoon savory
¼ teaspoon oregano
2 tablespoons chopped parsley
1 tablespoon minced celery
¼ cup butter

4 cups cubed cooked roast beef
4 cups diced boiled potatoes
2 tablespoons soy sauce
½ cup red wine
½ cup heavy cream
¼ teaspoon paprika

Heat oven to 350° F. Sauté onions, marjoram, thyme, savory, oregano, parsley, and celery in butter until vegetables are tender, about 5 minutes. Add beef and potatoes and stir. Combine soy sauce, wine, and cream; blend into meat mixture. Pour into a greased 1½-quart baking pan. Sprinkle with paprika. Bake 30 minutes. Makes 6 servings.

Strathmoor Yorkshire Squares

1 cup flour
⅓ teaspoon salt
1 cup milk
2 eggs
pinch nutmeg
dash cayenne
dash mace
dash paprika
3½ cups finely chopped roast beef

1½ tablespoons grated onion
1 teaspoon minced parsley
1 teaspoon minced celery
1 teaspoon finely cut chives
½ clove garlic, minced
½ teaspoon salt
½ teaspoon onion salt
⅛ teaspoon pepper
pinch ground cloves
Mushroom Sauce (see below)

Heat oven to 425° F. To make the batter, combine flour with the ⅓ teaspoon salt; gradually blend in milk until smooth. Add eggs, one at a time, beating vigorously after each addition. Add nutmeg, cayenne, mace, and paprika; beat 3 minutes. Set aside. Combine beef, onion, parsley, celery, chives, garlic, salt, onion salt, pepper, and cloves and mix well. Grease a 9-inch square pan or shallow casserole; heat it in the oven to piping hot. Pour in half the batter. Quickly and evenly spread meat mixture over batter. Gently pour remaining batter over meat. Bake about 20 minutes or until topping has risen and begins to be firm to the touch. Reduce heat to 350° F. and bake 20 minutes longer. Cut in squares; serve at once with Mushroom Sauce. Makes 6 servings.

Mushroom Sauce

1 can (2 ounces) sliced mushrooms, with liquid
1 tablespoon minced onion
1 tablespoon butter

1 can (10½ ounces) cream of mushroom soup
4 drops Worcestershire sauce

Drain mushrooms; reserve liquid. In a medium skillet sauté mushrooms and onion in butter until light brown. Add mushroom soup, mushroom liquid, and Worcestershire sauce. Cook over medium heat, stirring occasionally, until hot. Makes 2 cups.

Mexican Beef and Rice

¼ cup finely chopped onion
¼ cup chopped green pepper
1 small clove garlic, minced
2 tablespoons butter
3 cups cooked rice
2 cups cut-up cooked roast beef

2 cups cooked tomatoes
1½ teaspoons salt
⅛ teaspoon pepper
⅛ teaspoon oregano

In a 10-inch skillet sauté onion, pepper, and garlic in butter until onion is yellow. Add remaining ingredients and cook, uncovered, over low heat about 12 minutes, or until hot. Makes 4 servings.

Beef Casserole Patras Style

1 large onion, chopped
2 tablespoons olive oil
1 clove garlic, minced
2 cups ground roast beef
½ teaspoon salt
¼ teaspoon pepper
2 tablespoons minced parsley
1 teaspoon chopped fresh mint
2 tablespoons minced celery

¼ teaspoon cinnamon
½ bay leaf, crushed
4 cups potatoes, pared, thinly
  sliced
¼ cup tomato paste
1 cup leftover gravy, thinned
¼ cup hot water
Patras Topping (*see below*)
¼ cup grated Parmesan Cheese

Heat oven to 375° F. Sauté onion in oil until soft, but not brown. Add garlic and meat; cook, stirring, over medium heat until meat is lightly browned, about 6 to 8 minutes. Add all seasonings; blend. Layer mixture alternately with potato slices in a 1½-quart glass baking dish, ending with potato slices on top. Combine tomato paste with gravy in a small saucepan; add hot water. Cook, stirring until heated. Pour over potato mixture. Bake 30 minutes or until most of the liquid has been absorbed. Remove from oven. Reduce heat to 350° F. Pour Patras Topping carefully over baking dish; sprinkle with cheese. Bake 15 minutes or until custard is set and top is lightly browned. Makes 6 servings.

Patras Topping

2 teaspoons flour
1 cup light cream

2 egg yolks, beaten
dash paprika

Make paste with flour and some of the cream; blend until smooth. Blend paste with remaining cream, egg yolks, and paprika.

Beef Hash Andalusian

1 medium onion, chopped
4 tablespoons butter
¾ cup leftover beef gravy
1 teaspoon wine vinegar
2 tablespoons Madeira wine
3 cups diced roast beef

1 egg
2 cups leftover mashed
  potatoes, seasoned
2 tablespoons fine dry bread
  crumbs
½ teaspoon rosemary

Heat oven to 425° F. Sauté onion in 2 tablespoons of the butter until soft but not browned. Add gravy, vinegar, wine, and roast beef. Heat gently just to boiling. Pile in center of a well-greased, shallow 1-quart baking dish. Beat egg and mashed potatoes together. Spread in a ring around edge of baking dish to form a border. Melt remaining butter; stir in bread crumbs and rosemary. Spread mixture over potatoes. Bake 20 minutes or until hot and lightly browned. Makes 4 servings.

Beef Bones Diavolo

A zingy glaze that will appeal to men.

12 rib roast beef bones
2 teaspoons dry mustard
½ cup prepared mustard
2 tablespoons molasses
2 tablespoons vinegar

1 tablespoon brown sugar
½ cup Worcestershire sauce
1 teaspoon Tabasco
1 teaspoon salt
¼ teaspoon curry powder

When carving ribs leave a fair amount of meat on them. Save leftover ribs, wrapping them in foil and freezing them, until you have 12. Defrost. Heat oven to 400° F. Combine remaining ingredients, blending them well. Brush each rib generously with mixture. Bake 15 to 20 minutes until they are glazed. Serve hot. Makes 6 servings.

Swiss Beef

My son, Ralph, brought back this recipe from his European travels.

2 tablespoons shortening
2 tablespoons chopped onion
¾ teaspoon salt
¼ teaspoon pepper
2 tablespoons flour
2 cups canned tomatoes
½ teaspoon Worcestershire sauce

1½ cups chopped cooked leftover beef
1 cup diced leftover cooked carrots
1 cup leftover cooked green beans
Cheese Puff (*see below*)

Heat oven to 350° F. Grease an 8-inch square pan. Melt shortening in a skillet; add onion and brown lightly. Add salt, pepper, flour, tomatoes, and Worcestershire sauce. Cook 6 to 8 minutes or until slightly thickened. Add beef, carrots and beans; cook 3 minutes. Pour into prepared pan. Spread Cheese Puff dough over meat mixture evenly. Bake 20 to 25 minutes. Makes 6 servings.

Cheese Puff

1 cup flour
1½ teaspoons baking powder
½ teaspoon dry mustard
½ teaspoon salt

2 tablespoons butter
¼ cup grated sharp cheese
¼ cup milk

Combine flour, baking powder, mustard, and salt. Cut in butter. Add cheese and milk; blend to a soft dough.

Mr. Chen's Beef Suey

3 tablespoons butter
½ cup chopped onion
½ cup chopped celery
1 tablespoon flour
1 can (3 ounces) sliced
  mushrooms, with liquid
1 cup evaporated milk

¼ cup water
4 teaspoons soy sauce
2 cups diced cooked beef
1 can (5 ounces) water
  chestnuts, drained, sliced
1 can (3 ounces) chow mein
  noodles

Melt butter in a skillet. Add onion and celery; cook over low heat until almost tender, about 4 minutes. Blend in flour. Drain liquid from mushrooms and combine it with evaporated milk, water, and soy sauce. Gradually stir into skillet. Cook over moderate heat until thickened, stirring constantly. Add mushrooms, beef, and water chestnuts. Heat thoroughly. Serve over chow mein noodles. Makes 4 servings.

Beef Burgundy Delight

½ pound mushrooms, sliced
2 tablespoons butter
1¼ cups leftover beef gravy
½ cup dry red wine
2 teaspoons steak sauce
dash Tabasco
dash Worcestershire sauce
4 cups cooked beef, cut in
   1-inch cubes

½ teaspoon salt
⅛ teaspoon pepper
2 cups leftover mashed
   potatoes
2 egg yolks
1 tablespoon chopped parsley

Sauté mushrooms in butter 5 minutes. Add gravy, red wine, steak sauce, Tabasco, and Worcestershire sauce; simmer 5 minutes. Add beef and simmer 3 minutes. Season with salt and pepper. Heat oven to 450° F. Combine potatoes with egg yolks and beat well. Pour beef mixture into a 1½-quart baking dish. Surround with potato mixture. Bake 10 minutes or until potatoes are lightly browned. Sprinkle with parsley. Makes 4 servings.

Athenian Casserole

3 cups chopped cooked beef
2 tablespoons grated onion
1 small clove garlic, minced
1 tablespoon chopped parsley
1 tablespoon chopped celery
½ teaspoon salt
¼ teaspoon onion salt
¼ teaspoon pepper

⅛ teaspoon nutmeg
¼ teaspoon marjoram
¼ teaspoon thyme
1 medium eggplant, cut in
   ½-inch slices
3 tablespoons olive oil
1 cup canned tomato sauce

Heat oven to 375° F. Mix beef with onion, garlic, parsley, celery, salt, onion salt, pepper, nutmeg, marjoram, and thyme; set aside. Sauté eggplant slices in olive oil. Grease as 1½-quart casserole and arrange alternate layers of meat mixture and eggplant, adding a tablespoon of tomato sauce to each eggplant layer. Top with remaining sauce; bake 20 minutes. Makes 6 servings.

Russian Medley

½ cup chopped onion
2 tablespoons margarine
2 cups ground cooked beef
2 tablespoons flour
6 tablespoons ketchup
1 tablespoon prepared mustard

¼ teaspoon salt
¼ teaspoon celery salt
⅛ teaspoon pepper
⅛ teaspoon paprika
1 cup commercial sour cream
4 toasted buns

Brown onion in margarine. Add beef; cook 2 minutes. Drain off excess fat. Mix in remaining ingredients except sour cream and buns. Simmer 6 to 8 minutes or until thoroughly heated. Stir in sour cream. Serve hot on buns. Makes 4 servings.

Beef Casserole Provençale

The topping of Herb Biscuits is the perfect complement to this dish.

¼ cup chopped onion
2 tablespoons shortening
2 cups coarsely ground cooked beef
½ teaspoon salt
⅛ teaspoon pepper
⅛ teaspoon paprika
1½ cups tomato juice

3 stalks celery, chopped
1 tablespoon chopped parsley
2 medium carrots, diced
3 drops Tabasco
¼ cup ketchup
¼ cup chili sauce
¼ cup flour
Herb Biscuits (*see below*)

Heat oven to 375° F. Sauté onion in shortening. Add beef and seasonings. Cook over medium heat 6 minutes. Add 1 cup of the tomato juice, the celery, parsley, carrots, and Tabasco. Simmer, covered, 6 minutes. Add remaining tomato juice, ketchup, and chili sauce to flour and stir into meat mixture. Cook until thick, stirring constantly. Pour into a 2-quart baking dish. Top meat mixture with Herb Biscuits. Bake 20 to 25 minutes. Makes 6 servings.

Herb Biscuits

1 cup flour
1½ teaspoons baking powder
½ teaspoon salt
⅛ teaspoon dry mustard

¼ teaspoon crumbled dry sage
¾ teaspoon caraway seeds
2 tablespoons shortening
6 tablespoons milk

Combine flour with dry ingredients in a bowl. Cut in shortening with a pastry blender or two knives until mixture looks like meal. Stir in milk. Round into a ball on a lightly floured, cloth-covered board. Knead lightly 20 to 25 times. Roll dough or pat out to ½-inch thickness. Cut with floured biscuit cutter. Makes 10 biscuits.

Macaroni Frascati

In the vineyard country of Frascati, just outside Rome, I was served this dish with a crisp salad and chunks of Italian garlic bread.

2 cups elbow macaroni
1 teaspoon salt
⅛ teaspoon pepper
⅛ teaspoon oregano
⅛ teaspoon basil
2 cups diced cooked beef
1 small onion, sliced,
  separated into rings
1 cup finely diced processed
  American cheese

¼ cup grated Parmesan cheese
2 cups thin leftover cream
  sauce
1 tomato cut in sixths
2 tablespoons fine dry crumbs
⅛ teaspoon thyme
butter

Cook macaroni in boiling salted water 8 minutes or until just tender. Drain; sprinkle with mixture of salt, pepper, oregano, and basil. Heat oven to 350° F. In a 1-quart baking dish alternately layer half the beef, the onion, macaroni, cheeses, and cream sauce. Repeat layers. Bake 30 minutes. Arrange cut tomato on top. Sprinkle with combined crumbs and thyme. Dot with butter. Bake 10 minutes. Makes 6 servings.

Pacific Burger Casserole

The California method of serving a hearty casserole.

8 slices stale bread
2 cups ground cooked beef
¼ cup chopped onion
2 tablespoons chopped celery
1 teaspoon chopped parsley
1½ tablespoons prepared
   mustard
¼ teaspoon Worcestershire
   sauce

dash Tabasco
½ teaspoon salt
1 cup grated sharp Cheddar
   cheese
1 egg, beaten
¾ cup light cream
⅛ teaspoon dry mustard
⅛ teaspoon pepper
¼ teaspoon onion salt

Heat oven to 350° F. Toast bread lightly. Butter both sides and cut
diagonally. Mix beef, onion, celery, parsley, prepared mustard,
Worcestershire sauce, Tabasco, and salt in a medium frying pan.
Cook over medium heat until thoroughly heated, about 8 minutes.
Arrange toast slices, cheese, and meat mixture in alternate layers
in a greased 9-inch square pan, with cheese as the top layer.
Mix egg, cream, dry mustard, pepper, and onion salt. Pour mix-
ture over layers in pan. Bake 30 to 35 minutes. Makes 4 servings.

Calcutta Beef

An unusual way of serving beef with apple, raisins, and curry.

1 tablespoon butter
1 large apple, pared, cored,
   and diced
1 large onion, chopped
1 cup chopped celery
1 tablespoon curry powder
1 cup leftover beef broth
¼ cup seedless raisins

2 cups diced cooked beef
1 egg, slightly beaten
2 cups hot fluffy cooked rice
condiments: English chutney,
   toasted coconut, roasted
   pistachio nuts, curried lemon
   slices, toasted almonds

Melt butter in a heavy saucepan. Add apple, onion, and celery
and sauté over medium heat 5 minutes, stirring occasionally. Sprinkle in curry powder; sauté 3 minutes, stirring frequently. Stir in

broth, raisins, and beef. Cover and simmer 15 minutes. Remove from heat; stir in egg. Serve with rice and condiments. Makes 4 servings.

Southern Beef Fritters

In Kentucky these fritters are served with lima beans, corn, and applesauce.

1½ cups chopped cooked beef
2 tablespoons chopped parsley
1 tablespoon Worcestershire
   sauce
1 tablespoon chopped celery
1½ cups flour
1 teaspoon baking powder

¼ teaspoon salt
¼ teaspoon paprika
1 egg
1¼ cups milk
vegetable oil for frying
¾ cup heated leftover beef
   gravy

Combine chopped beef, parsley, Worcestershire sauce, and celery; set aside. Combine flour, baking powder, salt, and paprika; set aside. Beat together egg and milk and combine with flour mixture; blend until smooth. Add beef mixture. Drop batter by spoonfuls into hot oil, 360° F., and sauté until brown. Serve with heated gravy. Makes 4 servings.

Beef Hash D'Armand

2 cups leftover beef pot roast,
   cut in ¼-inch cubes
2 cups boiled, peeled, cubed
   potatoes
¼ cup finely chopped
   Bermuda onion
¼ cup finely chopped green
   onion
2 tablespoons coarsely
   chopped green pepper

2 tablespoons coarsely
   chopped red pepper
¾ teaspoon salt
¼ teaspoon pepper
½ teaspoon monosodium
   glutamate
4 tablespoons butter
2 cups hot, cooked asparagus
   tips
4 strips pimiento

Combine beef, potatoes, onions, peppers, and seasonings; blend well. Heat butter in a 10-inch skillet until very hot. Add beef mixture; cook over medium heat 5 minutes. With a large spatula carefully turn mixture over; cook 5 minutes. Turn over again; pat hash firmly with a spoon. Cook 5 minutes longer. Flip hash, or transfer carefully with spatula, onto a serving platter. Arrange asparagus tips in four bunches around hash; circle with pimiento strips. Serve with leftover pot roast gravy, if desired. Makes 4 servings.

Savory Southern Macaroni

2 medium onions, minced
2 tablespoons butter
1 tablespoon vegetable oil
1 cup finely chopped cooked beef
1 can (6 ounces) tomato purée
1 teaspoon crushed rosemary
1 teaspoon minced parsley

bit of bay leaf, crushed
½ cup leftover cooked string beans
½ cup leftover cooked carrots
1 cup meat stock
1 package (8 ounces) macaroni, cooked according to package directions
grated Parmesan cheese

Sauté onions in butter and oil. Add beef and cook 5 minutes. Add tomato purée, rosemary, parsley, and bay leaf; simmer 15 minutes. Add vegetables and meat stock. Heat mixture thoroughly; pour over hot, cooked macaroni on a heated platter. Sprinkle with cheese. Serve immediately. Makes 4 servings.

Pizza Siciliano

A good way to use leftover spaghetti sauce and meat balls.

1 envelope active dry yeast
2 tablespoons lukewarm water
1 cup boiling water
1 tablespoon shortening
1 teaspoon salt
½ cup sugar
3 cups flour
6 ounces sliced provolone cheese
1½ cups canned tomatoes, drained

¼ cup chopped green onions
¼ cup finely chopped onions
½ teaspoon basil
¼ teaspoon oregano
¼ teaspoon marjoram
½ cup spaghetti sauce, leftover or canned
1 can (2 ounces) anchovies, drained
6 leftover cooked meat balls, sliced

Heat oven to 425° F. Grease a 14-inch pizza pan or round shallow pan. Soften yeast in lukewarm water in a small bowl; let stand 5 minutes. Stir until dissolved. Pour boiling water over shortening in a mixing bowl. Add salt and sugar. Stir until smooth; cool to lukewarm. Stir in dissolved yeast. Gradually add flour, beating well to make a soft dough. Knead on a lightly floured board until smooth. Roll out dough ¼ inch thick. Pat into shape in prepared pan. Cover dough with a cloth. Let rise in a warm place 15 minutes. Arrange cheese slices across dough. Top with tomatoes. Sprinkle with onions and spices. Spread spaghetti sauce evenly on top. Garnish with anchovies and sliced meatballs. Bake 25 minutes or until crust is golden brown. Cut pizza into wedges. Makes 6 servings.

Munich Soup

⅔ cup diced lean bacon
4 small white onions, chopped
3 green onions, chopped
2 tablespoons flour
6 cups leftover beef broth
4 medium potatoes, pared, thinly sliced

¾ cup commercial sour cream
¼ cup light cream
2 egg yolks
dash nutmeg
1 tablespoon minced parsley
1½ teaspoons minced chervil

In a deep, heavy saucepan, sauté bacon 3 minutes. Add white and green onions; cook 5 minutes or until soft but not brown. Blend in flour. Gradually stir in beef broth. Add potatoes, cover, and simmer 45 minutes. Let sour cream stand 45 minutes at room temperature. Mix sour cream with light cream, egg yolks, and nutmeg. Spoon a little hot soup into cream mixture; mix well. Slowly stir back into hot soup. Simmer over very low heat 10 minutes, stirring frequently. Add herbs. Makes 8 servings.

Elegant Tongue Mold

1 tablespoon unflavored gelatin
1 cup broth
¼ cup prepared horseradish, drained
½ cup mayonnaise
2 cups finely chopped cooked tongue
¼ cup minced green pepper
1 tablespoon minced onion
1 teaspoon minced pimiento
1 teaspoon minced celery
½ teaspoon dry mustard
dash Tabasco
lettuce or water cress

Soak gelatin in ¼ cup of the broth. Heat remaining broth and dissolve gelatin in it. Cool to lukewarm. Combine remaining ingredients; stir into gelatin mixture. Turn into a 5-cup mold and chill until set. Serve over bed of lettuce or water cress. Makes 6 servings.

Tongue Tillyria

2 kosher-style gherkins, finely chopped
3 green onions, finely chopped
1 teaspoon finely chopped parsley
1 teaspoon finely chopped capers
¼ cup bread crumbs
¼ cup dry white wine
½ teaspoon salt
⅛ teaspoon white pepper
3 tablespoons butter, melted
12 thin slices cooked tongue
hot buttered noodles
2 tablespoons chopped parsley

Heat oven to 350° F. Combine gherkins, onions, parsley, capers, bread crumbs, wine, salt, and pepper. Pour half the butter in the bottom of a shallow 1½-quart baking dish. Spread over it half the gherkin mixture. Arrange slices of tongue over; top with remaining gherkin mixture. Top with remaining butter. Bake 20 minutes. Serve with hot buttered noodles garnished with chopped parsley. Makes 4 servings.

Americana Red Flannel Hash

1½ cups finely chopped
   leftover corned beef
1½ cups cooked, cold beets,
   chopped
3 cups cooked, cold potatoes,
   chopped
2 tablespoons finely chopped
   onion

1 teaspoon salt
½ teaspoon onion salt
⅛ teaspoon pepper
1 teaspoon Worcestershire
   sauce
3 tablespoons light cream
¼ cup shortening

Combine beef, beets, potatoes, onion, salts, pepper, and Worcestershire sauce. Add cream and mix lightly. Melt shortening in a
heavy skillet. Spread meat mixture evenly in bottom; cook over
low heat without stirring for 30 minutes. Loosen around edges with
a spatula; shake skillet occasionally to prevent mixture from stick-
ing. When crust forms on the bottom, make a shallow crosswise
cut in the top. Tip skillet and slide hash onto a heated platter,
folding it in half like an omelet. Makes 4 servings.

LAMB

Olympian Cabbage Roll-Ups

1 large head cabbage, about
    3½ pounds
4 cups ground cooked lamb
8 slices crisp bacon, crumbled
¾ cup cracker crumbs
1 medium onion, chopped
1 small clove garlic, minced
1 cup tomato juice

2 eggs, slightly beaten
½ teaspoon salt
⅛ teaspoon pepper
3 tablespoons butter
1 beef bouillon cube
1 cup hot water
1 tablespoon flour
1 tablespoon cold water

Cut core out of cabbage with a sharp knife. Pull off and discard
any coarse outer leaves; carefully remove 18 whole leaves, one at
a time. (Save any remaining cabbage for another meal.) Steam
leaves, covered, in a small amount of boiling salted water in a
large, heavy skillet 8 minutes or just until limp; drain well.
Combine lamb, bacon, cracker crumbs, onion, garlic, tomato juice,
eggs, salt, and pepper in a large bowl; mix lightly with a fork
until blended. Lay steamed cabbage leaves flat; place 2 to 3
tablespoons meat mixture in center of each. Fold thick end up over
filling; fold both sides toward middle. Roll up, jelly-roll fashion,
to cover filling completely; fasten with wooden pick. Brown rolls,
a few at a time, in butter in a large, heavy skillet or saucepan.
Pile all browned rolls back into the pan. Dissolve bouillon cube
in hot water; pour over cabbage rolls. Cover. Simmer 20 minutes
or until cabbage is tender. Remove rolls to a heated platter
and keep hot. Pour off drippings from pan and measure 1 cup;
add water, if needed. Return to pan. Blend flour with cold water
until smooth; stir into liquid in pan. Cook over low heat, stirring
constantly, until thickened. Serve with cabbage rolls. Makes 8 to
10 servings.

Risotto Milanese

A posh dish with the flavor of saffron.

4 tablespoons butter
½ medium onion, minced
¼ cup minced celery
1 cup brown rice
2 cups lamb broth or
  consommé
1 cup chopped cooked lamb

½ teaspoon salt
¼ teaspoon pepper
¼ cup slivered almonds
¼ to ½ teaspoon powdered
  saffron
½ cup grated Parmesan cheese

Melt butter in a large, heavy skillet; add onion and celery and sauté until soft. Add rice and sauté 6 minutes, stirring constantly. Add liquid and meat and stir well. Cover tightly and simmer over very low heat 35 minutes or until rice is tender. Season with salt and pepper. Add almonds, saffron, and cheese. Continue cooking 5 to 7 minutes or until cheese is melted. Makes 4 servings.

Company Hash

Plan to serve this at an informal party and surprise all that you dared serve hash—it's delicious!

1 cup raw potato, pared,
  diced
⅓ cup coarsely chopped onion
⅓ cup diced green pepper
1 tablespoon chopped celery
2 cups diced cooked lamb
1 cup cold lamb gravy

½ cup canned tomato sauce
¼ teaspoon seasoned salt
¼ teaspoon salt
1 teaspoon steak sauce
3 tablespoons diced pimiento
½ cup grated Cheddar cheese
1 tablespoon butter

Heat oven to 375° F. Combine potato, onion, green pepper, and celery in a saucepan. Add water to cover and cook 10 minutes. Reduce heat and cook 5 minutes longer. Drain. Return to saucepan. Add lamb, gravy, tomato sauce, salts, steak sauce, and pimiento. Blend well. Divide among 4 individual casserole dishes; sprinkle with cheese and dot with butter. Bake 20 to 25 minutes or until lightly browned. Makes 4 servings.

Devon Shepherd's Pie

2 tablespoons minced onion	½ teaspoon salt
1 small clove garlic, minced	⅛ teaspoon pepper
¾ cup celery, thinly sliced	3 egg yolks, beaten
2 tablespoons butter	3 cups leftover mashed
3 cups cubed cooked lamb	potatoes
3 cups leftover gravy	¼ teaspoon paprika
¼ cup chopped parsley	

Heat oven to 350° F. Sauté onion, garlic, and celery in butter until tender. Add lamb, gravy, parsley, salt, and pepper. Add egg yolks to mashed potatoes; beat well. With back of a spoon, spread potato mixture on sides of a 1½-quart baking dish to ½-inch thickness. Gently pour in lamb mixture. Spoon remaining potatoes around top edge of baking dish. Sprinkle with paprika. Bake 30 to 35 minutes. Makes 6 servings.

Bonnie Scotch Broth

Serve this hearty soup with chunks of Irish bread.

bone from lamb roast	⅛ teaspoon pepper
4 tablespoons butter	½ cup barley
2 cups diced cooked lamb	½ cup chopped parsley
3 leeks, thinly sliced	1 cup diced carrots
2 quarts water	1 cup chopped celery with
4 chicken bouillon cubes	leaves
½ teaspoon salt	

Crack lamb bone. Melt butter in a heavy skillet; add bone, lamb, and leeks. Cook 10 minutes, stirring frequently, until meat is browned. Add water, bouillon cubes, salt, and pepper and bring to a boil. Reduce heat, cover, and simmer 1 hour. Add barley and continue simmering 1 hour longer. Add parsley, carrots, and celery and simmer 30 minutes. Makes 6 servings.

Lamb Cassoulet

A streamlined adaptation of a French classic.

¼ cup diced salt pork
1½ cups dried lentils
2 cups chicken broth
1 cup beef consommé
1½ cups canned tomatoes
4 tablespoons finely chopped
   onion

1 clove minced garlic
1 tablespoon chopped parsley
1 small bay leaf
⅛ teaspoon basil
½ teaspoon salt
½ teaspoon Tabasco
2 cups cooked, cubed lamb

Brown salt pork in a medium skillet. Add all remaining ingredients except lamb and bring to a boil. Cover, reduce heat and simmer 2 hours. Heat oven to 350° F. Grease a 1½-quart casserole. Add lamb to mixture and stir. Pour into casserole. Bake 20 minutes. Makes 6 servings.

Tunisian Lamb

2 tablespoons butter
½ cup finely chopped onion
1 cup coarsely chopped celery
1 tablespoon minced parsley
3 cups cubed cooked lamb
½ cup lamb gravy or canned
   mushroom gravy

1 cup water
½ cup chopped dried apricots
¼ teaspoon ground poultry
   seasoning
½ teaspoon salt
¼ teaspoon pepper
1½ tablespoons flour

Melt butter in a medium saucepan. Add onion, celery, and parsley; cook 5 minutes or until tender, stirring occasionally. Add lamb, gravy, water, apricots, poultry seasoning, salt, and pepper. Cover and simmer 25 minutes. Blend flour with a little cold water to form a paste; add to lamb mixture. Cook and stir until thickened. Makes 6 servings.

Down-under Lamb Tarts

3 tablespoons butter
1 clove garlic, minced
⅓ cup chopped onion
2 tablespoons flour
¼ teaspoon marjoram
1 teaspoon salt

¼ teaspoon celery salt
1½ cups milk
2 cups diced cooked lamb
2 tablespoons chopped parsley
Orange Pastry Tart Shells
  (*see below*)

Melt butter in a skillet. Add garlic and onion; cook over low heat 5 minutes. Blend in flour, marjoram, and salts. Gradually add milk. Cook over low heat, stirring constantly, until mixture thickens. Add lamb and parsley. Heat thoroughly. Spoon into Orange Pastry Tart Shells. Makes 4 servings.

Orange Pastry Tart Shells

Prepare ½ package prepared pie crust mix as directed on package, substituting orange juice for liquid called for. Heat oven to 425° F. Place pastry on a 12-inch square of heavy aluminum foil. Flatten pastry and cover with a sheet of wax paper. Roll pastry into a 9-inch square. Remove wax paper. Trim foil to edge of pastry; cut pastry and foil into four 4½-inch squares. Pinch together the corners of each square and shape a 1-inch standing rim all around to form a square tart shell inside the foil. Carefully prick pastry with a fork. Place on a cookie sheet and bake 5 minutes. Prick pastry again and bake 10 minutes longer, until golden brown. When cool, carefully remove shells from foil.

Stew de la Casa

lamb bones
1¼ cups water
2 tablespoons margarine
½ cup chopped onion
1 cup cooked pumpkin
2 cups cubed roast lamb
1⅔ cups diced cooked
  potatoes

1 cup canned tomatoes
1 teaspoon chili powder
1 teaspoon salt
⅛ teaspoon paprika
2 cups hot cooked rice
parsley sprigs

Simmer lamb bones in water in a large kettle for 30 minutes. Reduce liquid to 1 cup and set aside. Melt margarine in a large skillet. Add onion and cook over low heat 4 minutes until tender. Add lamb liquid, pumpkin, lamb, potatoes, tomatoes, chili powder, salt, and paprika. Cover and simmer over low heat, stirring occasionally, 15 minutes or until thoroughly heated. Serve over hot rice; garnish with parsley. Makes 4 servings.

Bombay Curried Lamb

1¼ cups uncooked rice
1 cup sliced onions
2 cups diced celery
¼ cup chopped parsley
3 tablespoons lamb fat
1 tablespoon flour

4½ cups cubed cooked lamb
2 teaspoons curry powder
1¼ cups leftover lamb gravy
½ cup hot water
½ teaspoon salt

Cook rice according to package directions; set aside. Sauté onions, celery, and parsley in lamb fat in a heavy skillet until tender. Stir in flour. Add lamb, curry powder, gravy, water, and salt and blend. Cover and cook over low heat 12 minutes. Serve with cooked rice. Makes 6 servings.

Lamb in Aspic

For the grand buffet—a cold dish ideal for all occasions.

3 cups tomato juice
4 beef bouillon cubes
2 tablespoons unflavored
 gelatin
½ cup cold water
1½ teaspoons Worcestershire
 sauce
¼ teaspoon Tabasco

2 teaspoons minced onion
2 cups cooked lamb, cut in
 julienne strips
½ cup finely chopped celery
1 cup leftover cooked baby
 lima beans
lettuce greens
parsley sprigs

Heat tomato juice to boiling. Add bouillon cubes; stir until dissolved. Soften gelatin in cold water. Add to hot tomato juice and stir until gelatin is dissolved. Add Worcestershire sauce and Tabasco. Stir in onion. Cool until mixture begins to thicken. Stir in lamb, celery, and lima beans. Turn into a 1½-quart ring mold which has been rinsed in cold water. Chill until firm. Unmold on bed of lettuce greens; garnish with parsley. Makes 8 servings.

Lamb Polonaise

1 medium onion, thinly sliced
1 tablespoon butter
2 cups cooked lamb, cut in
    1-inch cubes
1 tablespoon flour
¼ teaspoon paprika

⅛ teaspoon white pepper
½ cup water
1 chicken bouillon cube
½ cup commercial sour cream
1 tablespoon minced parsley

Sauté onion in butter 3 minutes until transparent. Add lamb and brown lightly. Stir in flour, paprika, and pepper. Add water and bouillon cube; cook over medium heat 10 minutes, stirring constantly, until thickened. Stir in sour cream; heat 1 minute. Add parsley. Makes 4 servings.

PORK AND HAM

Quiche du Jambon

A Swiss specialty perfect for serving six.

½ cup green onions, cut up
½ cup leeks, cut up
1 9-inch unbaked pie shell
¾ cup diced cooked shrimp
½ cup diced Gruyère cheese
½ cup diced processed
  American cheese

½ cup finely diced cooked
  ham
3 eggs
1 cup light cream
½ cup heavy cream
½ teaspoon salt
⅛ teaspoon pepper

Heat oven to 375° F. Parboil green onions and leeks in boiling salted water for 5 minutes; drain. Arrange all the shrimp in the pie shell to cover center. Combine cheeses and arrange in another layer to encircle shrimp. Arrange ham in another layer to fill pie shell. Sprinkle onion and leek mixture over all. Beat eggs with creams, salt, and pepper until frothy and well blended. Carefully spoon over mixture in pie shell. Bake 45 minutes or until top is golden and center is firm when pressed. Let cool 10 minutes before serving. Makes 6 servings.

Sherried Ham Ring

2 eggs, separated
2 cups finely ground cooked
  ham
⅛ teaspoon nutmeg
dash mace
dash cayenne
½ teaspoon minced parsley

½ teaspoon minced pimiento
1 cup heavy cream
2 tablespoons dry sherry
1½ cups cooked green peas,
  well buttered
2 cups mashed potatoes

Heat oven to 300° F. Combine well-beaten egg yolks with ham, nutmeg, mace, cayenne, parsley, pimiento, cream, and sherry. Beat egg whites until stiff but not dry. Gently fold into ham mixture. Turn into a well-greased 1½-quart ring mold. Set mold in a pan of hot water. Bake 35 minutes or until top is firm to the touch. Remove from oven; let stand 3 to 4 minutes. Unmold on round heated serving platter. Fill center with green peas and garnish border with hot mashed potatoes. Serve at once. Makes 6 servings.

Curried Ham Fritters

1 cup flour
1 cup boiling water
2 eggs
1 tablespoon curry powder
¾ cup finely ground cooked
    ham

dash coriander
vegetable oil
Mushroom Sauce—½ recipe
    (page 137)

Stir flour into rapidly boiling water and continue stirring vigorously until it leaves sides of pan. Decrease heat; beat in eggs, one at a time, beating vigorously after each addition. Remove from heat. Stir in curry powder, ham, and coriander. Heat vegetable oil in a deep skillet to 390° F.; drop batter by spoonfuls into oil. Cook until golden brown on all sides; drain on absorbent paper and keep warm until all batter is used. Serve at once with hot Mushroom Sauce. Makes 4 servings.

Mushrooms au Jambon

1 pound mushrooms, 1½
    inches in diameter
3 tablespoons butter
1 cup ground cooked ham
¼ cup commercial sour cream

½ teaspoon salt
dash pepper
¼ teaspoon paprika
1½ tablespoons parsley

Wash mushrooms and remove stems. Sauté mushroom caps lightly in butter in a heavy skillet 5 minutes, or until they are still quite firm and hold their shape. Stuff with mixture of ham, sour cream, and seasonings. Sprinkle with parsley. Refrigerate until serving time. Makes 6 servings.

Odds and Ends Salad Kebabs

When my children were teenagers they considered this their own creation.

cherry tomatoes
large stuffed green olives
whole pickled beets
cooked ham cubes
marinated artichoke hearts

squares of Jack cheese
burr sweet pickles
cooked chicken cubes
bibb lettuce leaves

For an unusual salad string one of each of the first 8 ingredients on 8-inch skewers repeating, if necessary, to fill skewers. Allow 1 skewer for each person. Place on beds of chilled lettuce leaves. Serve with favorite dressing.

Vevey Chef's Salad

1 cup olive oil
¼ cup wine vinegar
¼ cup lemon juice
1 tablespoon anchovy paste
1 teaspoon salt
½ teaspoon coarsely ground pepper
1 clove garlic
2 heads Belgian endive
1 bunch romaine
1 small head iceberg lettuce, broken up

2 tablespoons snipped parsley
½ teaspoon basil
⅛ teaspoon oregano
leftover cooked tongue, cut in julienne strips
leftover cooked ham, cut in julienne strips
leftover white meat chicken, cut in julienne strips
¼ pound Swiss cheese, cut in julienne strips

Combine the first seven ingredients in a jar. Cover tightly and shake well. Chill dressing slightly. Cut endive and romaine in bite-size pieces. Combine with lettuce, parsley, basil, and oregano. Toss with dressing until well coated. Arrange meats and cheese on top. Serve at once. Makes 6 servings.

Chinese Pork with Pimiento Rice

A delightful recipe from Hong Kong, served with my favorite rice.

2 tablespoons vegetable oil
1 medium clove garlic
1 medium onion, thinly
sliced
2 green onions, thinly sliced
2 medium green peppers,
chopped
2 tablespoons chopped celery
3 large mushrooms, thinly
sliced
¾ cup green peas

2 medium tomatoes, skinned,
chopped
¾ teaspoon salt
⅛ teaspoon pepper
1 cup finely chopped cooked
pork
1 teaspoon sugar
1 teaspoon soy sauce
1 tablespoon butter
2 teaspoons flour
Pimiento Rice (*see below*)

Heat oil in a medium skillet; sauté garlic and onions 5 minutes or until lightly browned. Remove garlic; add green peppers and celery; cook 3 minutes. Add mushrooms; cook 2 minutes longer. Add peas and tomatoes; cook 5 minutes. Season with salt and pepper. Add pork, sugar, and soy sauce; cook 4 minutes. Make a paste of butter and flour; blend in; cook until mixture is thickened. Serve with Pimiento Rice. Makes 4 servings.

Pimiento Rice

2 chicken bouillon cubes
3½ cups water
1 teaspoon instant minced
onion
1½ teaspoons salt

1½ cups rice
1 jar (4 ounces) pimientos,
chopped
1 tablespoon vegetable oil

Combine bouillon cubes, water, minced onion, and salt in a medium saucepan. Bring to a boil; add rice, stir, cover, and cook over low heat 25 minutes or until rice is tender and liquid is absorbed. Sir in pimentos and oil. Serve hot.

Lanai Pork and Chicken

1 cup diced cooked pork
1 cup diced cooked chicken
½ teaspoon monosodium
  glutamate
⅓ cup mayonnaise
¼ cup stuffed green olives,
  chopped

2 black pitted olives, finely
  chopped
1 teaspoon lemon juice
1 teaspoon lime juice
pinch salt
2 egg whites, stiffly beaten

Place pork and chicken in 4 individual heatproof dishes. Sprinkle with monosodium glutamate. Broil 3 to 4 inches from source of heat 5 minutes. Combine remaining ingredients except egg whites; blend thoroughly. Fold into beaten egg whites. Spread over hot pork and chicken. Broil 3 to 4 inches from source of heat 1 to 2 minutes or until puffed and lightly browned. Serve immediately. Makes 4 servings.

Island of Bali Curry

2 cups cubed cooked pork
½ cup chopped green onion
½ cup diced carrot
¼ cup chopped celery
1 tablespoon minced parsley
2 medium apples, pared, diced
1 large banana, diced
½ cup raisins
2 dried figs, chopped
1½ tablespoons lemon juice

1 tablespoon honey
1 cup leftover thick gravy
2 cups water
2 tablespoons curry powder
dash nutmeg
2 cups cooked fluffy rice
¼ cup chutney
4 slices lemon
4 slices orange

Combine meat, vegetables, fruits, lemon juice, and honey in a large, heavy skillet. Blend gravy thoroughly with water and add to meat mixture. Blend in curry powder and nutmeg. Cover and simmer 1¾ hours, stirring occasionally. Remove cover and simmer 15 minutes longer. Serve over hot rice. Garnish with chutney and lemon and orange slices. Makes 4 servings.

Memphis Meat Casserole

2 cans (20 ounces each)
stewed tomatoes
3 tablespoons Minute tapioca
1 teaspoon salt
¼ teaspoon paprika
⅛ teaspoon thyme
⅛ teaspoon basil
1 tablespoon sugar

2 teaspoons Worcestershire
sauce
2 tablespoons margarine
⅔ cup chopped onion
⅔ cup thinly sliced celery
2 cups cubed cooked pork
1 recipe Baking Powder Biscuit
Dough (page 189)

Heat oven to 400° F. Drain juice from tomatoes into a medium saucepan. Add tapioca, salt, paprika, thyme, basil, sugar and Worcestershire sauce. Simmer slowly over medium heat until sauce is clear, stirring constantly. Melt margarine in a medium skillet; add onion and celery and sauté 5 minutes, stirring frequently. Add pork and sauce; heat just to boiling point. Turn into a greased 1-quart baking dish. Roll biscuit dough to ½-inch thickness and cut into rounds with a biscuit cutter. Top baking dish with biscuits. Bake 20 to 25 minutes. Makes 4 servings.

Eggs Benedict

4 English muffins
8 thin slices cooked ham
8 poached eggs
1 cup Hollandaise Sauce
(see below)

1 tablespoon chopped
parsley

Split muffins; toast, butter, and keep warm. Broil ham slices. Place 1 ham slice on each muffin half. Top with 1 poached egg. Spoon Hollandaise Sauce over all. Serve immediately, with a sprinkling of parsley. Makes 8 servings.

Hollandaise Sauce

2 egg yolks
1 tablespoon lemon juice
¼ teaspoon salt

pinch pepper
½ cup butter, heated to
bubbling

Place egg yolks, lemon juice, salt, and pepper in blender jar, cover, and turn blender on high speed for 2 seconds. With machine still running, remove cover, and pour butter very slowly in a steady stream into whirling blades. Use at once or keep warm in pan of warm water, or refrigerate and heat gradually over warm water.

Old Irish Ham Rolls

12 slices day-old white bread
2 tablespoons soft butter
6 slices processed American
   cheese
4 eggs
1 teaspoon salt
¼ teaspoon Tabasco

1 tablespoon prepared mustard
1 tablespoon Worcestershire
   sauce
¾ cup beer
6 slices cooked ham
6 2-inch strips cooked chicken
1 tablespoon chopped parsley

Grease an oblong shallow 1½-quart baking dish. Remove crusts from bread and butter slices. Arrange half the slices in the baking dish. Cover with cheese slices; top with remaining bread. Beat eggs until frothy. Blend in salt, Tabasco, mustard, and Worcestershire sauce. Stir in beer. Pour over bread in baking dish. Let stand 1 hour. Heat oven to 350° F. Bake, uncovered, 35 minutes. Roll each ham slice around a strip of chicken. Top baking dish with ham rolls and bake 5 minutes longer or until custard is puffy and lightly browned. Sprinkle with parsley. Makes 6 servings.

Ham du Chef

1 tablespoon butter
¼ cup chopped green onion
¼ cup chopped green pepper
2 cups diced cooked ham
3 cups diced cooked potatoes
¼ teaspoon salt

dash pepper
dash paprika
¼ cup mayonnaise
½ teaspoon prepared mustard
1½ cups sharp processed
   American cheese

Melt butter in a medium skillet. Add onion, green pepper, and ham and sauté until lightly browned, stirring occasionally. Add potatoes, salt, pepper, paprika, mayonnaise, and mustard. Heat, mixing lightly. Stir in cheese; heat just until it begins to melt. Serve immediately. Makes 4 servings.

Maine Ham Bake

In Bangor, Maine, a friend of mine serves this dish with French fries and asparagus.

4 cups diced cooked ham	2 tablespoons grated orange
3 tablespoons butter	rind
½ cup water	¼ teaspoon salt
½ cup sugar	pinch pepper
1¼ cups fresh cranberries	½ teaspoon lemon juice

Heat oven to 350° F. Sauté ham in butter until lightly browned. Combine water and sugar in a medium saucepan. Heat until sugar is dissolved. Add ¾ cup of the cranberries; simmer, covered, 15 minutes. Add orange rind. Season sauce with salt and pepper. Combine ham and cranberry sauce in a 1-quart baking dish. Bake, uncovered, 20 minutes. Add remaining cranberries; sprinkle with lemon juice. Bake 10 to 15 minutes longer. Makes 6 servings.

Ham à la Madeleine

An adaptation of a Bretagne recipe which I streamlined by using ingredients readily available in American stores.

1 pound dried lima beans	¼ cup ketchup
6 cups water	1 teaspoon dry mustard
4 strips bacon	½ teaspoon ginger
2 cups cooked ham, cut into	1½ teaspoons Worcestershire
1½-inch cubes	sauce
1 onion, sliced	¼ cup brown sugar
3 tablespoons molasses	1 tablespoon butter

Combine lima beans and water in a large saucepan; bring to a boil. Boil 2 minutes. Cover and let stand 1 hour. Cook 30 minutes or until tender. Drain; reserve ½ cup liquid. Heat oven to 350° F. Line bottom of a 2-quart baking dish with bacon. Combine lima beans, ham cubes, onion, molasses, ketchup, dry mustard, ginger, Worcestershire sauce and reserved bean liquid; mix lightly. Pour mixture into the baking dish. Sprinkle with brown sugar; dot with butter. Bake, uncovered, 1 hour. Makes 6 servings.

Dutch Treat Ham Loaf

3 cups ground cooked ham
½ cup cracker crumbs
½ cup milk
¼ cup buttermilk
1 egg
1½ cups cooked rice
4 tablespoons minced parsley

1½ tablespoons minced celery leaves
1 tablespoon butter, melted
dash pepper
¾ cup commercial sour cream
1 tablespoon drained prepared horseradish

Heat oven to 350° F. Combine ham, cracker crumbs, milk, buttermilk and egg and blend thoroughly. Spread half the mixture in a 9×5×2¾-inch loaf pan. Mix rice with parsley, celery leaves, butter, and pepper. Spread rice mixture over ham mixture. Top with remaining ham mixture. Bake 35 to 40 minutes. Combine sour cream with horseradish. Serve with ham loaf. Makes 6 servings.

Cherokee Corn And Ham Patties

2 cups flour
2 teaspoons baking powder
1 teaspoon salt
dash white pepper
2 eggs, well beaten
1¼ cups milk

1 cup leftover whole kernel corn
1 cup finely chopped cooked ham
shortening for frying

Combine flour with baking powder, salt, and pepper. Beat eggs with milk; add dry ingredients and beat until smooth. Fold in corn and ham. Melt shortening in a medium skillet to a depth of ¼ inch. Spoon ¼ cupfuls of batter into skillet. Cook over moderate heat until patties are golden brown on one side; turn and brown other side. Makes 6 servings.

Winterland Bean Soup

1 pound dried kidney beans
3 quarts water
1 meaty ham bone
½ cup chopped onion
½ cup chopped celery
½ cup chopped carrot

1 teaspoon minced parsley
4 whole cloves
1 bay leaf
1 teaspoon salt
¼ teaspoon pepper
pinch thyme

Place beans and water in a large kettle. Bring to a boil over moderate heat. Remove from heat; cover and let stand 1 hour. Add ham bone and remaining ingredients. Simmer 2 hours or until beans are very tender. Remove ham bone from soup; cut off any meat remaining on bone, cube it, and set aside. Remove bay leaf from kettle and put soup through a sieve. Add cubed ham; heat. Makes 8 to 10 servings.

Baton Rouge Ham

A savory Louisiana dish, served as a gumbo.

¼ cup butter	1½ cups water
1 cup chopped onion	¼ teaspoon chili powder
1 clove garlic, minced	1 teaspoon salt
½ cup chopped green pepper	⅛ teaspoon pepper
½ cup rice	1 can (4½ ounces) shrimp,
1 cup canned tomatoes	undrained
1 can (8 ounces) tomato	1½ cups ground cooked ham
sauce	

Melt butter in a large skillet. Add onion, garlic, and green pepper; cook over low heat until just tender, about 5 minutes. Add rice, tomatoes, tomato sauce, water, chili powder, salt, and pepper. Cover and cook 25 minutes, stirring occasionally, until rice is tender. Stir in shrimp and ham. Heat through. Makes 4 servings.

Eggs with Ham Chasseur

1 package (3 ounces) cream	dash pepper
cheese	5 eggs
2 tablespoons butter, softened	1 cup diced cooked ham
½ cup milk	1 teaspoon chopped chives
¼ teaspoon salt	4 slices toast

In top of a double boiler combine cheese, butter, milk, salt, and pepper. Place over boiling water and stir until cheese is softened. Beat eggs slightly; gradually add to cheese mixture, beating constantly until blended. Add ham and cook until eggs are set, stirring occasionally. Stir in chives just before serving. Serve over toast. Makes 4 servings.

Green Peppers Hawaiian

When I visited friends in Hilo, I was given the recipe for this satisfying luncheon dish.

6 large green peppers
1 cup boiling water, salted
  with 1 teaspoon salt
3 cups coarsely chopped
  cooked ham
1¼ cups cooked rice
½ cup raisins

¼ teaspoon pepper
¼ cup butter
1 cup sliced onions
4 peppercorns
6 whole cloves
1 cup condensed tomato soup
2½ cups canned tomatoes

Wash peppers; cut off stem ends and remove all seeds. Cook peppers in boiling salted water 5 minutes in a covered saucepan. Drain; reserve liquid. Combine ham, rice, raisins, and pepper. Fill drained green peppers with mixture. Melt butter in a heavy deep kettle; add onions and sauté until golden brown. Tie peppercorns and cloves in a small piece of cheesecloth. Add tomato soup, canned tomatoes, spice bag, and reserved liquid from peppers to onions; blend. Stand peppers upright in sauce; cover and simmer over low heat 25 to 30 minutes. Makes 6 servings.

Peking Sweet Sour Pork

Prepare this ahead of time and serve it in a chafing dish.

1½ cups cubed cooked pork
1 cup cubed cooked ham
½ cup water
⅓ cup vinegar
¼ cup brown sugar
2 tablespoons cornstarch
½ teaspoon salt
1 cup pineapple juice, drained
  from chunks

1 cup canned pineapple
  chunks
1 medium green pepper,
  thinly sliced
2 medium onions, thinly sliced
Fried Rice (page 181)

In a large skillet brown pork and ham lightly in a little pork fat. Combine water, vinegar, sugar, cornstarch, salt, and pineapple juice.

Cook in a medium saucepan until liquid is clear and slightly thickened; pour sauce over meats. Cover and cook 25 minutes. Add pineapple chunks, green pepper and onion; cook 5 minutes longer. Serve with Fried Rice. Makes 4 servings.

Ham Allemand

2 tablespoons butter
2 tablespoons flour
¼ teaspoon salt
⅛ teaspoon pepper
1 cup milk
2 cups leftover cooked macaroni

1 cup cooked ham
1 cup cubed Cheddar cheese
1 teaspoon prepared mustard
1 teaspoon horseradish
¼ cup buttered bread crumbs

Melt butter over low heat in a medium saucepan. Blend in flour, salt and pepper. Cook over low heat, stirring constantly, until mixture is smooth and bubbly. Remove from heat; stir in milk. Bring to a boil, stirring constantly; boil 1 minute. Heat oven to 400° F. Combine sauce with remaining ingredients except bread crumbs. Pour mixture into 4 greased individual heatproof casseroles; top with bread crumbs. Bake 20 minutes. Makes 4 servings.

Hearty Ham Casserole

1 can (15½ ounces) green beans, drained
8 slices cooked ham
1 can (10½ ounces) cream of celery soup
¼ cup mayonnaise

1 teaspoon prepared mustard
¼ cup fine bread crumbs
1 teaspoon chopped parsley
pinch of nutmeg
½ cup grated sharp Cheddar cheese

Heat oven to 350° F. Place green beans in bottom of a 9-inch square baking dish. Add ham in a single layer. Combine soup, mayonnaise, and mustard and pour over ham and beans. Combine remaining ingredients and sprinkle over top. Bake 30 minutes. Makes 8 servings.

Navajo Corn Bake

2 cups cream-style corn *(1 can)*
1 egg, slightly beaten
¼ cup milk
¼ cup light cream *(½ & ½)*
½ cup bread crumbs
1¼ cups diced cooked ham
¼ cup chopped onion

¼ cup chopped green pepper
1 teaspoon chopped pimiento ?
1 teaspoon margarine ⎱ *3 tsp marg*
2 teaspoons butter   ⎰ *¼ tsp butter flavor*
¼ teaspoon salt
⅛ teaspoon paprika

Heat oven to 350° F. Combine all ingredients. *(grease casserole)* Pour into a 1½-quart baking dish. Bake 30 to 35 minutes. Makes 4 servings.

Quickie Ham Treat

2 cups diced cooked potatoes
2 cups cubed cooked ham
¼ cup grated Cheddar cheese
¼ cup chopped Swiss cheese

2 tablespoons chopped
  pimiento
½ cup heavy cream

Heat oven to 350° F. Combine all ingredients; turn into a 1½-quart baking dish. Cover and bake 40 to 45 minutes. Makes 4 servings.

Maurice's Salad

1 clove garlic, cut in half
1 head lettuce
½ bunch endive
½ cup chopped green onion
¼ cup sliced celery
¼ cup chopped green pepper
1 cup julienne strips of Swiss
  cheese

½ cup julienne strips of
  cooked tongue
½ cup julienne strips of
  cooked ham
1 can (2 ounces) flat fillets
  of anchovies
½ cup mayonnaise
¼ cup French dressing

Rub a large salad bowl with cut clove of garlic then discard garlic. Tear greens into bite-size pieces. Toss greens, onion, celery, pepper, cheese, meats, and anchovies in the bowl. Just before serving, blend mayonnaise and dressing; add to salad and toss lightly. Makes 6 servings.

Peruvian Soup

Make this ahead of time and let it stand a while to develop the flavor fully.

1½ pounds dried lima beans, washed
2 tablespoons butter
4 large onions, chopped
1 large clove garlic, chopped
6 sprigs parsley
½ teaspoon thyme
¼ teaspoon marjoram

1½ large bay leaves
1 carrot, chopped
½ lemon, sliced
1 ham bone
1 cup chopped cooked ham
2 teaspoons salt
¼ teaspoon pepper

Put beans in a large bowl, cover with water, and let soak overnight. Drain beans and rinse well under hot water. Put beans in a heavy kettle and add 3 quarts water. Melt butter in a saucepan; add onions and garlic and sauté 5 minutes or until transparent. Add to kettle. Tie parsley, thyme, marjoram, bay leaves, carrot, and lemon in cheesecloth; add to kettle. Add ham bone and cooked ham. Bring to a boil and cover. Cook over low heat 3 hours or until liquid is reduced by half and beans are soft. Discard cheesecloth bag. Remove bone and let cool. Remove 2 cups beans with a little liquid; purée through a sieve. Return to soup. Remove any meat left on ham bone; cut into small pieces and discard bone. Add ham pieces to soup; season with salt and pepper. Reheat thoroughly. Makes 8 servings.

Chinese Egg Petal Soup

½ cup lean, shredded cooked pork
1½ teaspoons sherry
1½ teaspoons soy sauce
1½ teaspoons cornstarch
2 tablespoons vegetable oil

6 cups chicken broth
1 green onion, sliced
1 cucumber, sliced
½ teaspoon salt
⅛ teaspoon pepper
1 egg, lightly beaten

Combine pork, sherry, soy sauce and cornstarch. Heat oil in a heavy saucepan. Add pork mixture and brown quickly. Add broth;

bring to a boil and simmer 10 minutes. Add onion and cucumber and season with salt and pepper. Simmer 5 minutes longer. Bring to a fast rolling boil. Slowly add egg, stirring constantly. Remove from heat at once. Makes 6 servings.

Monte Cristo Sandwiches

2 eggs
2 tablespoons flour
½ cup milk
1 teaspoon salt
⅛ teaspoon pepper
⅛ teaspoon paprika
8 slices white bread, buttered

4 slices cooked ham
4 thin slices cooked chicken
4 slices American cheese
⅓ cup butter
¼ cup commercial sour cream
3 tablespoons strawberry
   preserves

Blend eggs, flour, milk, salt, pepper, and paprika in a bowl. Arrange on 4 slices of bread 1 slice each of ham, chicken, and cheese. Cover with remaining bread slices. Dip sandwiches into egg mixture, coating both sides well. Melt butter in a large heavy skillet. Brown sandwiches on both sides. Serve at once topped with sour cream and strawberry preserves. Makes 4 servings.

Ham Soufflé Sandwiches

1 package (10 ounces) frozen
   asparagus spears
4 slices cooked ham
4 slices white bread, toasted
⅔ cup mayonnaise
¼ cup grated sharp Cheddar
   cheese

¼ cup stuffed green olives,
   sliced
¼ teaspoon salt
2 tablespoons finely chopped
   green pepper
2 egg whites

Cook asparagus spears according to package directions; drain and set aside. Preheat broiler. Line broiler pan with aluminum foil. Place 1 slice of ham on each slice of toast. Arrange on broiler pan. Put 2 or 3 asparagus spears on each slice of ham. Blend mayonnaise, cheese, olives, salt, and green pepper. Beat egg whites until stiff but not dry. Fold into mayonnaise mixture. Spread over asparagus and ham. Broil 4 inches from heat for 5 minutes, or until golden brown. Makes 4 servings.

Hot French Roll Gourmet Sandwiches

1½ cups ground cooked ham
½ pound Cheddar cheese,
    shredded
1 medium onion, grated
2 medium carrots, grated
2 tablespoons sweet pickle
    relish
2 tablespoons chili sauce
¼ cup commercial sour cream

1½ tablespoons mayonnaise
1½ tablespoons prepared
    mustard
½ teaspoon garlic salt
½ teaspoon celery salt
½ teaspoon pepper
½ teaspoon sugar
dash of cayenne
12 French rolls

Heat oven to 400° F. Combine all ingredients, except rolls. Slice
rolls lengthwise; scoop out centers and fill with sandwich mixture.
Wrap in aluminum foil. Bake in oven 20 minutes. Serve hot. Makes
12 servings.

Wontons

Another time-honored oriental delicacy. This version is quick and
easy to make.

2 cups flour
2 teaspoons salt
1 egg
⅓ cup water
1 tablespoon bacon drippings
3 green onions, chopped
1 medium onion, chopped
2 cups coarsely chopped
    mushrooms

2 cups coarsely chopped
    cooked pork
8 cooked shrimp, chopped
⅛ teaspoon pepper
¼ teaspoon monosodium
    glutamate
1 egg, beaten
shortening for frying
hot mustard

Combine flour and 1 teaspoon of the salt in a medium bowl. Add
egg and water a few drops at a time; mix to a smooth dough. Turn
onto a lightly floured board. Knead until smooth. Cover; let stand
20 minutes. Roll out dough until paper thin. Cut into 2-inch squares;
set aside. Heat bacon drippings in a heavy skillet; add onions and
sauté 6 minutes or until transparent. Add mushrooms and pork.
Sauté 5 minutes, stirring occasionally. Add shrimp, remaining salt,

pepper, and monosodium glutamate; cook over low heat 5 minutes. Place 1 teaspoon of filling in middle of each wonton pastry square. Moisten edges with egg. Bring ends to center to enclose filling; press to seal. Fry wontons 4 or 5 at a time in deep shortening, 365° F., until golden. Drain on absorbent paper; keep warm in oven. Serve with mustard. Makes 4 dozen.

Ham Roly Polies

1 cup chopped cooked ham
¾ cup grated Cheddar cheese
2 tablespoons grated onion
1 egg
¼ cup dry cracker crumbs
½ cup milk
1 cup crushed cornflakes
shortening for frying

Combine ham, cheese, onion, egg, and crumbs in bowl; mix well. Shape into 1½-inch balls. Dip balls into milk; coat with cornflakes. Fry in deep fat, 365° F., for 4 minutes or until golden brown. Drain on absorbent paper; Serve at once. Makes 16 balls.

Oahu Ham Loaf

A Hawaiian masterpiece of flavor blends.

3 cups ground cooked ham
1 medium carrot, grated
½ cup soft bread crumbs
½ cup leftover mashed
  potatoes
1 egg, slightly beaten
1½ teaspoons chopped parsley
1½ teaspoons chopped celery
1 small onion, chopped
1½ teaspoons butter
1 teaspoon prepared mustard
¼ teaspoon salt
dash paprika
8 whole cloves
1 tablespoon frozen
  concentrated orange juice
1 tablespoon honey
Pineapple Relish Rings (see
  below)

Heat oven to 400° F. Combine ham, carrot, bread crumbs, potatoes, egg, parsley, and celery in a large bowl. Toss lightly to mix. Sauté onion in butter in a small skillet until transparent; stir in mustard, salt, and paprika. Add to ham mixture; mix lightly. Pack into a 9×5×3-inch loaf pan, then turn out onto a greased shallow baking pan. Stud top with cloves. Mix concentrated orange juice and honey;

brush half the mixture over ham loaf. Bake 20 minutes. Brush remaining orange-honey mixture on loaf; bake 20 minutes longer, or until richly glazed. Carefully transfer loaf onto a heated platter; garnish with Pineapple Relish Rings. Makes 4 servings.

Pineapple Relish Rings

1 can (8½ ounces) pineapple, with syrup
2 tablespoons cider vinegar
½ teaspoon mixed pickling spices
1 tablespoon chopped parsley

Drain syrup from a small can of pineapple slices into a small saucepan; stir in vinegar and spices. Heat syrup to boiling. Reduce heat; simmer 5 minutes. Place pineapple in a small bowl. Strain syrup over pineapple; chill 4 hours. When ready to serve, drain pineapple slices well; roll edges in chopped parsley. Cut through one side of each pineapple slice, then twist slice to make a loop. Arrange around ham loaf on platter.

Dixie Ham Puff

I use pancake mix to streamline this old southern favorite.

2 medium sweet potatoes, pared, sliced thin
3 medium tart apples, pared, cored, sliced
3 cups diced cooked ham
3 tablespoons brown sugar
½ teaspoon salt
¼ teaspoon pepper
¼ teaspoon curry powder
⅛ teaspoon mace
⅓ cup apple juice
1 cup pancake mix
½ teaspoon dry mustard
1 cup milk
2 tablespoons butter, melted

Heat oven to 375° F. Layer half each of sweet potatoes, apples and ham in a 1½-quart baking dish. Mix brown sugar, salt, pepper, curry powder, and mace in a bowl; sprinkle half the mixture on top of layers in the baking dish. Repeat with remaining sweet potatoes, apples, ham, and seasoning mixture; pour apple juice over and cover dish. Bake 40 minutes or until sweet potatoes are tender. While ham mixture bakes, combine pancake mix, mustard, milk, and butter in a medium bowl; blend well to make a thin batter;

pour over ham mixture. Bake, uncovered, 20 minutes longer, or until pancake topping is puffed and golden brown. Makes 6 to 8 servings.

Hungarian Pork Casserole

2 tablespoons butter
1 small onion, minced
2 cups ground leftover smoked
  pork
¼ cup fine dry bread crumbs
1 pound creamed cottage
  cheese

¼ teaspoon dried basil
½ teaspoon salt
dash pepper
3 eggs
paprika

Heat oven to 375° F. Melt butter in a medium skillet; add onion and pork and cook, stirring, 3 minutes. Add crumbs. Spread mixture in bottom of a shallow 1½-quart baking dish. Beat cheese until almost smooth; add seasonings and beat in eggs, one at a time. Pour over meat mixture; sprinkle with paprika. Bake 35 to 40 minutes. Makes 4 servings.

South Seas Pork Pie

2 tablespoons minced onion
3 tablespoons butter
3 tablespoons flour
¼ teaspoon poultry seasoning
dash of nutmeg
dash of allspice
½ teaspoon salt
½ teaspoon celery salt
⅛ teaspoon pepper

2 cups milk
1½ cups leftover sweet
  potatoes, cut in chunks
2 cups diced cooked pork
1 package prepared pastry
  mix
1 egg yolk
2 teaspoons water

Heat oven to 450° F. Sauté onion in butter in a medium skillet 3 minutes. Blend in flour and seasonings. Gradually add milk and cook over medium heat, stirring constantly, until thickened. Put potato chunks and pork in 2-quart baking dish. Pour sauce over mixture. Prepare pastry mix; roll to ¼-inch thickness; cut in strips ¾ inch wide. Arrange, lattice-fashion, on pie. Beat egg yolk with water; brush on pastry. Bake 10 minutes. Reduce heat to 350° F. and bake 15 minutes longer. Makes 6 servings.

Panhandle Pork Pie

A Texas he-man's meal—hearty, wholesome and tasty.

2 cups cooked pork, cut in
  ½-inch cubes
¼ cup chopped green pepper
¼ cup chopped onion
2 tablespoons chopped celery
3 large mushrooms, chopped
1 tablespoon bacon drippings
2 cups canned whole-kernel
  corn, drained
2 cups canned tomato sauce

½ teaspoon sage
¾ cup flour
2 teaspoons baking powder
¾ teaspoon salt
1 tablespoon sugar
¾ cup yellow corn meal
1 egg, well beaten
¾ cup milk
dash Worcestershire sauce
3 tablespoons butter, melted

Heat oven to 400° F. Brown pork, pepper, onion, celery, and mushrooms in bacon drippings. Stir in corn, tomato sauce, and sage. Turn into a 2-quart baking dish. Combine flour, baking powder, salt, sugar, and corn meal. Combine egg, milk, Worcestershire sauce, and butter. Blend with dry ingredients; stir until smooth. Pour over meat mixture. Bake 30 to 35 minutes. Makes 8 servings.

VEAL

Stuffed Peppers à la Greque

6 green peppers
2 cups chopped cooked veal
2 cups cooked buckwheat
  groats
1 teaspoon salt
⅛ teaspoon pepper
2 tablespoons grated onion
2 tablespoons chopped parsley
1 tablespoon chopped celery
3 cups canned tomatoes

⅛ teaspoon thyme
⅛ teaspoon marjoram
¼ teaspoon basil
2 teaspoons chili powder
2 teaspoons Worcestershire
  sauce
2 tablespoons grated Parmesan
  cheese
½ teaspoon paprika

Heat oven to 350° F. Cut off tops of peppers; remove seeds and fibers. Parboil for 10 minutes. Drain thoroughly. Combine veal, buckwheat groats, salt, pepper, onion, parsley, celery, 1 cup of the tomatoes, thyme, marjoram, basil, chili powder, and Worcestershire sauce. Stuff peppers with this mixture. Set in a greased baking dish. Sprinkle tops of peppers with cheese and paprika. Pour remaining tomatoes around them. Bake 30 minutes. Makes 6 servings.

Veal Hash à la Drake

An easy-to-make dish, often served at the Drake Hotel in Chicago.

1 tablespoon chopped onion
3 tablespoons butter
3 cups diced cooked veal
1 cup diced cooked potato
1 hard-cooked egg, chopped
1 tablespoon chopped pimiento
1 cup veal stock
1 cup undiluted evaporated
  milk

½ teaspoon salt
¼ teaspoon onion salt
¼ teaspoon pepper
2 egg yolks, slightly beaten
4 slices bread, toasted and
  buttered
1 teaspoon chopped parsley

Cook onion in butter until soft but not browned. Add veal and potato and cook 4 minutes over low heat. Add egg, pimiento, veal stock, evaporated milk, and seasonings. Heat slowly just to boiling point. Add egg yolks and stir over low heat until thickened. Serve immediately on hot toast. Garnish with parsley. Makes 4 servings.

Veal Goulash au Vin

2 cups thinly sliced onions
¼ cup butter
3 cups diced cooked veal
½ teaspoon thyme
⅛ teaspoon basil
1 tablespoon paprika
1 teaspoon grated lemon rind
½ teaspoon salt

¼ teaspoon Tabasco
1 teaspoon Worcestershire
  sauce
½ cup dry white wine
3 tablespoons flour
2 cups beef bouillon
2½ cups hot cooked buttered
  noodles

Sauté onions in butter in a large skillet until transparent. Add veal, thyme, basil, paprika, lemon rind, salt, Tabasco, and Worcestershire sauce. Cook 10 minutes, stirring constantly. Add wine and stir. Combine flour with beef bouillon and add gradually to veal mixture. Cook, stirring constantly, until thickened. Serve over noodles. Makes 6 servings.

Veal Sandwiches Neapolitan

½ cup butter
1 teaspoon dry mustard
1 teaspoon anchovy paste
1 teaspoon oregano
12 slices white bread, toasted

12 thin slices cooked veal
12 thin slices Mozzarella
  cheese
tomato wedges

Cream butter with mustard, anchovy paste, and oregano. Spread mixture on each slice of toast. Top with slice of veal and slice of cheese. Broil 5 inches from heat until cheese melts. Serve with tomato wedges. Makes 6 servings.

Veal Stroganoff

3 cups cooked veal, cut in
 strips
2 tablespoons butter
1¼ cups leftover gravy
1 tablespoon tomato paste
1½ teaspoons Worcestershire
 sauce
dash Tabasco
½ teaspoon bottled gravy
 seasoning

1 can (4 ounces) button
 mushrooms, with liquid
2 cups cooked noodles, hot
2 tablespoons toasted sesame
 seed
¼ cup commercial sour cream
¼ teaspoon paprika

Gently brown veal in butter. Remove veal; in the same pan heat
gravy, tomato paste, Worcestershire sauce, Tabasco, bottled gravy
seasoning and mushrooms with liquid. Cook 5 minutes. Return veal
to mixture and heat thoroughly, about 3 minutes. Combine noodles
and sesame seed and place in a serving dish. Pour Veal Stroganoff
over noodles. Top with sour cream; sprinkle with paprika. Makes 6
servings.

Veal and Cheese Soufflé

The original Cordon Bleu recipe calls for shoulder of veal twice
ground.

¼ cup butter
¼ cup flour
2 cups milk
½ cup grated Cheddar cheese
1 cup chopped cooked veal
¼ cup minced celery
¼ cup minced parsley
¾ teaspoon curry powder

1 can (4 ounces) chopped
 mushrooms
1 tablespoon minced onion
½ teaspoon salt
⅛ teaspoon pepper
4 egg yolks
5 egg whites, stiffly beaten

Heat oven to 350° F. Thoroughly grease a 2-quart soufflé dish; dust with some of the grated cheese. Set aside. Melt butter in a medium saucepan; stir in flour. Gradually add milk and cook, stirring constantly, until thick. Continue cooking over medium heat. Stir in remaining cheese. Blend in veal, celery, parsley, curry powder, mushrooms, onion, salt, and pepper. Gradually beat in egg yolks. Remove from heat; cool slightly. Gently fold mixture into beaten egg whites. Turn into prepared soufflé dish. Bake 35 to 40 minutes or until a knife inserted in the center comes out clean. Makes 6 servings.

Southern Veal Loaf

1 cup herb stuffing mix
¾ cup leftover veal gravy
4 cups ground cooked veal
2 eggs, well beaten
1 can (5⅓ ounces)
  evaporated milk
½ cup chopped celery
½ cup chopped green pepper
1 tablespoon chopped parsley
1 small onion, minced
2 tablespoons butter, melted

½ teaspoon salt
¼ teaspoon paprika
½ cup dry bread crumbs
1 tablespoon butter
1 package (4 servings)
  scalloped potatoes
1 tablespoon coarsely chopped
  pimiento
1 tablespoon coarsely chopped
  sweet pickle

Heat oven to 400° F. Soak stuffing mix in gravy. Combine with veal, eggs, evaporated milk, celery, green pepper, parsley, onion, melted butter, salt, and paprika and mix well. Pat into a greased 1½-quart loaf pan. Sprinkle with bread crumbs; dot with butter. Bake 45 minutes. Prepare scalloped potatoes according to package directions, in a shallow heatproof dish. Unmold loaf on potatoes. Top with pimiento and pickle. Makes 6 servings.

Veal Chop Suey

Who can resist this oriental dish with succulent water chestnuts and fried rice?

1 package (9 ounces)
  French-style green beans
1 package (10 ounces)
  frozen peas
1 cup sliced celery
½ cup boiling water
3 cups cooked veal, cut in
  thin strips
¼ cup diced green pepper
¼ cup diced red pepper

¼ cup sliced water chestnuts
1 large onion, sliced
1 chicken bouillon cube
3 tablespoons soy sauce
1 can (1 pound 3 ounces)
  bean sprouts, drained
2 tablespoons cornstarch
2 tablespoons cold water
Fried Rice (*see below*)

Combine green beans, peas, and celery in a large saucepan; pour boiling water over them and cook 5 minutes. Add veal, green and red peppers, water chestnuts, onion, bouillon cube, soy sauce, and bean sprouts; cook until liquid boils, about 10 minutes. Stir in cornstarch blended with cold water. Cook until thickened, stirring frequently. Serve with Fried Rice. Makes 6 servings.

Fried Rice

2 cups rice, cooked and
  frozen in freezer for 2
  hours
10 slices bacon
½ cup thinly sliced water
  chestnuts
½ cup finely diced bamboo
  shoots

½ cup minced onion
½ cup finely chopped green
  pepper
1 tablespoon soy sauce
1½ teaspoons Worcestershire
  sauce
peanut oil

Keep rice in freezer until needed. Fry bacon in skillet until crisp; drain on absorbent paper. Crumble bacon and mix with rice and all remaining ingredients except peanut oil. Pour enough oil into a large skillet to cover bottom. Heat and add rice mixture. Cook over moderate heat, turning with spatula, until very hot. Makes 6 servings.

Siberian Soup

leftover veal bones
1 medium onion
1 clove garlic
1 bay leaf
1 celery top (leaves)
1 sprig parsley
½ teaspoon salt
2 cups cubed cooked veal
2 onions, sliced
2 stalks celery, sliced
3 carrots, sliced

½ small head cabbage, cut
   in chunks
1 can (16 ounces) tomatoes
1 can (16 ounces) shoestring
   beets, drained, liquid
   reserved
1 teaspoon sugar
juice of 1 lemon
½ teaspoon celery salt
¼ teaspoon white pepper
½ cup commercial sour cream

Cover veal bones with water in a large kettle. Add onion, garlic, bay leaf, celery top, parsley, and salt. Simmer, covered, 2 hours. Strain; measure 2 quarts stock and return to kettle. Add veal, onions, celery, carrots, cabbage, tomatoes and liquid from beets. Cover; simmer 1 hour. Add sugar, lemon juice, celery salt, pepper, and drained beets; simmer 15 minutes. Top each serving with a dollop of sour cream. Makes 8 servings.

Veal Crêpes Gregory

4 eggs
½ cup milk
½ cup water
2 tablespoons butter, melted
1 cup flour
¾ teaspoon salt
1 onion, chopped
1 tablespoon margarine

2 cups chopped cooked veal
¼ cup chopped pimiento
½ teaspoon salt
⅛ teaspoon pepper
¼ cup leftover gravy
1 cup canned cheese sauce
¼ cup sautéed, slivered
   almonds

Beat eggs, milk, water, butter, flour, and salt until smooth. Let stand 1 hour. Meanwhile sauté onion in margarine in a medium skillet. Add veal, pimiento, salt, and pepper. Add enough gravy to moisten mixture; set aside. Heat oven to 400° F. Heat an 8-inch skillet and brush it with butter. Pour batter into pan by scant ¼ cup-

fuls. Turn and tip pan so batter covers entire area. Turn crêpes
after a few seconds. Fill cooked crêpes with veal mixture and roll
up. Place rolls in a shallow baking pan. Top with cheese sauce and
almonds. Bake 10 minutes or until brown and bubbly. Makes 6 servings.

Veal Goulash Friand

¼ cup butter
2 cups chopped onion
3 cups diced cooked veal
2 beef bouillon cubes
1½ cups hot water
¼ cup chili sauce
4 teaspoons paprika
1 teaspoon caraway seeds

½ teaspoon fennel seeds
½ teaspoon dried marjoram
⅛ teaspoon pepper
⅓ cup cold water
2 tablespoons flour
Parsley Rice Ring (see
   below)

Melt butter in a skillet. Add onion and cook until almost tender,
about 4 minutes. Add veal and cook 4 minutes or until lightly
browned. Dissolve bouillon cubes in hot water. Add bouillon, chili
sauce, paprika, caraway and fennel seeds, marjoram, and pepper to
skillet; cover and simmer 10 minutes, stirring occasionally. Blend
cold water and flour. Stir into the skillet and cook over low heat,
stirring constantly, until thickened. Serve in Parsley Rice Ring.
Makes 6 servings.

Parsley Rice Ring

1 cup uncooked rice
2 tablespoons butter

3 tablespoons chopped
parsley

Cook rice according to package directions. Add butter and parsley;
toss until butter is melted. Spoon into buttered 1-quart ring mold.
Let stand 1 minute. Turn out on warm platter. Spoon veal mixture
into center.

Veal Salad Jardinière

2 cups cooked, cooled   ¾ cup mayonnaise
    macaroni   ½ teaspoon salt
1 cup diced cucumber   ⅛ teaspoon pepper
1½ cups diced cooked veal   ⅛ teaspoon paprika
1 tablespoon grated onion   lettuce leaves
1 tablespoon minced parsley   1 tablespoon chopped chives
1 tablespoon chopped celery

Combine all ingredients except lettuce and chives. Chill thoroughly.
Serve on lettuce leaves; garnish with chives. Makes 4 servings.

Kentucky Veal Shortcake

A quick-to-prepare dish, perfect for unexpected guests.

2 cups cubed cooked veal   ½ cup light cream
3 tablespoons flour   ¾ teaspoon salt
¼ cup butter   ¾ teaspoon Worcestershire
2 tablespoons minced onion   sauce
¾ cup diced celery   ¼ teaspoon Tabasco
¼ cup diced green pepper   8 hot baking powder biscuits
1½ cups milk

Roll veal in flour; brown lightly in butter with onion, celery, and
green pepper. Add milk and light cream slowly. Cook over low
heat, stirring constantly, until thickened. Add salt, Worcestershire
sauce, and Tabasco. Split hot biscuits and butter them generously;
place on heated platter. Pour meat mixture between halves. Makes
4 servings.

Veal au Gratin

3 tablespoons butter
4 tablespoons flour
2 cups milk
½ teaspoon salt
⅛ teaspoon pepper
¼ teaspoon nutmeg
⅛ teaspoon mace
¼ teaspoon ginger

2 cups diced cooked veal
1 cup stuffed green olives,
  quartered
½ cup canned mushrooms
2 tablespoons dry bread
  crumbs
4 tablespoons Parmesan
  cheese

Heat oven to 375° F. Melt butter in a saucepan over low heat; add flour, stirring constantly, until blended. Add milk and cook, stirring constantly, until thickened. Add salt, pepper, nutmeg, mace, and ginger; stir until blended. Combine veal with olives and mushrooms. Place in a greased 1½-quart casserole. Pour creamed mixture over meat mixture. Sprinkle with bread crumbs and cheese and bake 35 to 40 minutes. Makes 6 servings.

Egg Rolls à la Chinois

½ cup flour
2 teaspoons cornstarch
¼ teaspoon salt
1 egg, lightly beaten
dash of sugar
1 cup water
¾ cup finely chopped celery
1 cup finely shredded
  cabbage
½ cup warm water

2 tablespoons butter
½ cup diced shrimp
½ cup diced cooked veal
¾ cup finely chopped water
  chestnuts
4 green onions, finely
  chopped
1 tablespoon flour
2 tablespoons beef broth
vegetable oil for frying

Combine the ½ cup flour, cornstarch, and salt in a bowl. Add egg and sugar and beat well. Slowly add the 1 cup water; beat until smooth. Heat a little of the vegetable oil in a 6-inch skillet to coat the bottom; pour 3 tablespoons of batter evenly over bottom. Place skillet over medium heat; cook until batter shrinks from sides of pan. Turn and cook 1 to 2 minutes longer. Remove from pan; repeat with remaining batter. Set aside until needed. Combine celery, cabbage, and the ½ cup water in a small saucepan; bring to boil, then drain well. Heat butter in a medium skillet. Add shrimp and veal; cook 3 minutes over medium heat, stirring constantly. Add celery mixture, water chestnuts, and green onions. Cook over medium heat, stirring constantly, until delicately brown. Remove from heat; cool. Place about 4 tablespoons filling on each egg roll. In a small bowl, blend flour and beef broth to a paste; use to brush edges of rolls; fold in 2 sides of rolls, then roll up; press lightly to seal. Heat vegetable oil in a large, heavy skillet to 1 inch depth. Fry egg rolls, turning them carefully and frequently, until golden on all sides. Drain on absorbent paper; serve at once. Makes 8 servings.

Veal Eiffel Tower

½ cup butter, melted
3 tablespoons flour
1½ cups consommé
½ cup dry white wine
¾ teaspoon salt
⅛ teaspoon white pepper
⅛ teaspoon paprika
1 small bay leaf
½ clove garlic, minced
½ small onion, minced
1 green onion, minced

2 tablespoons minced parsley
1 tablespoon minced celery
3 cups cooked veal, cut in 1-inch cubes
6 small white onions
1 cup mushrooms, thickly sliced
2 tablespoons sherry
2 cups cooked noodles, buttered

Combine butter and flour to make a smooth paste; cook slowly in a heavy skillet but do not brown. Stir in consommé and white wine gradually, stirring constantly until smooth and thickened. Season with salt, pepper, and paprika. Add bay leaf, garlic, minced onions, parsley, celery, and veal. Cover; simmer 5 minutes. Add white onions; simmer 12 minutes. Add mushrooms; simmer 10 minutes longer. Remove bay leaf. Add sherry; stir. Serve over hot buttered noodles. Makes 6 servings.

Veal Ragout Polonaise

This is the Polish version of a great favorite.

3 cups cooked veal, cut in
  1-inch cubes
2 tablespoons flour
2 tablespoons butter
½ teaspoon salt
¼ teaspoon pepper
¾ cup boiling chicken broth
12 small white onions
¾ cup coarsely chopped
  carrots

1 cup sliced mushrooms
½ cup coarsely chopped
  celery
2 teaspoons minced parsley
¼ teaspoon nutmeg
1 teaspoon pickle liquid
1 cup commercial sour cream

Heat oven to 375° F. Place veal cubes and flour in a paper bag and shake until meat is well coated. Brown cubes in butter in a heavy skillet. Season with salt and pepper. Pour chicken broth over meat. Add onions, carrots, mushrooms, celery, parsley, nutmeg, and pickle liquid. Blend well. Turn into a 1½-quart baking dish. Cover; bake 35 minutes. Remove from oven; stir in sour cream. Bake 5 minutes longer. Makes 6 servings.

Veal à la Liege

2 tablespoons butter
1 large Bermuda onion,
  sliced
1 clove garlic
2 cups cooked veal, cut in
  ¾-inch cubes
¾ teaspoon curry powder
½ cup boiling water
2 tablespoons crisp bacon,
  crumbled
½ cup condensed tomato soup

½ cup sliced mushrooms,
  sautéed
¼ cup sliced water chestnuts,
  sautéed
¼ cup beer
½ cup commercial sour cream
2 cups cooked noodles,
  buttered
1 teaspoon poppy seed
2 tablespoons chopped
  toasted almonds

Melt butter in a medium, heavy skillet; add onion and garlic and sauté until tender; add veal and delicately brown on all sides. Stir in curry powder, boiling water, bacon, and tomato soup. Cover; simmer 20 minutes. Add mushrooms, water chestnuts, and beer. Simmer 5 minutes. Just before serving, stir in sour cream. Lightly toss noodles with poppy seed and almonds. Serve veal mixture over noodles. Makes 6 servings.

CHICKEN

Chicken And Oyster Pie Louisiana

¼ cup butter
¼ cup flour
¼ teaspoon paprika
2 cups chicken broth
¾ teaspoon salt
⅛ teaspoon pepper
2 hard-cooked eggs, sliced

¼ cup finely chopped celery
¼ cup finely chopped parsley
1 pint oysters, freshly
   shucked, drained
3 cups diced cooked chicken
Baking Powder Biscuit
   Dough (*see below*)

Heat oven to 400° F. Grease a 2-quart casserole. Melt butter in a saucepan; stir in flour and paprika. Gradually stir in broth. Cook over low heat, stirring constantly, until thickened and smooth. Season with salt and pepper. Stir in eggs, celery, parsley, oysters, and chicken. Pour into casserole. Set aside. Prepare Baking Powder Biscuit Dough and turn out onto lightly floured board. Knead gently 10 times; roll out approximately ½ inch thick to fit top of casserole and place dough over chicken mixture. Bake 20 minutes or until golden. Makes 6 servings.

Baking Powder Biscuit Dough

2 cups flour
½ teaspoon salt
4 teaspoons baking powder
½ teaspoon cream of tartar

2 teaspoons sugar
½ cup shortening
⅔ cup milk

Combine dry ingredients in a mixing bowl. With pastry blender or two knives cut in shortening until mixture resembles corn meal. Add milk. Stir gently with a fork until dough holds together. Gather dough into a ball. Roll or pat to ½-inch thickness and cut as desired.

Olè Tomato Soup

8 medium tomatoes, sliced
3 cups chicken broth
1 teaspoon lemon juice
1 teaspoon lime juice
¼ teaspoon basil
2 teaspoons sugar

2 drops garlic juice
1 teaspoon salt
½ teaspoon onion salt
¼ teaspoon pepper
2 teaspoons minced parsley
4 celery leaves, chopped

Combine all ingredients and place in blender jar; blend 2 minutes. Strain. Chill at least 3 hours before serving. Makes 6 servings.

Simple Simon Chicken Divan

1 package frozen asparagus
6 slices cooked chicken
2 tablespoons butter
1 can (10½ ounces) cream of
  chicken soup

¼ cup light cream
⅛ teaspoon basil
⅛ teaspoon rosemary
2 tablespoons sherry
½ cup grated Cheddar cheese

Cook asparagus according to package directions; drain. Heat oven to 350° F. Place chicken in one layer in an oblong, shallow, greased 1-quart baking dish. Top with cooked asparagus. Dot with butter. Heat soup with cream, stirring in basil, rosemary, sherry, and cheese. Heat until cheese is melted. Pour over chicken mixture. Bake 20 minutes or until bubbling. Makes 4 servings.

Poulet Onion Soup

2 tablespoons butter
3 cups thinly sliced onions
1 small clove garlic, minced
2½ cups leftover chicken
  stock

1 cup heavy cream
½ teaspoon salt
¼ teaspoon pepper
toasted croutons
grated Parmesan cheese

Melt butter in a heavy saucepan. Add onions and garlic and cook over low heat until onions are soft but not browned. Add chicken stock. Cover and simmer over low heat for about 2 hours. Just

before serving, stir in cream and reheat but do not boil. Season
with salt and pepper. Serve soup garnished with croutons. Sprinkle
grated cheese over it. Makes 4 to 6 servings.

Heirloom Chicken Croquettes

6 tablespoons flour
6 tablespoons butter, melted
2 cups milk
1¾ teaspoons salt
¼ teaspoon onion salt
⅛ teaspoon pepper
¼ cup minced onion
1 tablespoon parsley

3 cups chopped cooked
chicken
1 cup ground walnuts
8 ½-inch cubes canned
jellied cranberry sauce
2 cups cracker crumbs
1 egg, well beaten
cooked noodles

Blend flour into melted butter in a medium skillet; slowly add milk,
stirring constantly until thickened. Season with salts, pepper, onion,
and parsley. Mix in chicken and ¼ cup of the ground walnuts
Remove mixture from heat and cool thoroughly. Chill several hours
or overnight. Shape into 8 croquettes, placing 1 cube of cranberry sauce in center of each. Combine remaining walnuts with
cracker crumbs. Roll croquettes in crumb mixture, then in beaten
egg, then in crumbs again. Fry in deep hot fat, 375° F., until
golden brown. Serve with noodles. Makes 4 servings.

Southern Delight Biscuits

These biscuits are sometimes served with a rich mushroom sauce.

1½ cups flour
½ teaspoon salt
4 teaspoons baking powder
¼ teaspoon nutmeg
2 tablespoons shortening
1 cup leftover mashed
potatoes

¾ cup diced cooked chicken
1 egg
¼ cup milk
melted butter
1 tablespoon minced parsley

Heat oven to 450° F. Combine flour, salt, baking powder, and
nutmeg in a mixing bowl. Cut in shortening and mashed potatoes.
Add chicken; cut in until blended and flour mixture is the size of

peas. Mix egg with milk; add to flour mixture and stir only until blended. Knead dough lightly on floured board. Pat to ¾-inch thickness. Cut into 3-inch squares, then into triangles. Place on a greased baking sheet and bake 10 minutes. Brush with melted butter and sprinkle with parsley; bake 5 minutes longer. Makes about 16 biscuits.

Jiffy Chicken Salad

1½ cups coarsely chopped
   cooked chicken
1 cup diced celery
¼ cup chopped walnuts

¼ cup mayonnaise
2 tablespoons chopped sweet
   pickle
1½ tablespoons lemon juice

Lightly toss together all ingredients. Season to taste with salt and pepper. Chill. Serve in scooped-out fresh tomatoes, or atop crisp lettuce. Makes 4 servings.

Chicken Strata

An adaption of an internationally popular dish.

2 slices day-old white bread,
   buttered
6 slices day-old white bread
2 cups diced cooked chicken
½ cup chopped onion
½ cup chopped green pepper
½ cup finely chopped celery
1 tablespoon finely chopped
   parsley
½ cup mayonnaise
¾ teaspoon salt

dash pepper
⅛ teaspoon paprika
2 eggs, slightly beaten
1 cup milk
½ cup light cream
1 can (10½ ounces)
   condensed cream of
   mushroom soup
½ cup shredded sharp
   Cheddar cheese

Cut buttered bread into ½-inch cubes; set aside. Cut unbuttered bread into 1-inch cubes. Place half of these in bottom of an 8-inch square baking dish. Combine chicken, vegetables, mayonnaise, and seasonings; spoon over bread cubes. Sprinkle remaining unbuttered cubes over chicken mixture. Combine eggs, milk, and cream and pour over all. Cover and chill 1 hour or longer.

Spoon soup over chicken mixture. Sprinkle with buttered cubes. When ready to cook, heat oven to 325° F. Bake 40 minutes. Sprinkle cheese over top and bake another 10 minutes, or until set. Makes 6 servings.

Chicken Salad Savarin

1½ cups diced cooked chicken
1 cup diced cooked potatoes
½ cup chopped cooked carrots
¼ cup cooked leftover peas
¼ cup cooked leftover green beans
1 teaspoon salt
½ teaspoon pepper
½ teaspoon paprika
¼ teaspoon confectioners' sugar
¼ teaspoon dry mustard
dash cayenne
3 tablespoons vinegar
¼ cup vegetable oil
¼ cup olive oil
2 sweet pickles, finely chopped
½ cup mayonnaise
1 hard-cooked egg, chopped
sliced pickled beets
parsley

Mix chicken and vegetables; set aside. In a small bowl combine seasonings; beat in vinegar and oils until well blended. Pour over chicken mixture. Chill in refrigerator 2 hours. Stir occasionally. Just before serving add chopped pickles and mayonnaise; mix lightly. Garnish with egg, pickled beets, and parsley. Makes 4 servings.

Chicken Croquettes Cumberland

3 tablespoons butter
⅓ cup flour
½ teaspoon salt
dash pepper
1 cup milk
1¾ cups minced cooked chicken
2 tablespoons sherry
1 egg, slightly beaten
1 tablespoon dried tarragon
1 tablespoon chopped chives
1 tablespoon chopped parsley
1 teaspoon chopped celery
1 egg
2 tablespoons water
1 cup fine dry bread crumbs
vegetable oil for frying

Melt butter in a medium saucepan. Blend in flour, salt, and pepper. Gradually add milk and cook, stirring constantly, until thickened. Add chicken, sherry, beaten egg, tarragon, chives, parsley, and celery; mix well and cook until mixture comes to a boil. Cool quickly, then chill at least 1 hour. Shape ¼-cup portions of chicken mixture into cone-shaped croquettes. Beat remaining egg and water together. Dip each croquette in bread crumbs, then beaten egg, and again in bread crumbs. Chill 30 minutes. Heat oil in a deep pan to 380° F. Fry croquettes until golden brown. Drain on paper. Makes 6 servings.

Chicken à la King Supreme

2 tablespoons chopped green pepper
1 pimiento, chopped
3 tablespoons butter
½ cup sliced mushrooms, canned or fresh
1½ tablespoons flour
1½ cups light cream
¼ teaspoon salt

¼ teaspoon onion salt
dash pepper
¼ teaspoon paprika
2 cups diced leftover cooked chicken
2 egg yolks
2 tablespoons sherry
6 slices white bread, toasted

Sauté green pepper and pimiento in butter for 5 minutes in a heavy saucepan. Add mushrooms. Move vegetables to side of pan; blend flour with butter. Add cream and cook over medium heat until thickened, stirring constantly. Season with salts, pepper, and paprika. Add chicken. Beat egg yolks slightly and add some of the sauce to them; stir and return this mixture to sauce. Cook over low heat 2 minutes, stirring constantly. Remove from heat; add wine. Serve on toasted bread. Makes 6 servings.

Louisiana Chicken Loaf

This loaf may also be served cold. Place slices on lettuce leaves and decorate with rounds of cranberry sauce.

2 cups hot chicken broth
3 eggs, slightly beaten
1½ cups soft bread crumbs
1½ teaspoons salt
¼ teaspoon paprika
¼ teaspoon rosemary
1 teaspoon Worcestershire
  sauce

½ cup minced celery
⅓ cup chopped green pepper
1 tablespoon minced parsley
1 teaspoon grated onion
1½ teaspoons lemon juice
Fresh Mushroom Sauce (*see below*)

Pour chicken broth over eggs, stirring constantly. Add bread crumbs; mix well. Add all remaining ingredients except sauce; mix well. Heat oven to 350° F. Grease a 9×5×2¾-inch loaf pan. Pat chicken mixture evenly into pan. Set in pan of hot water; bake 1½ hours or until knife inserted comes out clean. Remove pan from hot water; let stand 10 minutes before unmolding. Serve with Fresh Mushroom Sauce. Makes 8 servings.

Fresh Mushroom Sauce

½ pound mushrooms
½ cup butter, melted
6 tablespoons flour
1½ cups milk
½ cup light cream
1 teaspoon salt

½ teaspoon paprika
⅛ teaspoon white pepper
1 small clove garlic, crushed
1 beef bouillon cube
¼ cup hot water

Wipe mushrooms, chop stems, and slice caps thin. Sauté caps and stems in 2 tablespoons of the butter in a skillet until tender. Do not brown. In a saucepan make cream sauce by blending remaining butter with flour and slowly adding milk and cream, stirring constantly. Season with salt, paprika, pepper, and garlic. Add bouillon cube which has been dissolved in hot water. Add contents of skillet to the sauce; mix well. Keep hot over simmering water until ready to use. Makes 3½ cups.

Hot Chicken Salad Supreme

2 cups cubed cooked chicken
2 cups thinly sliced celery
1 cup toasted bread cubes
1 cup mayonnaise
½ cup chopped toasted
  almonds

2 tablespoons lemon juice
2 teaspoons minced onion
½ teaspoon salt
½ cup grated sharp Cheddar
  cheese
1 cup crushed potato chips

Heat oven to 450° F. Combine all ingredients except cheese and potato chips. Pile chicken mixture lightly into 6 individual baking dishes. Sprinkle each with cheese and potato chips. Bake 10 to 12 minutes or until bubbly. Makes 6 servings.

Chicken Caliente

This is a Mexican dish which I learned to enjoy by streamlining the original version.

2 cups boiling salted water
2 cups white corn meal
2 teaspoons bacon drippings
1 tablespoon butter
2 tablespoons minced onion
2 medium tomatoes, chopped
2 cups chopped cooked
  chicken
½ teaspoon salt

⅛ teaspoon pepper
vegetable oil
1 can (5 ounces) green
  chili peppers, drained,
  chopped
1 pound Monterey Jack
  cheese, shredded
4 chicken bouillon cubes
1 cup light cream

Combine boiling salted water, corn meal, and bacon drippings. Pat mixture into 6 very thin, flat cakes (tortillas) about 6 inches in diameter. Set aside until needed. Melt butter in a saucepan and sauté onion. Add tomatoes; simmer 5 minutes. Add chicken, salt, and pepper; simmer 20 minutes. Remove from heat; set aside. Heat oven to 350° F. Heat oil in deep pan; dip tortillas in oil for 30 seconds, but do not brown. Drain on absorbent paper. Put a few spoonfuls of chicken mixture on each tortilla; sprinkle each with chili peppers. Roll up and fasten with wooden picks. Arrange in a 2-quart baking pan; top with cheese. Sprinkle any remaining chili peppers on top. Dissolve bouillon cubes in cream; pour over tortillas. Bake 25 minutes. Makes 6 servings.

Chicken Monterey

1 can (10½ ounces)
condensed cream of
chicken soup
2 tablespoons dry sherry
1 cup diced, cooked chicken
1 cup leftover green peas
1 tablespoon chopped parsley
1 tablespoon lemon juice
1½ tablespoons chopped
pimientos

2 teaspoons chopped green or
black olives
½ teaspoon salt
⅛ teaspoon pepper
2 tablespoons butter
1 cup fresh bread crumbs
3 avocados, halved lengthwise
½ cup water

Heat oven to 375° F. Grease an 11×7×1½-inch baking pan. Blend
soup and sherry in a medium saucepan; bring to a boil, stirring
frequently. Add chicken, peas, parsley, lemon juice, pimientos, and
olives; blend carefully. Season with salt and pepper. Simmer 2
minutes, stirring occasionally. Melt butter in a small skillet; add
bread crumbs and sauté over medium heat, tossing frequently,
until golden. Arrange avocados, cut side up, in prepared pan.
Add water to pan. Fill avocados with chicken mixture and sprinkle
buttered crumbs on top. Bake 15 minutes. Makes 6 servings.

Mai Kai Chicken Croquettes

6 tablespoons flour
6 tablespoons butter, melted
1½ cups milk
½ cup light cream
1½ teaspoons salt
½ teaspoon celery salt
dash pepper
¼ cup minced onion

⅛ teaspoon ground ginger
3 cups chopped, cold cooked
chicken
1 cup finely chopped
blanched almonds
2 cups cracker crumbs
1 egg, well beaten
cooked rice

Blend flour into melted butter in a medium skillet; slowly add
milk and cream, stirring constantly until thickened. Season with
salts, pepper, onion, and ginger. Mix in the chicken. Remove
from heat and cool. Chill several hours or overnight. Shape into

8 croquettes. Add almonds to cracker crumbs and mix well. Roll croquettes in the crumbs, then in beaten egg, then in crumbs again. Fry in deep hot fat, 375° F., until golden brown. Serve with rice. Makes 4 servings.

Devonshire Chicken Sandwiches

I enjoyed these sandwiches when I was visiting in England.

3 cups diced cooked chicken
1½ cups chopped celery
1 cup grated sharp Cheddar
  cheese
¼ cup stuffed green olives,
  chopped

½ cup finely chopped walnuts
1 teaspoon salt
¼ teaspoon pepper
1 cup mayonnaise
8 slices bread

Preheat broiler. In a mixing bowl combine chicken, celery, cheese, olives, and walnuts. Season with salt and pepper; add mayonnaise. Blend well. Arrange bread on broiler pan; spread with chicken mixture. Broil 5 inches from heat for 8 minutes, or until golden. Makes 8 servings.

Chicken Lanai

2 cups fresh bread crumbs
4 cups diced cooked chicken
1 cup leftover cooked rice
1½ teaspoons salt
1 tablespoon finely chopped
  pimiento

1 teaspoon minced parsley
2 cups milk
1 cup chicken broth
4 eggs, lightly beaten
Mushroom Sauce (page 137)

Heat oven to 325° F. Grease a 10×6×1½-inch baking pan. Combine bread crumbs, chicken, and rice in a mixing bowl. Add salt, pimiento, parsley, milk, and broth and mix well. Add eggs; mix well. Turn into prepared pan and bake 1 hour. Cut into squares; serve with Mushroom Sauce. Makes 8 servings.

Chicken Pie Rockefeller

3 cups diced cooked chicken
1 cup diced cooked carrots
6 small white onions, boiled
1 tablespoon chopped parsley
1 tablespoon chopped celery
1 cup plus 2 tablespoons
  flour
1½ teaspoons salt
⅛ teaspoon pepper

⅛ teaspoon paprika
1 cup evaporated milk
1 cup chicken broth
1 teaspoon baking powder
1 cup cooled, cooked, mashed
  sweet potatoes
2 tablespoons butter, melted
1 egg, well beaten

Put chicken in a shallow 1½-quart baking dish. Sprinkle with carrots, onions, parsley, and celery. Combine 2 tablespoons of the flour with 1 teaspoon of the salt, the pepper and paprika in a saucepan. Gradually stir in evaporated milk and broth. Bring to a boil. Cook, stirring constantly, for 2 minutes. Pour sauce over chicken mixture.

To make the dough for the topping, combine remaining 1 cup flour, baking powder, and remaining salt. Combine sweet potatoes, butter, and egg in a bowl. Stir in dry ingredients. Chill thoroughly, at least 1 hour. Heat oven to 350° F. Roll out dough ¼ inch thick on a lightly floured board; cut a little larger than the baking dish. Place over baking dish and flute edge. Bake 40 minutes or until top is lightly browned. Makes 6 servings.

Hong Kong Egg Drop Soup

3 cups chicken broth
2 egg yolks

1 tablespoon slivered celery
few grains salt

Heat chicken broth over moderate heat until boiling. Beat egg yolks slightly. Slowly pour egg into broth, stirring constantly. Sprinkle celery and salt over soup. Serve at once. Makes 4 servings.

Luzerne Potato Soup

4 leeks
1¼ cups sliced fresh
  mushrooms
¼ cup butter
4 cups leftover chicken
  broth
5 sprigs parsley
¼ teaspoon crushed bay leaf

¼ teaspoon thyme
⅛ teaspoon basil
2 cups diced cooked potatoes
¾ teaspoon salt
¼ teaspoon white pepper
1 cup light cream
2 tablespoons chopped chives

Slice thinly the white and tender green part of the leeks. Sauté
with mushrooms in butter, stirring frequently, 5 minutes. Add
broth, parsley, bay leaf, thyme, and basil. Bring to a boil; cook
5 minutes. Add potatoes; season with salt and pepper. Cover
and simmer 15 minutes or until potatoes are mushy. Force mixture
through a food mill. Return to saucepan and heat to boiling point.
Stir in cream; heat gently 5 minutes. Serve hot, sprinkled with
chives. Makes 6 servings.

Chicken and Stuffing Scallop

1 package (8 ounces) herb-
  seasoned bread stuffing
3 cups diced cooked chicken
½ cup butter
½ cup flour
¼ teaspoon salt
⅛ teaspoon pepper
4 cups chicken broth

6 eggs, lightly beaten
1 can (10½ ounces)
  condensed cream of
  mushroom soup
¼ cup milk
1 cup commercial sour cream
¼ cup chopped pimientos

Heat oven to 325° F. Grease a 13×9½×2-inch baking pan. Sprinkle stuffing into pan and cover area; top with chicken. Melt butter
in a saucepan; blend in flour. Season with salt and pepper. Gradually
stir in broth. Cook over medium heat, stirring constantly, until
sauce is thick and smooth. Combine eggs with a little sauce. Return to rest of sauce and blend well. Pour over chicken in baking

pan. Bake 45 minutes or until knife inserted in center comes out clean. Let stand for 5 minutes. To make the sauce, combine remaining ingredients in a saucepan and heat thoroughly, but do not boil. Cut scallop into squares and serve with hot sauce. Makes 8 servings.

TURKEY

Turkey Pilau

6 slices bacon
1 large pepper, chopped
1 medium onion, chopped
1 tablespoon minced celery
1 package (10 ounces)
   frozen cut okra, thawed
3 teaspoons salt
4½ cups Turkey Broth (*see below*)

2⅓ cups rice
¾ teaspoon Tabasco
1 can (1 pound 3 ounces)
   whole tomatoes
dash Worcestershire sauce
3 cups diced cooked turkey

Sauté bacon until golden; remove from skillet and break into pieces. Reserve 2 tablespoons bacon drippings in the skillet. Add pepper, onion, celery, okra, and 1 teaspoon of the salt and sauté 5 minutes. In a large saucepan, heat Turkey Broth to boiling; add rice, the remaining 2 teaspoons salt, and Tabasco. Add sautéed mixture, bacon, tomatoes, and Worcestershire sauce. Simmer, covered, 25 minutes or until liquid is absorbed. Toss with turkey. Fluff up rice with fork before serving. Makes 6 servings.

Turkey Broth

leftover turkey bones
1½ quarts water
1 carrot, sliced
1 medium onion, sliced

1 stalk celery
2 teaspoons salt
⅛ teaspoon pepper

In a large kettle combine all ingredients; simmer, covered, 2 hours. Strain and use. Makes about 4½ cups.

Newburg Supreme

1 tablespoon butter
2 tablespoons flour
1 cup heavy cream
¼ cup mushroom liquid (from canned mushrooms)
1 egg yolk, slightly beaten
⅛ teaspoon white pepper
¼ teaspoon paprika

⅛ teaspoon nutmeg
1 cup diced cooked turkey
½ cup diced cooked ham
½ cup sliced canned mushrooms
2 tablespoons sherry
toast triangles

Melt butter in a heavy saucepan. Add flour and mix until smooth. Add cream and mushroom liquid; cook, stirring constantly, until just thickened. Remove from heat. Add a little of the hot mixture to the beaten egg yolk and stir vigorously. Pour back into remaining hot cream mixture, stirring constantly. Season with pepper, paprika, and nutmeg. Add turkey, ham, and mushrooms. Stir in sherry. Cook over low heat, stirring occasionally, until meat is thoroughly heated. Do not boil. Stir well. Serve at once over toast triangles. Makes 4 servings.

Turkey Mousse Parisienne

1 envelop unflavored gelatin
1½ cups turkey stock
1½ cups ground cooked turkey
¼ teaspoon curry powder
¼ cup mayonnaise
1 teaspoon celery salt
2 teaspoons grated onion
1 teaspoon finely chopped celery

½ teaspoon salt
⅛ teaspoon white pepper
¾ cup heavy cream, whipped, unsalted
lettuce leaves
¾ cup heavy cream, whipped, salted
6 slices pineapple
6 slices jellied cranberry sauce

Soften gelatin in ½ cup cold turkey stock. Dissolve over hot water. Combine remaining stock, turkey, curry powder, mayonnaise, celery salt, onion, and celery. Add dissolved gelatin; mix well. Season with salt and pepper. Chill until thick and syrupy. Beat chilled mixture until light and foamy; fold in the unsalted whipped cream. Pour mousse into a melon-shaped 1-quart mold. Chill until firm, 6 hours or overnight. Unmold on lettuce leaves on a serving platter. Using a pastry tube, garnish mousse with the salted whipped cream. Arrange pineapple slices around mousse. Top each pineapple slice with a cranberry sauce slice. Makes 6 servings.

Turkey Vôtre Goût

1 envelope sour cream mix
1 envelope cheese sauce mix
1½ cups milk
½ package (8 ounces)
   medium noodles

2 tablespoons butter
2 cups diced cooked turkey
1 tablespoon minced parsley
⅛ teaspoon paprika
⅛ teaspoon onion salt

Prepare the two mixes according to package directions, using ½ cup milk for the sour cream mix and 1 cup milk for the cheese sauce mix. Cook noodles in boiling salted water as directed on package until just done. Drain. Toss noodles with butter until well coated. Keep warm over very low heat. Add turkey to cheese sauce; heat until bubbly hot. Add sour cream mixture; heat 1 minute. Turn noodles around edge of a heated platter; sprinkle with parsley, paprika, and onion salt. Fill center with turkey in sauce. Makes 4 servings.

Turkey Pies à la Sharon

These individual pies will appeal to young and old alike.

1½ cups flour
1 envelope cheese sauce mix
½ teaspoon salt
½ teaspoon paprika
½ cup shortening
5 to 6 tablespoons cold water
2 cups leftover turkey gravy
3 cups diced cooked turkey
1 cup slant-sliced cooked
   celery

1 can (4 ounces) sliced
   mushrooms, drained, liquid
   reserved
1 tablespoon minced onion
   flakes
¼ teaspoon rosemary
⅛ teaspoon thyme

Heat oven to 425° F. In a mixing bowl combine flour, cheese sauce mix, salt, and paprika. With a pastry blender cut shortening into dry ingredients until mixture resembles corn meal. Add just enough water to moisten flour particles. Press dough together. Divide into 6 portions. Roll each portion ⅛ inch thick. Cut each to fit individual round serving dishes. Flute edges. Place rounds on an ungreased baking sheet. Carefully cut a small star in center of each round; remove center dough and reserve to bake separately. Prick pastry rounds. Bake 10 to 15 minutes or until baked through. Cool on rack. In a saucepan combine gravy, turkey, celery, drained mushrooms and half the mushroom liquid, the onion flakes, rosemary, and thyme. Heat until bubbly hot. Divide evenly among the 6 individual serving dishes. Top with baked crust rounds. Heat in a 350° F. oven 10 minutes or until heated through. Makes 6 servings.

New Orleans Turkey Scallop

The Turkey Liver Sauce provides an interesting contrast in flavors.

⅓ cup rice	2 eggs, well beaten
2 cups turkey broth	½ teaspoon salt
2½ cups diced cooked turkey	¼ teaspoon celery salt
⅓ cup chopped celery	⅛ teaspoon poultry seasoning
¼ cup chopped pimiento	Turkey Liver Sauce (*see*
1 tablespoon minced celery	*below*)

Heat oven to 325° F. Cook rice in broth 10 minutes or until partially tender. Combine with remaining ingredients, except Turkey Liver Sauce. Turn into a greased 1-quart baking dish. Bake 40 to 45 minutes or until set. Serve hot with Turkey Liver Sauce. Makes 6 servings.

Turkey Liver Sauce

¼ cup minced onion	¾ cup sliced mushrooms,
3 tablespoons butter	drained
3 tablespoons flour	¾ cup cooked chopped turkey
1 cup turkey broth	liver
½ cup heavy cream	

Sauté onion in butter until soft but not brown. Blend in flour. Stir in turkey broth and heavy cream. Cook, stirring constantly, over medium heat until thick. Add mushrooms and turkey liver. Heat thoroughly. Makes 2½ cups.

Turkey à l'Orange

2 tablespoons orange
  marmalade
¼ teaspoon instant minced
  onion
1 teaspoon grated lemon rind
½ teaspoon grated orange rind

2 tablespoons lemon juice
1 tablespoon cornstarch
¾ cup ginger ale
4 thick slices cooked turkey
  breast

Mix orange marmalade, onion, grated lemon and orange rinds, and lemon juice in a medium skillet. Cook 5 minutes over moderate heat. Combine cornstarch and ginger ale; stir gradually into orange marmalade mixture. Cook, stirring constantly, 6 minutes or until thickened and clear. Lay turkey slices in sauce; cover and cook over very low heat 5 minutes. Makes 4 servings.

Divine Turkey Divan

¼ cup margarine
¼ cup flour
1 chicken bouillon cube
1½ cups boiling water
2 tablespoons sherry
dash nutmeg
dash mace
½ cup heavy cream, whipped
¾ cup grated Parmesan
  cheese

2 packages (10 ounces each)
  frozen broccoli spears,
  cooked and drained
5 large slices cooked turkey
  breast
¼ cup grated sharp Cheddar
  cheese

In a medium saucepan, melt margarine over low heat. Blend in flour and cook over low heat, stirring constantly, until smooth and bubbly. Remove from heat. Dissolve chicken bouillon cube in boiling water. Gradually stir broth into flour mixture. Heat to boiling, stirring constantly. Boil 1 minute. Remove from heat. Stir in sherry and spices; gently fold in whipped cream and ½ cup of the Parmesan cheese. Place hot cooked broccoli in an oblong, shallow baking dish. Top with slices of turkey. Pour sauce over turkey. Sprinkle with remaining ¼ cup Parmesan cheese and Cheddar cheese. Set oven control at broil. Place baking dish 3 inches to 5 inches from heat and broil until cheese is bubbly and lightly browned. Makes 4 servings.

Turkey Amandine

1 cup flour	6 large slices cold cooked
1 teaspoon baking powder	turkey
½ teaspoon salt	shortening for frying
1 egg, lightly beaten	¼ cup butter
¾ cup milk	½ cup chopped almonds

In a mixing bowl combine flour, baking powder, and salt. Combine egg and milk; stir into dry ingredients to make a batter. Dip turkey slices in batter. Fry in shortening heated to 365° F. until golden brown. Drain on absorbent paper. Melt butter in a small saucepan; add almonds and sauté until golden brown. Pour almonds over turkey slices and serve immediately. Makes 6 servings.

Curried Turkey Benares

½ cup butter	2 teaspoons salt
1½ cups chopped onions	½ cup orange marmalade
1 cup diced green pepper	2 tablespoons lemon juice
2 tablespoons curry powder	4 cups diced cooked turkey
¾ cup flour	Almond Ti-Ti Rice (*see*
6 cups turkey or chicken broth	*below*)

Melt butter in a large, heavy saucepan; add onions and pepper and sauté 5 minutes. Stir in curry powder; sauté 2 minutes. Stir in flour. Gradually add broth and cook, stirring constantly, until mixture is thickened and smooth. Add salt, marmalade, and lemon juice. Cover and simmer 15 minutes. Add turkey and heat to serving temperature, stirring occasionally. Serve with Almond Ti-Ti Rice. Makes 8 servings.

Almond Ti-Ti Rice

2¾ cups instant rice   4 tablespoons butter
1 teaspoon salt   ½ cup slivered blanched
⅓ cup currants   almonds

Bring 2⅔ cups water to a boil in a medium saucepan; stir in rice, salt, and currants. Stir in 2 tablespoons of the butter. Cover and removed from heat; let stand 5 minutes. Melt the remaining 2 tablespoons butter in a skillet; add almonds and sauté over low heat, stirring frequently, until golden. Stir almonds into rice.

DUCK

Duck Fricassee Jong

A San Francisco dish adapted from the South.

1 carcass of roast duck
3 cups hot water
1 onion, sliced
1 stalk celery, cut up
1 carrot, cut up
2 teaspoons salt
¼ teaspoon rosemary
2 whole cloves
dash Tabasco

¼ cup orange marmalade
2 tablespoons currant jelly
¼ teaspoon Worcestershire sauce
1 tablespoon flour
2 cups roast duck meat, cut up
1 tablespoon chopped parsley

Break up carcass of duck and place in a large, heavy kettle. Pour hot water over duck bones. Add onion, celery, carrot, salt, rosemary, cloves, and Tabasco. Cover and simmer 1½ hours. Remove bones. Strain broth and skim off fat. Reduce broth to 1⅔ cups of liquid; pour into a heavy skillet. Add marmalade, currant jelly, and Worcestershire sauce. Bring to boil, stirring. Add flour, stirring constantly until mixture is smooth and thickened. Add duck meat; heat through. Serve on heated platter. Sprinkle with parsley. Makes 4 servings.

FISH AND SHELLFISH

Bavarian Fish Casserole

1 large onion, chopped
¼ cup butter
2 tablespoons flour
dash sage
1 cup light cream
1 cup milk
¾ teaspoon salt
2 tablespoons capers
½ teaspoon lemon juice
3 tablespoons grated
   Parmesan cheese

6 medium potatoes, pared,
   thinly sliced
3 cups any leftover firm
   cooked fish, flaked
2 tablespoons fine dry bread
   crumbs
½ teaspoon paprika
1 tablespoon margarine

Heat oven to 350° F. Sauté onion in butter 3 minutes or until soft but not brown. Stir in flour and sage. Gradually add combined cream and milk, cooking over low heat and stirring frequently until sauce bubbles and thickens. Add salt, capers, lemon juice, and cheese. Layer potatoes and fish alternately in a 2-quart baking dish, ending with potatoes. Pour sauce over all. Combine bread crumbs and paprika and sprinkle over casserole; dot with margarine. Bake 1 hour or until potatoes are tender. Makes 6 to 8 servings.

Halibut Droyel

2½ pounds fresh or frozen
   halibut steaks
16 medium mushrooms
1 small onion, chopped
¼ cup chopped celery
½ cup fine dry bread crumbs
½ cup butter, melted
3 tablespoons lemon juice

¾ teaspoon salt
⅛ teaspoon pepper
16 small shrimp, cooked,
   shelled, deveined
1 cup commercial sour cream
¼ teaspoon paprika
1 tablespoon chopped parsley

If fish is frozen, let stand at room temperature 30 minutes. Heat oven to 375° F. Wash and trim mushrooms. Carefully pull out stems and chop, reserving caps. Mix chopped stems with onion, celery, and bread crumbs. Combine butter, lemon juice, salt, and pepper. Add half this mixture to crumb mixture and mix well. Fill mushroom caps loosely with it; reserve leftover. Press a shrimp into each mushroom. Grease a heatproof platter large enough to hold halibut steaks. Sprinkle remaining crumb mixture on platter. Lay steaks on top; arrange stuffed mushrooms around fish. Pour remaining butter mixture over all. Spread fish steaks with sour cream; add a dab on each mushroom. Bake 30 minutes or until fish flakes easily with fork. Sprinkle with paprika and parsley. Makes 4 servings with leftovers.

East Indian Fish Puff

2 cups cooked rice
1½ cups leftover cooked
   haddock, flaked
4 hard-cooked eggs, sliced

2 tablespoons chopped parsley
2 tablespoons chopped celery
1½ cups light cream
2 tablespoons curry powder

Heat oven to 350° F. In a 1-quart baking dish alternately layer rice, fish, sliced eggs, parsley, and celery. Combine cream with curry powder; pour over all. Bake 20 to 30 minutes. Makes 4 servings.

Noodle Ring Supreme

1 package (6 ounces)
  noodles
1½ cups milk
1 cup grated Cheddar cheese
½ teaspoon salt
½ teaspoon paprika
dash seasoned pepper
dash white pepper
½ cup finely chopped onion

3 eggs, beaten
1 cup soft bread crumbs
1 canned pimiento, chopped
4 mushrooms, chopped
2 tablespoons chopped parsley
½ cup chopped cooked carrots
2 cups hot creamed leftover
  halibut cubes

Cook noodles according to package directions; drain and keep warm. Heat oven to 350° F. Heat milk in top of double broiler; stir in cheese, seasonings, and onion. Add mixture to beaten eggs, stirring constantly. Stir in crumbs, pimiento, mushrooms, parsley, and carrots; lightly stir in hot cooked noodles. Turn into a greased 4-cup ring mold. Set mold in pan of hot water. Bake 25 to 30 minutes. Turn out onto heated platter. Fill center with hot creamed halibut; serve immediately. Makes 4 servings.

Italian Stuffed Cheese Balls

1 cup grated sharp Cheddar
  cheese
3 tablespoons butter
½ cup flour

½ teaspoon salt
⅛ teaspoon cayenne
12 cooked shrimp, cut up
paprika

Heat oven to 400° F. Combine cheese, butter, flour, salt, and cayenne and mix thoroughly. Shape into small balls around shrimp pieces. Sprinkle with paprika. Arrange on baking sheet and bake 15 minutes or until golden brown. Makes 1 dozen appetizers.

Fish Soufflé with Pecan Sauce

1 cup fresh bread crumbs
2 cups cooked fish, boned
  and flaked
1 teaspoon salt
¼ teaspoon pepper

½ cup milk
½ cup heavy cream
4 egg whites
Pecan Sauce (*see below*)

Heat oven to 350° F. Grease a 1½-quart casserole. In top of double boiler combine bread crumbs, fish, salt, pepper, milk, and cream. Cook over hot water, stirring frequently, until creamy; cool slightly. Beat egg whites until stiff but not dry. Fold into fish mixture. Turn into casserole. Place in shallow pan containing 1 inch hot water. Bake 45 minutes. Cut into slices; serve with Pecan Sauce. Makes 6 servings.

Pecan Sauce

2 tablespoons butter
¼ cup chopped pecans
2 tablespoons flour

1 cup light cream
¼ teaspoon salt

Melt butter in a saucepan; brown pecans lightly, stirring frequently. Blend in flour; gradually stir in cream. Cook over low heat, stirring constantly, until thickened. Remove from heat; season with salt. Makes 1½ cups.

Pamplona Española

1 pound salt codfish
2 tablespoons vegetable oil
1½ cloves garlic, minced
2 tomatoes, sliced
1 large onion, thinly sliced
1 green pepper, chopped
2 tablespoons chili sauce
1 bay leaf
¼ teaspoon basil
½ teaspoon sugar
¼ teaspoon cumin seeds
¼ teaspoon oregano

¼ teaspoon marjoram
¼ teaspoon pepper
½ cup white wine
½ cup cooked crab meat, flaked
1 cup cooked shrimp
1 cup cooked chicken, chopped
1 can (4 ounces) whole mushrooms, drained
1 cup cooked black beans
1¼ cups cooked rice

One day before, cover codfish with cold water; let stand 20 minutes, then drain. Cut into pieces. Add cold water to cover and soak overnight. Next day, bring fish and water to boil; reduce heat and simmer 45 minutes. Rinse in warm water; drain thoroughly. Heat oil in a large, heavy skillet. Add garlic, tomatoes, onion, green pepper, chili sauce, bay leaf, basil, sugar, cumin seeds, oregano, marjoram, and pepper. Blend in wine and bring to boil. Cover; simmer 30 minutes. Add codfish; simmer 20 minutes longer. Add crab meat, shrimp, chicken, and mushrooms; simmer 10 minutes longer. Serve with black beans and rice which have been heated and tossed lightly. Makes 6 servings.

Deep Sea Haddock Pie

¼ cup butter, melted
2 cups fresh bread crumbs
1 tablespoon grated onion
¾ teaspoon salt
½ teaspoon celery salt
⅛ teaspoon pepper

⅛ teaspoon sage
3 tablespoons shortening
3 tablespoons flour
1 cup milk
1 cup cooked, flaked haddock
1 cup bread crumbs, buttered

Heat oven to 375° F. Grease a 1½-quart baking pan. In mixing bowl combine butter, fresh crumbs, onion, ½ teaspoon of the salt and half the quantities of celery salt, pepper, and sage; mix well. Press mixture onto bottom and sides of baking pan. Bake 25 minutes. Increase oven temperature to 425° F. Melt shortening in a medium skillet; blend in flour. Gradually stir in milk. Cook over medium heat, stirring constantly, until thick and smooth. Remove from heat. Stir in remaining seasonings and fish. Pour onto prepared crust. Top with buttered bread crumbs. Bake 20 minutes or until lightly browned. Makes 4 servings.

Crab and Shrimp Newburg

¼ cup butter
¼ cup flour
¼ teaspoon salt
¼ teaspoon onion salt
⅛ teaspoon paprika
1½ cups milk
½ cup light cream

2 egg yolks, beaten
1 cup cooked crab meat, flaked
1 cup shrimp, halved
1 tablespoon lemon juice
6 patty shells

Melt butter over low heat in a saucepan. Blend in flour and seasonings; cook over low heat, stirring, until mixture is smooth and bubbly. Remove from heat; stir in milk and cream gradually.

Return to heat and bring to boil, stirring constantly. Boil 1 minute. Stir half the hot sauce into the egg yolks; blend mixture into remaining sauce. Just before serving, stir in crab, shrimp, and lemon juice. Serve hot in patty shells. Makes 6 servings.

Virgin Islands Fish Salad

The original recipe for this refreshing salad called for raw fish, which is popular in many countries.

2 cups cold cooked rice
¼ cup French dressing
1½ cups cooked fish, boned, flaked
1 tablespoon lemon juice
¼ cup mayonnaise
½ teaspoon curry powder
½ cup chopped celery

1 tablespoon chopped chutney
½ cup cooked peas
1 tablespoon chopped almonds
½ teaspoon salt
dash paprika
salad greens

Fold together rice and French dressing; chill and marinate 1 hour. Sprinkle fish with lemon juice and chill. Mix mayonnaise and curry powder. Toss together rice, fish, mayonnaise, and remaining ingredients, except salad greens. Serve on salad greens. Makes 6 servings.

Lobster Romandeaux

¼ cup minced green onions
2 tablespoons butter
2 tablespoons flour
¼ teaspoon salt
¼ teaspoon onion salt
⅛ teaspoon pepper
⅛ teaspoon paprika
¼ teaspoon dry mustard

1½ cups milk
1½ cups shredded mild Cheddar cheese
¼ cup sherry
2 cups cooked wide noodles
2 cups cooked lobster meat, cut up
2 tablespoons lemon juice

Heat oven to 375° F. Cook onion in butter until soft; remove from heat. Blend in flour and seasonings. Cook over low heat, stirring constantly, until mixture is bubbly. Remove from heat. Slowly stir in milk. Heat to boiling, stirring constantly; boil 1 minute. Add 1 cup of the cheese; stir over low heat until cheese is melted. Stir in wine. Arrange noodles around sides of baking dish, 10× 6×1½-inch. Place lobster meat in center and sprinkle with lemon juice. Pour sauce over all. Sprinkle with remaining cheese. Bake 20 to 25 minutes or until mixture is bubbly and lightly browned. Makes 4 servings.

Shrimp Bisque

2 tablespoons butter
1 teaspoon minced onion
2 tablespoons flour
1 cup chicken broth
1½ cups light cream
½ teaspoon salt

⅛ teaspoon white pepper
1 cup finely chopped cooked
   shrimp
dash cayenne
1 teaspoon minced parsley

Melt butter in a medium skillet; add onion and sauté until soft but not brown. Stir in flour; cook 2 minutes. Slowly add combined chicken broth and cream; stir until smooth. Season with salt and pepper. Add shrimp. Turn into the top of a double boiler. Heat over boiling water 20 minutes. Pour into a soup tureen; sprinkle with cayenne and parsley. Makes 4 servings.

VEGETABLES

Winter Garden Loaf

A dramatic salad mold, refreshing and delicious.

2 packages lemon-flavored
   gelatin
3½ cups hot water
3 tablespoons vinegar
¼ teaspoon salt
¼ teaspoon seasoned salt
16 canned whole green beans
4 long strips pimiento

1 cup cooked cauliflowerets
¼ cup cooked sliced carrots
¼ cup cooked, diced green
   pepper
¼ cup diced celery
¼ cup sliced radishes
¼ cup sliced green onions
lettuce leaves

Dissolve gelatin in hot water; add vinegar and salts. Pour about
½ inch gelatin mixture in an 8½ × 4½ × 2½-inch loaf pan. Chill until set. Divide beans in bundles of 4. Circle each bundle with a
pimiento strip. Arrange on gelatin in pan. Chill remaining gelatin
until partially set; pour enough over beans to cover. Chill until
firm. Combine remaining gelatin with remaining vegetables. Pour
over firm gelatin in pan; chill until set. Unmold on bed of lettuce.
Makes 8 servings.

Fried Rollies

2 eggs, separated
2 cups leftover mashed
   potatoes
¼ pound processed American
   cheese, cubed
1 teaspoon baking powder

½ teaspoon curry powder
⅛ teaspoon garlic salt
¼ teaspoon paprika
2 tablespoons water
1 cup fine bread crumbs
shortening for frying

Add egg yolks to mashed potatoes; mix well. Add cheese, baking powder, and seasonings. Form into 12 1-inch balls. Combine egg whites with water. Dip balls into egg white mixture. Roll in bread crumbs. Fry in hot shortening, 375° F., 4 minutes or until golden brown. Serve hot. Makes 4 servings.

Potato Cups Madeleine

3 cups leftover mashed
  potatoes
melted butter
1 can (8 ounces) cheese
  sauce

2 strips bacon, crisp-fried,
  crumbled
6 strips pimiento

Heat oven to 400° F. Shape mashed potatoes into 6 mounds on a greased baking sheet. Make a hollow in the center of each mound with a tablespoon; brush with melted butter. Bake 10 minutes. Fill mounds with cheese sauce; place under broiler for a few minutes to brown. Sprinkle with bacon; decorate with pimiento. Serve hot. Makes 6 servings.

Chantilly Potato Cups

2 cups leftover mashed
  potatoes
1 egg yolk
2 tablespoons butter
¼ cup finely chopped green
  pepper
2 tablespoons finely chopped
  onion

½ teaspoon salt
⅛ teaspoon pepper
⅛ teaspoon paprika
½ cup heavy cream
¼ cup grated cheese
1 egg white, stiffly beaten

Heat oven to 350° F. Combine potatoes and egg yolk and blend well. Melt butter in a skillet. Add green pepper and onion and cook over low heat until tender. Add to mashed potatoes and mix well. Season mixture with salt, pepper, and paprika. Spoon mixture into 6 greased custard cups. Whip cream until stiff. Fold in cheese and egg white. Spoon over potato mixture. Bake 30 minutes or until a knife inserted in the center comes out clean. Serve immediately. Makes 6 servings.

Cordon Bleu Pancakes

1½ cups cold mashed potatoes
3 tablespoons flour
¾ teaspoon salt
⅛ teaspoon pepper

⅛ teaspoon paprika
½ cup chopped Bleu cheese
butter

Mix potatoes, flour, and seasonings. Shape into 8 thin patties about 2 inches wide. Sprinkle 4 patties with cheese; cover with remaining patties. Press together to thoroughly enclose cheese. Sauté over low heat in a small amount of butter until browned on both sides. Makes 4 servings.

Pink Luncheon Salad

1 cup slivered cooked beets
2 cups coarsely chopped celery
1 teaspoon instant minced onion

¼ cup French dressing
1 teaspoon sesame seed
salad greens

Combine beets and celery in a bowl. Mix onion, dressing, and sesame seed; add to beet mixture and toss lightly. Chill and serve on salad greens. Makes 4 servings.

Carrots Louisa

1½ cups diced cooked carrots
3 soda crackers, crushed
½ teaspoon onion salt
2 tablespoons chopped green pepper

⅛ teaspoon pepper
1 tablespoon butter, melted
¼ cup grated sharp cheese

Heat oven to 425° F. Grease a 1-quart baking dish. Place a layer of carrots in the bottom. Combine crackers, onion salt, green pepper, and pepper. Spread mixture over carrots and alternate layers until all ingredients are used. Pour butter over mixture and sprinkle with cheese. Bake 15 to 20 minutes or until cheese melts. Makes 4 servings.

Peas and Celery au Coq

2 cups sliced celery
1 tablespoon instant minced
 onion
½ cup chicken broth
2 teaspoons flour
¼ cup light cream

1 to 1½ cups leftover cooked
 peas
1 tablespoon butter
½ teaspoon salt
⅛ teaspoon pepper

Combine celery, onion, and chicken broth in a medium saucepan; cover and simmer 15 minutes. Blend flour and cream; stir into mixture. Cook, stirring constantly, until slightly thickened. Add peas and butter. Heat 2 minutes. Season with salt and pepper. Makes 4 servings.

Frankfurters à la Patoush

6 strips bacon
6 frankfurters
1½ cups leftover mashed
 potatoes
1 egg
1½ tablespoons chopped
 onion

½ teaspoon celery salt
⅛ teaspoon paprika
1 teaspoon prepared mustard
2 teaspoons horseradish

Heat oven to 425° F. Fry bacon until limp. Cut frankfurters almost through lengthwise; lay open. Mix together remaining ingredients. Spoon potato mixture into frankfurters; close halves. Wrap each frankfurther with bacon and fasten with wooden pick. Place in shallow baking pan. Bake 10 to 15 minutes or until bacon is crisp. Makes 6 servings.

Puff and Bacon

4 strips bacon
¾ cup milk
¾ cup grated American
 cheese
½ teaspoon Worcestershire
 sauce

dash Tabasco
¼ teaspoon chili powder
3 cups leftover mashed
 potatoes
4 eggs, separated
1 tablespoon chopped parsley

Heat oven to 350° F. Partially fry bacon in a skillet, saving the drippings. Heat milk in a saucepan; add cheese, stirring thoroughly until cheese is melted. Add bacon drippings, Worcestershire sauce, Tabasco, and chili powder. Combine milk mixture with mashed potatoes and blend. Add egg yolks and beat well. Beat egg whites until stiff but not dry. Fold into potato mixture. Turn into an ungreased 2-quart baking dish and top with bacon strips. Bake 45 to 50 minutes. Sprinkle with parsley. Makes 6 servings.

Sweet Potato Casserole Delight

2 cups mashed leftover sweet potatoes
2 tablespoons butter, melted
2 tablespoons flour
½ cup grated Swiss cheese
½ cup grated Parmesan cheese

½ cup milk
¼ cup light cream
3 eggs, separated
½ teaspoon salt
¼ teaspoon nutmeg
dash mace

Heat oven to 375° F. Combine sweet potatoes, butter, flour, cheeses, milk, and cream; blend well. Beat in egg yolks, one at a time. Season with salt, nutmeg, and mace. Beat egg whites until stiff but not dry. Fold into sweet potato mixture. Turn into a buttered 1-quart baking dish. Bake 45 minutes or until puffed and lightly browned. Makes 6 servings.

Pomme de Terre Provençale

8 slices bacon, diced
½ cup diced green pepper
½ cup finely chopped green onion
1½ cups diced cooked potato
½ teaspoon salt

¼ teaspoon pepper
6 eggs
¼ cup heavy cream
¼ cup milk
paprika

Fry bacon in a large, heavy skillet until browned. Remove and set aside. Pour off all but 3 tablespoons drippings. Add green pepper and onion; cook 5 minutes. Add potato; cook until lightly browned, stirring occasionally. Season with salt and pepper. Beat eggs with cream and milk just enough to mix. Pour egg mixture carefully into the pan over the vegetables. Cook over low heat, stirring lightly, until eggs are set but still moist and creamy. Sprinkle with paprika and reserved bacon and serve immediately. Makes 4 servings.

Gnocchi di Brindisi

This Italian specialty is an international dish.

1 cup flour	1 cup grated Parmesan cheese
2 cups mashed potatoes	2 cups Mornay Sauce (*see*
2 tablespoons butter	*below*)
1 egg, beaten with 1 egg	½ cup grated Gruyère cheese
yolk	1 tablespoon minced parsley
dash nutmeg	

Sprinkle a wooden board or flat surface generously with some of the flour. Place potatoes on board. With a fork, quickly work in butter, egg, ¾ cup of the flour, and nutmeg. Knead mixture lightly with remaining flour and ½ cup of the Parmesan cheese, until dough is smooth and pliable. Cut off egg-size knobs of dough; roll into finger-sized rolls. Cut in 1-inch pieces. With the back of a floured fork, press in lightly and roll fork forward to simulate shell indentation. Place prepared dough on a towel and let stand 1 hour. Drop gnocchi, a few at a time, into a large, heavy kettle of boiling salted water. Cook gently 4 to 6 minutes or until light and slightly puffed. Remove with a slotted spoon. Continue until all are cooked. Heat oven to 400° F. Layer drained, cooked gnocchi in a buttered, shallow 2-quart baking dish with Mornay Sauce and the remaining ½ cup Parmesan cheese in between. Sprinkle Gruyère cheese and parsley on top. Bake 15 to 20 minutes or until bubbly hot and browned on top. Makes 8 servings.

Mornay Sauce

2 tablespoons butter	⅛ teaspoon pepper
3 tablespoons flour	dash cayenne
2 cups milk, scalded	2 tablespoons grated Swiss
½ teaspoon salt	cheese

Melt butter in a medium saucepan; blend in flour. Stir over low heat 2 minutes. Do not allow to brown. Gradually stir in scalded milk. Cook over moderate heat, stirring constantly, until mixture comes to a boil. Season with salt, pepper, and cayenne. Blend in Swiss cheese. Makes about 2 cups.

Prospector's Soufflé

¾ teaspoon salt
dash pepper
4 eggs, separated
1½ cups cooked vegetables, drained, chopped
1 tablespoon chopped parsley

1 tablespoon chopped celery
2 tablespoons minced onion
3 tablespoons grated Parmesan cheese
1 teaspoon mixed herbs
2 tablespoons vegetable oil

Add salt and pepper to egg yolks and beat until thick. Fold in vegetables, parsley, celery, onion, cheese, and herbs. Heat oven to 350° F. Beat egg whites until stiff. Fold into vegetable mixture. Heat vegetable oil in a large, heavy skillet until hot. Pour in mixture; bake 20 minutes. Makes 4 servings.

Beets à l'Orange

¼ cup orange juice
½ teaspoon grated orange rind
1 tablespoon lemon juice
2 tablespoons sugar

1½ teaspoons cornstarch
¼ teaspoon salt
1½ cups cooked beets
1 tablespoon butter

Combine orange juice, rind, and lemon juice in a small saucepan; heat thoroughly. Combine sugar, cornstarch, and salt; add to hot liquid, stirring constantly, until smooth and thickened. Add beets and butter; heat through and serve at once. Makes 4 servings.

Mashed Potatoes Royale

1½ cups mashed potatoes
2 tablespoons butter
1 egg
½ cup light cream, hot

½ teaspoon salt
dash pepper
⅛ teaspoon paprika

Heat oven to 375° F. Combine all ingredients except paprika. Beat well. Turn into a greased 1-quart baking dish. Sprinkle with paprika. Bake until top is lightly browned, about 10 minutes. Makes 4 servings.

Garden Vegetable Ring

1 package lemon-flavored
  gelatin
1½ cups boiling water
1 tablespoon vinegar
¾ cup shredded cabbage
¼ cup chopped parsley

½ cup diced celery
2 tablespoons chopped green
  pepper
½ cup cooked peas
½ cup diced cooked carrot
¼ teaspoon salt

Dissolve gelatin in boiling water; cool. Add remaining ingredients. Stir well and turn into a 6-cup ring mold. Chill in refrigerator overnight or until firm. Unmold and serve. Makes 6 servings.

Three-Spice Patties

At our PTA circle we called this our 1-2-3 quick meal.

1 cup leftover mashed
  potatoes
½ pound ground beef
1 egg
½ teaspoon salt
⅛ teaspoon pepper
¼ teaspoon oregano
⅛ teaspoon thyme

⅛ teaspoon basil
2 tablespoons minced onion
¼ cup dry milk solids
flour
shortening
1 can (10½ ounces)
  condensed tomato soup

Mix potatoes with beef, egg, seasonings, spices, onion, and dry milk solids. Form into 6 patties about 1 inch thick. Coat with flour. Brown patties on both sides in shortening. Add tomato soup; cover and simmer 25 minutes. Makes 6 servings.

SANDWICHES

Suggestions for Sandwich Making

To make sandwich fillings use your imagination and whatever is on hand. Even if the leftover ingredient quantity is small, don't throw it away. Make individual sandwiches and label them with small flags on wooden picks for easy identification and offer several varieties of one-of-a-kind.

Use white, whole wheat, rye, nut, date, pumpernickel, whole-grain dark, cheese, garlic, cracked wheat, or corn bread and almost any type of roll.

Spread soft butter or margarine to the edge on both slices of bread to prevent filling from soaking in. Season filling before spreading.

Lettuce leaves, tomato slices, pickles, and bacon should be added to sandwiches just before serving. Use colorful garnishes to complement the flavor of the filling, such as olives, pickles, celery sticks, radishes, carrot sticks, pickled onions, tiny cherry tomatoes, green pepper cut into thin strips, and thinly sliced cucumbers.

Sandwich Fillings

Cheese
Cream cheese, chopped stuffed olives, and chopped walnuts.
Cream cheese, drained crushed pineapple, and chopped almonds.
Cream cheese, Roquefort cheese, crumbled bacon, and chopped pecans.
Cream cheese, apricot juice, and mayonnaise.
Cream cheese, finely shredded cucumber, minced onion tops.
Cream cheese, dried beef pieces, grated onion, and diced celery.
Cottage cheese, minced green pepper, chopped parsley, and minced onion.

Roquefort cheese, chopped chicken, and crumbled bacon.

Blue cheese, finely chopped almonds, and grated onion.

Shredded American cheese, chopped pimiento, onion, pickle, hard-cooked eggs, and mayonnaise.

Shredded American cheese, bacon pieces, chopped pickles, olives, Worcestershire sauce, and mayonnaise.

Cottage cheese, bacon pieces, horseradish, salt, pepper, and mayonnaise.

Eggs

Chopped hard-cooked egg, chopped ham, minced green pepper, and green onion with salad dressing.

Chopped hard-cooked egg, pickle relish, pimiento, and mayonnaise.

Chopped hard-cooked egg, chopped stuffed olives, chopped celery, salt, pepper, and mayonnaise.

Chopped hard-cooked egg, finely minced celery, onion, parsley, green pepper, crumbled crisp bacon, salt and pepper, and mayonnaise.

Chopped hard-cooked egg, deviled ham, Worcestershire sauce, and chopped pickle.

Chopped hard-cooked egg, chopped onion, pickle, and crumbled crisp bacon.

Chopped hard-cooked egg, crumbled bacon, drained pickle relish, finely chopped radish, carrot, with mayonnaise.

Fish

Flaked salmon, chopped celery, sweet pickle, and mayonnaise.

Crab meat, chopped celery, parsley, dash of lemon juice, and mayonnaise.

Chopped cooked lobster meat, chopped mushrooms, green pepper, curry powder, Worcestershire sauce, and mayonnaise.

Red caviar, chopped cucumber (drained), riced hard-cooked egg, onion juice, and salad dressing.

Flaked tuna fish, chopped celery, egg, pimiento, sweet pickle, salt, pepper, and mayonnaise.

Minced cooked shrimp, onion, lemon juice, salt, and mayonnaise.

Minced tuna, horseradish, cream cheese, lemon juice, and mayonnaise.

Chopped cooked lobster, minced onion, diced celery, lemon juice, salt, paprika, and salad dressing.

Meat

Leftover ground roast beef, chopped pickle and celery, horseradish, and mayonnaise.

Chopped corned beef, grated onion, chopped kosher pickle, celery, parsley, and tomato purée.

Chopped cooked beef, chili sauce, minced celery, water cress, salt, pepper, and prepared mustard.

Mashed leftover baked beans with chopped frankfurter, minced onion, prepared mustard, and mayonnaise.

Ground cooked chicken, ground blanched almonds, drained pineapple, and mayonnaise.

Ground ham, chopped gherkins, prepared mustard, and mayonnaise.

Chopped almonds, ground cooked ham, hard-cooked egg, horseradish, and mayonnaise.

Ground cooked ham, minced green pepper, prepared mustard, minced onion, and mayonnaise.

Chopped cooked ham, chopped celery, chopped red apple, and salad dressing.

DESSERTS

Orange Delight Sponge

1 cup cake flour
1 teaspoon baking powder
¼ cup butter, melted
½ teaspoon vanilla
½ cup milk, scalded

6 egg yolks
1 cup sugar
Orange Delight Frosting (*see below*)

Heat oven to 350° F. Mix flour and baking powder. Add butter and vanilla to scalded milk; keep hot. Beat egg yolks until thick and lemon-colored; gradually beat in sugar. Quickly add flour mixture. Stir in the hot milk mixture. Pour into a greased 9-inch square pan. Bake 30 to 35 minutes or until done. Cool thoroughly. Frost with Orange Delight Frosting.

Orange Delight Frosting

¼ cup butter
2 cups sifted confectioner's sugar
2 teaspoons grated orange rind

1 to 2 tablespoons orange juice
9 walnut halves

Thoroughly cream butter with confectioners' sugar. Add orange rind. Stir in enough orange juice to make frosting of spreading consistency; beat until smooth. Spread on cooled cake; top with walnut halves.

Eskimo Soufflé

½ cup sugar
⅔ cup water
1 package (10 ounces)
    frozen raspberries, thawed

2 egg yolks
1½ cups heavy cream
green maraschino cherries,
    halved

Cook sugar and water together until mixture spins a thread or a candy thermometer registers 240° F. Beat egg yolks well; gradually add hot sugar syrup, beating constantly until blended. Rub raspberries through a sieve. Whip 1 cup of the heavy cream until it holds its shape. Fold raspberries and cream into egg-yolk mixture. Pour into a 1-quart soufflé dish. Cover surface with foil; freeze 3½ to 4 hours. Whip the remaining cream and garnish soufflé with whipped cream and cherries. Makes 6 servings.

Top Plum Pudding

1 cup stale bread crumbs
1 cup milk
¾ cup dried currants
6 eggs, separated
¾ cup sugar
1 cup flour
1 teaspoon salt
½ teaspoon cloves
½ teaspoon cinnamon
½ teaspoon nutmeg

¼ teaspoon mace
¼ teaspoon allspice
¾ pound fresh beef suet, very
    finely chopped
1 package (4 ounces) citron,
    chopped
1 pound seedless raisins
½ cup brandy
Hard Sauce (*see below*)

Soak bread crumbs in milk. Soak currants in warm water to plump. Beat egg yolks with sugar. Drain bread crumbs and add to egg yolk mixture. Combine flour with salt and spices; blend well. Add suet and blend. Stir flour mixture into egg yolk mixture. Drain currants; add with citron and raisins to pudding mixture. Beat egg whites until stiff. Fold into pudding mixture. Very slowly add brandy in a thin stream and mix well. Turn into a greased 3-cup mold and steam, on a rack, 3 to 4 hours. Serve with Hard Sauce. Makes 6 servings.

Hard Sauce

½ cup sweet butter, softened   1 tablespoon brandy
2 cups sifted confectioner's
  sugar

Combine all ingredients and beat until smooth. Chill thoroughly before serving.

Swedish Fruktsoppa

A streamlined version of a Swedish fruit soup.

1 apple, pared and diced   ½ cup apricot juice
10 cooked prunes, pitted   1 tablespoon lemon juice
6 canned whole apricots,   peel of ¼ lemon, thinly
  pitted   sliced
½ cup prune juice   1 cup finely cracked ice

Blend this soup in the electric blender 2 minutes. Serve very cold. Makes 4 servings.

Handorshire Cake

1 envelope unflavored gelatin   ⅛ teaspoon salt
1 cup canned fruit syrup   1 cup canned fruit cocktail,
¼ teaspoon grated lemon rind   drained
3 tablespoons lemon juice   2 egg whites
¾ teaspoon ground ginger   ½ cup heavy cream
dash nutmeg   1 9-inch yellow cake layer
½ cup sugar

Sprinkle gelatin over fruit syrup in a saucepan to soften. Dissolve gelatin over low heat, stirring constantly. Add lemon rind and juice, ginger, nutmeg, ¼ cup of the sugar, and the salt; mix well. Chill until mixture begins to thicken. Fold in fruit. Beat egg whites until soft peaks form; gradually add remaining ¼ cup sugar, beating until stiff but not dry. Whip cream until it holds its shape. Fold beaten egg whites and cream into gelatin mixture. Pour into an 8-inch layer cake pan; chill until set. Unmold on cake layer. Makes 8 servings.

Coffee Cake à la Reine

Add this special touch to your afternoon tea.

1½ cups prepared biscuit mix
1 cup sugar
¼ teaspoon baking soda
3 tablespoons butter, melted
1 egg

¾ cup soured heavy cream
1 teaspoon vanilla
¼ cup margarine, melted
½ cup soft bread crumbs
¼ cup chopped walnuts

Heat oven to 350° F. Grease and flour an 8-inch square pan. Combine biscuit mix, ¾ cup of the sugar, and soda. Add butter, egg, and ¼ cup of the soured cream. Beat vigorously with a wooden spoon 1 minute. Add remaining cream and vanilla; beat ½ minute. Pour into the prepared pan. Combine margarine, the remaining ¼ cup sugar, bread crumbs, and walnuts and sprinkle over cake. Bake 35 minutes. Serve warm. Makes 8 servings.

Zabaglione

This Italian favorite can be prepared a dozen different ways.

4 egg yolks
1 cup sugar

few grains salt
½ cup sherry

Beat egg yolks slightly with a rotary beater in the top of a double boiler. Gradually add sugar and salt, beating constantly until light and fluffy. Gradually add sherry, beating until blended. Place over gently boiling water. Cook until thickened, beating constantly, about 15 to 20 minutes or until mixture forms soft peaks. Chill in sherbet glasses. Makes 4 servings.

Petaluma Puffs

2 egg whites
⅔ cup sugar
2 cups flaked coconut

4 teaspoons cornstarch
¾ teaspoon almond extract

Heat oven to 300° F. Beat egg whites with a rotary beater until soft peaks form; gradually add sugar, beating constantly, until whites are stiff but not dry. Stir together coconut and cornstarch and fold into beaten egg whites. Add almond extract. Drop rounded teaspoonfuls about 1 inch apart on a greased cookie sheet. Bake 20 to 25 minutes or until light golden brown. Makes about 16 puffs.

Frosted Grapes Parisienne

1 egg white   1 cup sugar
grapes, washed and dried

Allow 1 small bunch grapes for each serving. Beat egg white until just foamy. Pour it on a platter; dip or roll grapes until well coated. Dip in sugar. Let dry at room temperature. When coating is firm, refrigerate.

Martha's Potato Candy

⅔ cup leftover mashed   1 teaspoon instant coffee
   potatoes   ¼ teaspoon salt
1 square (1 ounce)   1 pound confectioners'
   unsweetened chocolate,   sugar, sifted
   melted   ½ pound shredded coconut

Combine mashed potatoes with chocolate, instant coffee and salt; mix well. Add confectioner's sugar. Work in shredded coconut until well blended. Drop onto a waxed paper-lined cookie sheet and form into mounds. Refrigerate until hardened, at least 3 hours. Makes about 1½ pounds candy.

Hollywood Pie

1 cup graham cracker crumbs   ¼ teaspoon salt
½ cup chopped flaked   ½ teaspoon vanilla extract
   coconut   ½ teaspoon almond extract
¼ cup chopped walnuts   1 cup sugar
¼ cup chopped filberts   1 pint butter pecan ice cream
4 egg whites

Heat oven to 350° F. Combine graham cracker crumbs, coconut, and nuts. Beat egg whites, salt, and flavorings until soft peaks form; gradually add sugar, beating until all sugar has dissolved and whites are very stiff. Fold graham cracker mixture into egg white mixture. Spread in a well-greased 9-inch pie plate. Bake 30 minutes. Cool thoroughly. Cut in wedges; top with scoops of ice cream. Makes 6 servings.

Custard Empress Josephine

7 egg yolks, slightly beaten
¾ cup sugar
2 cups milk, scalded and
  slightly cooled

¼ teaspoon salt
¼ teaspoon vanilla extract
¼ teaspoon toffee flavoring
dash nutmeg

Heat oven to 325° F. Combine egg yolks, ¼ cup of the sugar, and the salt; slowly stir in milk. Add flavorings, blend, and set aside. Melt the remaining ½ cup sugar in a heavy skillet over low heat, stirring constantly. As soon as the sugar syrup turns a light golden brown, remove from heat. Spoon 1 tablespoon syrup into each of six 5-ounce custard cups. Quickly swirl syrup with the spoon to coat the bottom and sides of cup. Set custard cups in a shallow pan on the oven rack. Pour hot water 1 inch deep around them. Pour custard in the cups and sprinkle with nutmeg. Bake 40 to 45 minutes or until knife inserted comes out clean. Serve warm in cups, or chill thoroughly and unmold onto dessert dishes. Makes 6 servings.

Sherbet Tropicale

Serve this in tall parfait glasses with Crème de Menthe whipped cream.

½ envelope (1½ teaspoons)
  unflavored gelatin
2 tablespoons cold water
¾ cup buttermilk
1 cup sugar

1 can (9 ounces) crushed
  pineapple
½ teaspoon vanilla extract
½ teaspoon almond extract
1 egg white

Soften gelatin in cold water; dissolve over hot water. Combine buttermilk, ¾ cup of the sugar, the pineapple, vanilla, almond, and dissolved gelatin; mix well. Freeze in a refrigerator tray until firm. Break in chunks; turn into a chilled bowl; beat with an electric beater until smooth. Beat egg white until soft peaks form; gradually add remaining ¼ cup sugar and beat until stiff. Fold into pineapple mixture; return quickly to cold tray. Freeze firm. Makes 4 to 6 servings.

Blushing Baked Apples

4 large baking apples
¾ cup jellied cranberry sauce
½ cup water

¼ cup sugar
¾ cup heavy cream, whipped, sweetened

Heat oven to 400° F. Wash and core apples; pare down about ⅓ of the way from the stem end. Place apples in a deep casserole. Combine cranberry sauce, water, and sugar; beat until smooth. Pour over apples. Cover and bake 30 minutes, basting with cranberry mixture occasionally. Remove cover; continue baking until apples are fork tender. Baste occasionally. Remove from heat. Place baked apples in individual dessert dishes and spoon juice over apples. Serve warm or cold, topped with sweetened whipped cream. Makes 4 servings.

Crown Nesselrode Pie

2 cups fine chocolate cookie crumbs
⅓ cup butter, melted
1 envelope unflavored gelatin
¼ cup cold water
1½ cups milk, scalded
2 eggs, separated
1 cup sugar
½ teaspoon salt

2 tablespoons cornstarch
1 teaspoon vanilla extract
1 teaspoon almond extract
½ cup heavy cream
½ cup finely chopped semi-sweet chocolate pieces
½ cup heavy cream, whipped, sweetened

Heat oven to 325° F. Mix cookie crumbs and butter together until thoroughly blended. Press firmly against sides and bottom of a 10-inch pie pan. Bake 10 minutes. Cool. Soften gelatin in cold water; add scalded milk and stir until gelatin is dissolved. Beat egg yolks; add ½ cup of the sugar, the salt, and cornstarch and beat 5 minutes. Add gelatin mixture gradually, stirring constantly until smooth. Cook over very low heat, stirring constantly, until slightly thickened; remove from heat. Add flavorings and blend. Cool thoroughly. Beat with rotary beater until foamy. Beat egg whites until stiff but not dry; gradually beat in remaining ½ cup sugar. Whip ½ cup cream until stiff; add egg whites, whipped cream and chocolate pieces to custard mixture. Fold in gently. Pour into crumb crust; chill in refrigerator until set. Top with sweetened whipped cream and garnish with a sprinkling of chocolate. Makes 8 servings.

Uncooked De Luxe Fruitcake

My California friends and I developed the ideal no-cook fruitcake, which takes very little time to prepare.

2 cups dry leftover pound cake crumbs
2 cups finely cut marshmallows
dash of salt
¼ cup sweetened condensed milk
½ cup chopped almonds

¼ cup chopped walnuts
¼ cup chopped pecans
¼ cup finely cut dates
¼ cup coarsely chopped figs
½ cup finely cut red maraschino cherries
Orange Custard Sauce (*see below*)

Combine all ingredients except Orange Custard Sauce. With your hands, mix well and press into a 7½ × 3½ × 2½-inch loaf pan which has been lined with waxed paper. Chill 2 days in the refrigerator before serving. Cut in slices and serve with Orange Custard Sauce. Makes 8 servings.

Orange Custard Sauce

4 egg yolks
⅓ cup orange juice
1 tablespoon grated orange rind

1 tablespoon lemon juice
1 cup sugar
1 cup heavy cream, whipped

Beat egg yolks in the top of a double boiler. Stir in orange juice and rind, lemon juice, and sugar. Cook over hot water, stirring constantly, until thickened and smooth. Remove from heat; cool. Fold in whipped cream. Serve at once. Makes 2 cups.

Starlight Cheese Parfait

1 cup cottage cheese
1 cup heavy cream
1 egg white, stiffly beaten

½ teaspoon salt
crushed frozen strawberries

Beat cottage cheese with a rotary beater until smooth and fluffy. Whip cream until stiff. Fold cream, egg white, and salt into beaten cheese, blending thoroughly. Place alternate spoonfuls of cheese mixture and fruit in parfait glasses. Serve immediately or keep in refrigerator until ready to serve. Makes 8 servings.

Johnny Appleseed Dessert

6 slices stale white bread
soft butter
½ cup sugar
¼ teaspoon cinnamon
¼ teaspoon mace
1 can (1 pound) applesauce

⅓ cup raisins
2 tablespoons chopped
    toasted almonds
¼ cup maple-flavoring syrup
¾ cup heavy cream
dash of mint flavoring

Heat oven to 350° F. Trim crusts from bread slices. Cut each trimmed slice into 3 strips; butter both sides of bread strips. Combine sugar, cinnamon, and mace. Sprinkle 2 tablespoons of the sugar mixture in the bottom of an 8-inch square baking pan. Cover with half the bread strips. Sprinkle with 2 more tablespoons sugar mixture. Cover with applesauce; sprinkle with raisins and almonds. Top with remaining bread strips. Sprinkle remaining ¼ cup sugar mixture over them. Pour syrup over all. Bake 30 minutes or until bread strips are golden brown. Whip cream with mint flavoring. Serve dessert warm with whipped cream. Makes 6 servings.

Grandma's Maple Custard

I call this the compromise dessert—not filling but *so* satisfying.

6 egg yolks
⅓ cup sugar
¼ teaspoon salt
1½ cups milk, scalded

½ cup light cream, scalded
½ teaspoon vanilla extract
¼ teaspoon ground nutmeg
6 tablespoons maple syrup

Heat oven to 350° F. Beat egg yolks, sugar, and salt together slightly to mix. Stir in scalded milk and cream, vanilla, and nutmeg. Butter 6 custard cups; pour 1 tablespoon maple syrup into each cup. Pour custard mixture into cups carefully so as not to mix with the syrup layer. Set custard cups in a pan of hot water; bake 45 to 50 minutes or until knife inserted comes out clean. Makes 6 servings.

Angel's Bread Pudding

Pistachio nuts add a piquant flavor and a dash of color.

2¼ cups milk
2 eggs, slightly beaten
2 cups 1-inch, day-old bread
  cubes
½ cup brown sugar

1 teaspoon cinnamon
1 teaspoon vanilla extract
¼ teaspoon salt
½ cup seedless raisins
¼ cup chopped pistachio nuts

Heat oven to 350° F. Combine milk and eggs; pour over bread cubes. Add remaining ingredients; toss lightly to blend. Spread mixture in a greased 8-inch square baking pan. Set in shallow pan on oven rack. Pour hot water around it to 1 inch deep. Bake 35 to 40 minutes or until knife inserted in center comes out clean. Makes 6 to 8 servings.

Sunshine Sponge Cake

¾ cup cake flour
1 teaspoon baking powder
¼ teaspoon salt
3 egg yolks
½ cup sugar

¼ cup boiling water
1 teaspoon almond extract
¼ teaspoon vanilla extract
Daffodil Lemon Sauce (*see below*)

Heat oven to 350° F. Grease and flour a 9-inch layer cake pan. Mix flour, baking powder, and salt; set aside. Beat egg yolks until thick; beat in sugar. Blend in water and flavorings; add dry ingredients and blend well. Pour into prepared pan. Bake 30 minutes or until top springs back when touched lightly. Cool 10 minutes before removing from pan. Top each serving with warm Daffodil Lemon Sauce. Makes 8 servings.

Daffodil Lemon Sauce

½ cup sugar
2 teaspoons cornstarch
dash salt
dash nutmeg
dash mace

1 cup water
2 egg yolks, well beaten
2 tablespoons butter
½ teaspoon grated lemon rind
2 tablespoons lemon juice

Combine sugar, cornstarch, salt, nutmeg, and mace; gradually stir in water. Cook over low heat, stirring constantly, until thick and clear. Stir small amount of hot mixture into egg yolks, then stir egg yolks into hot mixture. Cook 1 minute, stirring constantly. Remove from heat. Add butter, lemon rind, and juice; blend thoroughly. Serve warm. Makes 1½ cups.

Heavenly Prune Whip

1 cup cooked prunes, cut-up
3 egg whites
⅓ cup sugar
¼ teaspoon salt

1 tablespoon lemon juice
¾ cup heavy cream, whipped, sweetened

Beat prunes, egg whites, sugar, and salt together until stiff enough
to hold shape, about 5 minutes. Fold in lemon juice. Fold in whipped
cream. Chill. Makes 6 servings.

Lemon Tapioca Fluff

2 egg whites
¼ teaspoon salt
1 cup sugar
⅓ cup quick-cooking tapioca
3 cups water

grated rind of 1 lemon
⅓ cup lemon juice
¾ cup heavy cream, whipped
½ teaspoon lemon flavoring

Beat egg whites with salt until frothy. Gradually add ¼ cup of the
sugar and beat until stiff but not dry. Set aside. In a medium saucepan combine remaining ¾ cup sugar, tapioca, and water. Let stand
8 minutes. Bring to a full rolling boil, stirring constantly. Remove
from heat. Add lemon rind and juice. Gradually pour over egg
whites, stirring constantly. Cool, stirring occasionally, and chill
thoroughly. Combine whipped cream and lemon flavoring and serve
on top of pudding. Makes 4 servings.

Almond Crunchies

3 egg whites
⅔ cup sugar
3 tablespoons flour
¼ teaspoon salt

1½ cups grated coconut
½ cup finely chopped almonds
½ teaspoon vanilla extract
½ teaspoon almond extract

Heat oven to 325° F. Beat egg whites until frothy. Gradually add
sugar, beating until stiff. Carefully fold in remaining ingredients.
Drop by spoonfuls onto a greased baking sheet; bake 15 minutes.
Makes 36 crunchies.

Meringue Pie Shell

3 egg whites
few grains salt

¼ teaspoon cream of tartar
¾ cup sugar

Heat oven to 350° F. Beat egg whites until frothy; add salt and cream of tartar. Beat until soft peaks form. Gradually add sugar, beating until stiff but not dry. Spread with a spoon over bottom and sides of 9-inch buttered pie plate. Bake 20 to 25 minutes or until lightly browned. Cool; fill with fresh fruits, ice cream, or cooled chocolate pudding. Makes 6 servings.

Dreamy Meringues

6 egg whites   2 cups sugar
½ teaspoon cream of tartar

Heat oven to 400° F. Beat egg whites with cream of tartar until frothy. Gradually beat in sugar, a little at a time. Beat until stiff and glossy. Drop by small spoonfuls in circles on a baking sheet covered with brown paper, or heap into high mounds and hollow out with back of spoon. Put into oven, close door, and turn off oven. DO NOT OPEN DOOR. Let stand overnight in oven. To serve, fill meringues with ice cream, top with fresh fruit or with chocolate sauce. Sprinkle with chopped almonds. Makes 12 meringues.

Confetti Snow

3 egg whites   ⅓ cup chopped candied
1 tablespoon vanilla extract   cherries
1 cup confectioners' sugar   ⅓ cup mixed candied fruit
2 cups heavy cream, whipped
⅓ cup chopped candied
   citron

Beat egg whites until frothy; add vanilla. Gradually add sugar, beating until stiff. Fold in whipped cream and candied fruits. Pour into a 1-quart mold and freeze until firm. Serve plain or with your favorite sweet sauce. Makes 6 servings.

Oranges Par Excellence

At the Cordon Bleu there are a dozen ways to serve this elegant dessert.

6 large thick-skinned oranges
pistachio ice cream, softened
2 tablespoons Drambuie
2 egg whites

dash of salt
¼ cup packed light brown
sugar

Cut about ⅓ off the top of each orange; scoop out pulp and reserve for other uses. Blend ice cream with Drambuie and fill orange shells with the mixture. Freeze until firm. Just before serving, heat oven to 450° F. Beat egg whites until frothy. Add salt. Gradually add sugar, beating continuously until stiff. Place oranges on a baking sheet. Lightly swirl meringue over tops, making sure ice cream is covered completely. Bake 3 to 4 minutes or until meringue is delicately browned. Serve at once. Makes 6 servings.

November Delight

1 cup sugar
½ cup orange juice
¼ teaspoon cinnamon
¼ teaspoon allspice
2 cups cranberries
½ cup butter, melted
3 cups bread crumbs from
day-old bread

1 egg yolk
2 tablespoons sugar
1 cup heavy cream, whipped
½ teaspoon vanilla extract
½ teaspoon almond extract
1 teaspoon chopped toasted
almonds

Heat oven to 350° F. Combine the 1 cup sugar with the orange juice, cinnamon, and allspice in a medium saucepan; bring to a boil. Add cranberries; cook over medium heat 2 minutes or until berries are softened. Mix butter and bread crumbs thoroughly. In a greased 1½-quart baking dish arrange alternate layers of crumbs and cranberries, ending with crumbs. Cover and bake 20 minutes. Uncover and continue baking 15 minutes longer, or until brown and crisp on top. Beat egg yolk and the 2 tablespoons sugar together. Fold in whipped cream. Blend in vanilla and almond flavorings. Serve pudding warm with the flavored whipped cream. Garnish top with almonds. Makes 4 servings.

Golden Autumn Pudding

4 cups day-old bread, cut in
½-inch cubes
1 apple, grated
1 can (1 pound) whole
cranberry sauce
½ teaspoon cinnamon

¼ teaspoon mace
¼ teaspoon nutmeg
½ cup raisins
1 teaspoon margarine, melted
½ cup water

Heat oven to 350° F. Combine all ingredients. Turn into a greased 2-quart baking pan. Bake 30 minutes. Makes 6 servings.

California Snow Pudding

1 envelope unflavored gelatin
¼ cup cold water
¼ cup hot water
¾ cup sugar
¼ teaspoon salt

1 tablespoon lemon juice
½ cup orange juice
½ cup grapefruit juice
2 egg whites

Soften gelatin in cold water. Add hot water; stir until gelatin is dissolved. Add ½ cup of the sugar, the salt, and the juices, and stir until well blended. Chill until partially set. Beat egg whites until frothy. Gradually add remaining ¼ cup sugar and beat until stiff but not dry. Beat gelatin mixture until light and fluffy. Fold in egg whites and chill until firm. Serve with lemon-flavored whipped cream or custard sauce. Makes 4 servings.

Eskimo Fruit Ice

12 marshmallows
1¼ cups syrup from any
canned fruit

3 tablespoons lemon juice
1 egg white, stiffly beaten

Melt marshmallows in ¼ cup syrup over low heat; cool. Fold in remaining 1 cup of syrup combined with lemon juice and beaten egg white. Freeze in refrigerator tray, stirring twice. Makes 4 servings.

Lemony Carrot Squares

1 cup margarine, melted, cooled
1¼ cups sugar
4 eggs
1 cup cooked carrots, mashed
2 cups flour
1 teaspoon baking powder
1 teaspoon vanilla extract
½ teaspoon almond extract
2¼ teaspoons lemon extract
dash nutmeg
2¼ cups confectioners' sugar
¼ cup water
½ teaspoon grated lemon rind

Heat oven to 350° F. Pour margarine into a mixing bowl; gradually beat in sugar. Add eggs, one at a time, beating thoroughly after each addition. Add carrots, flour, and baking powder; beat 2 minutes. Add vanilla, almond, ¾ teaspoon of the lemon flavoring, and the nutmeg. Spread in a greased 10×15×1-inch baking pan. Bake 25 minutes. Cool on rack. Beat together remaining 1½ teaspoons lemon flavoring, confectioners' sugar, water, and lemon rind. Spread on cooled cake. Cut in squares. Makes 35 squares.

Gingerbread with Lemon Sauce

4 servings leftover gingerbread
2 egg yolks
¾ cup milk
¼ cup light cream
3 tablespoons sugar
⅛ teaspoon salt
½ teaspoon grated lemon rind

Cut four pieces of aluminum foil large enough to wrap around gingerbread pieces. Heat oven to 325° F. Place wrapped gingerbread on a baking sheet; heat in oven 15 minutes or until warmed through. In the top of a double boiler beat egg yolks slightly. Add milk, cream, sugar, and salt. Cook over boiling water, stirring, until mixture is slightly thickened and coats a metal spoon. Remove from heat; stir in grated lemon rind. Cool slightly. Serve with hot gingerbread. Makes 4 servings.

Thanksgiving Bread Pudding

¼ cup butter
½ teaspoon salt
½ cup sugar
2 eggs, well beaten

⅓ cup light cream
2 cups soft white bread cubes
1 cup cranberries

Heat oven to 350° F. Cream butter; add salt and sugar. Combine with eggs. Slowly add cream. Fold in bread cubes and cranberries. Turn mixture into greased custard cups. Set cups in pan of hot water; bake 1 hour. Makes 6 servings.

Wedgewood English Trifle

1 package vanilla pudding
1½ cups milk
½ cup light cream
½ teaspoon almond extract
6 slices leftover cake, ½ inch
   thick
raspberry jam

1½ cups mixed fresh or
   canned fruit
¾ cup chopped pecans
½ cup heavy cream, whipped
¼ cup chopped toasted
   almonds

Prepare pudding with milk and cream according to package directions. Add almond extract; cool. Line a 7-inch loaf pan with waxed paper. Cover bottom of pan with slices of cake; spread with jam. Place half the fruit and pecans over cake; cover with half the pudding. Make second layer as above, ending with layer of cake. Spread whipped cream on top; sprinkle with almonds. Refrigerate 4 hours before serving. Makes 4 servings.

MINI-MEALS
FOR TWO

Even the best planner will sometimes be caught with leftovers in such small amounts—a cup of cooked chopped beef, half a cup of fish or chicken—that the temptation is to throw them away. But such small supplies, plus ingenuity, can be the basis of a creditable meal for two.

When a friend or neighbor drops in unexpectedly just at lunchtime, don't let your hospitable instincts be smothered—those oddments in the refrigerator will see you through, as the following recipes will show you.

BEEF

Boeuf à Deaux

1 tablespoon chopped onion
3 teaspoons butter
1½ teaspoons flour
¾ cup consommé
1½ teaspoons tomato purée
1 teaspoon chopped parsley
1 teaspoon chopped celery

1 cup coarsely chopped
   cooked beef
1 cup hot mashed potatoes
2 tablespoons grated
   Parmesan cheese
1 tablespoon fine bread crumbs
1 tablespoon chopped walnuts

Heat oven to 450° F. Sauté onion in 1½ teaspoons of the butter in a medium skillet until lightly browned. Blend in flour gradually; stir and cook 1 minute. Gradually add consommé and tomato purée and continue cooking, stirring constantly, until mixture is smooth and thickened. Stir in parsley and celery. Add beef; stir and bring just to boiling point. Turn into a 1-quart baking dish. Spread potatoes on top. Sprinkle with cheese and bread crumbs. Dot with remaining butter. Sprinkle walnuts on top. Bake 10 minutes or until top is delicately browned.

Tijuana Bake

I recommend this for a hungry twosome.

¾ cup milk
½ cup prepared pancake mix
2 tablespoons butter, melted
1 tablespoon chopped peanuts
1 egg yolk, well beaten
1 tablespoon finely chopped
   onion
3 tablespoons bacon fat
1 cup finely chopped cooked
   beef

½ teaspoon salt
⅛ teaspoon pepper
1 tablespoon minced parsley
¼ cup commercial sour
   cream
1 tablespoon grated
   Parmesan cheese
⅛ teaspoon thyme

Add milk to pancake mix in a medium-sized bowl; stir in 1 table-spoon of the butter, peanuts, and egg yolk. Beat well; let stand. Sauté onion in 1 tablespoon of the bacon fat. Stir in beef; cook 2 minutes. Season with salt and pepper and add to pancake batter. Warm the oven. Cook pancakes in remaining bacon fat, one at a time, in a heavy 6-inch skillet. Sprinkle each cooked pancake with parsley; roll each up, and lay in a shallow, well-greased 1½-quart baking dish, packing pancakes close together. Keep baking dish in warmed oven until all pancake batter is used up. Heat oven to 350° F. Brush pancake rolls with the remaining butter and the sour cream and sprinkle with Parmesan cheese. Sprinkle thyme over all. Bake 10 minutes or until cheese is melted. Place under broiler a moment to lightly brown top.

Pierrot Beef with Rice

The sauce makes the dish interesting.

1½ tablespoons butter
1½ teaspoons chopped green
  pepper
1½ teaspoons chopped onion
1 teaspoon chopped celery
1½ tablespoons flour
¾ cup consommé
¼ cup tomato purée
1 cup coarsely chopped
  cooked beef

½ teaspoon salt
⅛ teaspoon pepper
⅛ teaspoon paprika
dash Tabasco
½ teaspoon lemon juice
¼ teaspoon prepared
  horseradish, drained
fluffy hot rice

Melt butter in a medium skillet and sauté green pepper, onion, and celery until soft but not brown. Blend in flour. Gradually stir in consommé and tomato purée. Add beef; season with salt, pepper, paprika, and Tabasco. Stir in lemon juice and horseradish. Heat thoroughly. Serve on fluffy hot rice.

Caliente Corn Pie

A Mexican version toned down for mild palates.

2 strips bacon
1 cup coarsely ground cooked
  beef
1 small onion, sliced
¼ cup seedless raisins
¼ cup sliced stuffed olives
1 tablespoons chopped
  pimiento

½ cup cooked corn
½ teaspoon salt
⅛ teaspoon pepper
1 tablespoon chopped parsley
1½ teaspoons butter

Heat oven to 350° F. Sauté bacon in a skillet until crisp. Chop up and combine with beef. Discard all but 2 tablespoons bacon fat in the skillet, add onion and sauté until lightly brown. Add meat mixture and sauté over high heat until lightly browned. In a 1-quart baking dish place alternate layers of meat mixture and combined raisins, olives, and pimiento. Spread corn on top. Season with salt and pepper. Sprinkle with parsley; dot with butter. Bake 20 minutes.

Brazilian Beef Chili

I especially liked the contrast in texture and flavor of this Rio de Janeiro delicacy.

1 small onion, finely chopped
1 small green pepper, finely
  chopped
1 tablespoon margarine
1 cup canned tomatoes
2 tablespoons tomato paste
1 teaspoon chili powder
½ teaspoon salt

⅛ teaspoon pepper
¼ teaspoon paprika
1 teaspoon Worcestershire
  sauce
1 cup coarsely ground cooked
  beef
1 cup cooked kidney beans
1 cup cooked spaghetti

Brown onion and green pepper in margarine in a heavy skillet. Add tomatoes, tomato paste, and seasonings. Cover; simmer gently 40 minutes, stirring frequently. Add beef; continue cooking 15 minutes. Add kidney beans and spaghetti just before serving; heat thoroughly and serve at once.

Duo Roast Beef Hash

1 cup coarsely chopped
  cooked beef
¾ cup diced cooked potatoes
1 medium onion, chopped
½ teaspoon salt
⅛ teaspoon pepper

3 tablespoons leftover beef
  gravy
1 tablespoon bacon fat
parsley sprigs

Combine beef, potatoes, onion, salt, and pepper with enough gravy to moisten thoroughly. Heat bacon fat in a heavy 8-inch skillet. Turn in the hash and stir well; cover and cook over low heat until underside is browned. Fold over and slide onto a heated serving platter. Garnish with parsley sprigs.

Tongue Hash Marguerite

1 cup coarsely chopped
  cooked tongue
1 cup coarsely chopped
  cooked potatoes
¼ cup minced onion
1 teaspoon minced parsley
1 teaspoon minced celery

2 to 4 tablespoons tongue
  broth
¼ teaspoon marjoram
dash thyme
½ teaspoon salt
⅛ teaspoon pepper

Combine tongue, potatoes, onion, parsley, and celery in a medium, heavy skillet. Pour over enough broth in which tongue was boiled to moisten through. Cook over medium heat 5 minutes. Add marjoram, thyme, salt, and pepper and blend in. Cover; reduce heat and simmer 20 minutes or until thoroughly hot. Serve at once.

LAMB

Lamb Africaine

The original African recipe called for a "grass" lamb, which meant the young animal had grazed one season.

1 small onion, chopped
½ clove garlic, mashed
1 tablespoon olive oil
1 small eggplant, peeled, cut
  in 1-inch cubes
½ cup canned tomatoes
1 teaspoon tomato paste
1 small bay leaf

¼ teaspoon chervil
¼ teaspoon basil
⅛ teaspoon marjoram
½ teaspoon salt
¼ teaspoon pepper
1 cup coarsely chopped
  cooked lamb
1 cup hot fluffy rice

Sauté onion and garlic in olive oil in a medium, heavy skillet. Add eggplant; cook 5 minutes, stirring frequently. Add tomatoes, tomato paste, bay leaf, herbs, salt, and pepper. Cover; simmer 12 minutes or until eggplant is soft. Stir in lamb and heat thoroughly. Serve over hot fluffy rice.

Lamburgers De Luxe

1 cup finely chopped cooked
  lamb
2 tablespoons finely chopped
  green pepper
1 small onion, finely chopped
¼ cup chopped mushrooms
¼ cup chopped celery
1 pullet egg or 1 egg yolk
1 tablespoon butter, melted
1½ tablespoons sour cream

1 tablespoon fine bread
  crumbs
½ teaspoon salt
⅛ teaspoon pepper
¼ teaspoon paprika
½ teaspoon prepared mustard
1 teaspoon Worcestershire
  sauce
dash Tabasco
1 tablespoon bacon fat

Combine lamb, pepper, onion, mushrooms, celery, egg or yolk, butter, sour cream, bread crumbs, salt, pepper, paprika, mustard, Worcestershire sauce and Tabasco. Mix vigorously until well blended. Shape into small cakes. Chill 3 hours or until firm. Brown slowly in heated bacon fat in a heavy skillet.

Quickie Lamb Curry

An interesting quick dish with a touch of East Indian flavor.

½ cup sliced mushrooms
½ cup diced apple
3 tablespoons finely chopped onion
1½ tablespoons butter
1 teaspoon curry powder

1¼ cups condensed cream of celery soup
1½ cups cubed cooked lamb
1½ cups hot cooked rice
2 tablespoons shredded coconut

Sauté mushrooms, apple, and onion in butter 6 minutes or until soft. Add curry powder, soup, and lamb; simmer 15 minutes. Heap curried lamb on hot rice; sprinkle with coconut and serve.

Near Eastern Lamb Dolmas

In Turkey and Greece this is almost daily fare in the back country.

2 medium onions
¾ cup finely chopped cooked lamb
½ cup cooked rice
1 tablespoon butter, melted
1 teaspoon minced parsley

¼ cup pine nuts
¼ teaspoon salt
⅛ teaspoon pepper
⅛ teaspoon paprika
1 tablespoon ketchup
¾ cup consommé

Heat oven to 350° F. Cut the outer rings of the onions halfway down in four places so that the centers can be removed easily. Place onions in saucepan; cover with water and cook until just tender. Drain. Place onions in a 1-quart baking dish. Combine lamb with rice, butter, parsley, pine nuts, salt, pepper, and paprika; mix well. Remove centers of boiled onions. Heap lamb mixture into onions; place onion centers on top. Mix ketchup and consommé; pour over lamb mixture. Bake 20 minutes.

Lamb Puffs Grillier

leftover lamb gravy
1 cup chopped cooked lamb
1 small egg, well beaten
1 cup hot mashed potatoes
½ teaspoon salt

⅛ teaspoon pepper
⅛ teaspoon paprika
flour
melted butter

Heat oven to 400° F. Add enough gravy to lamb to make it spreadable. Blend egg, mashed potatoes, salt, pepper, paprika, and enough flour to make a mixture stiff enough to roll out on a floured board. Roll ¼ inch thick; cut with large biscuit cutter. Drop a spoonful of lamb mixture into center of each round; bring up edges to form a three-corned puff. Press edges together and brush with melted butter. Place puffs on a greased baking sheet; bake 10 to 12 minutes or until browned. Serve with more heated leftover gravy.

Lamb Armentiere

¼ cup rice
1 cup diced cooked lamb
1 small onion, chopped
¼ cup minced celery
½ cup minced green pepper
½ clove garlic, minced
1½ tablespoons vegetable oil

1 cup canned tomatoes
¼ teaspoon salt
dash pepper
2 dashes red hot sauce
⅛ teaspoon mace
⅛ teaspoon nutmeg

Cook rice in salted boiling water 15 minutes or until not quite done. Drain. Combine with lamb. Sauté onion, celery, green pepper, and garlic in vegetable oil in a medium skillet 5 minutes. Add tomatoes and meat mixture and mix well. Season with salt and pepper. Sprinkle with red hot sauce and spices. Heat oven to 350° F. Pour mixture in a 1-quart baking dish. Bake 15 minutes.

Lamb Espagnole

½ cup uncooked rice
2 tablespoons bacon
  drippings
1 small onion, chopped
½ cup diced celery
1 tablespoon chopped parsley

1 cup canned tomatoes
½ cup water
½ teaspoon salt
⅛ teaspoon pepper
1 cup cooked lamb, in small
  cubes

Brown rice lightly in bacon drippings, stirring frequently. Add onion, celery, and parsley; cook 5 minutes longer. Add tomatoes, water, salt, and pepper. Cook, covered, over low heat, stirring occasionally, until rice is tender, 20 to 25 minutes. Add lamb. Heat through but do not boil.

Italian Lamb Hash

A zingy, flavorful dish I had in Frascati.

½ cup diced eggplant
2 tablespoons olive oil
¼ cup minced onion
2 tablespoons coarsely
  chopped green pepper
½ clove garlic, minced
1 cup canned tomatoes,
  drained
¼ cup leftover gravy

¾ teaspoon salt
⅛ teaspoon pepper
pinch thyme
pinch rosemary
¾ cup diced cooked lamb
½ cup hot cooked rice
1 tablespoon butter
½ teaspoon grated lemon rind

Sauté eggplant slowly in olive oil until tender, about 6 minutes. Remove from pan; drain off excess oil. Add to the pan onion, green pepper, and garlic; sauté until onion is golden. Add tomatoes and gravy. Season with salt, pepper, thyme, and rosemary. Cover; simmer 10 minutes. Add lamb. Mix well; cover and cook 10 minutes longer. Combine rice with butter and lemon rind. Serve with hash.

VEAL

Veal Soufflé de Bramand

1 tablespoon butter
1 tablespoon flour
½ cup milk
½ cup light cream
½ teaspoon salt
⅛ teaspoon pepper

dash nutmeg
¼ cup soft bread crumbs
1 cup ground cooked veal
1 teaspoon minced onion
3 eggs, separated

Heat oven to 350° F. Melt butter in a medium skillet; remove from heat and blend in flour until smooth. Return to heat; add milk and cream and cook and stir until thickened. Season with salt, pepper, and nutmeg. Add bread crumbs; stir well. Remove from heat. Stir in veal, onion, and slightly beaten egg yolks; cool. Beat egg whites until stiff. Gently fold into meat mixture. Pour into a buttered 4-cup soufflé dish; set in pan of hot water. Bake 45 minutes or until set.

Veal Mont Blanc
A hearty meal for two which originated in the provinces of France.

2 cups diced cooked veal
3 small onions
1 stalk celery, cut up
2 carrots, cut into 1-inch
    pieces
2 medium potatoes, pared,
    quartered
1 teaspoon chopped parsley
1 teaspoon chopped celery

½ small clove garlic, minced
2 cloves
1 small bay leaf, crushed
3 cups consommé
½ teaspoon salt
dash pepper
2 tablespoons flour
Baking Powder Biscuit Dough
    (page 189)

Heat oven to 350° F. Combine veal, onions, celery, carrots, potatoes, parsley, celery, garlic, cloves, and bay leaf. Add 2½ cups of consommé, salt, and pepper. Make a paste with remaining ½ cup consommé and flour and stir into mixture. Turn into a 1-quart baking dish. Bake, covered, 40 minutes or until vegetables are tender. Remove from oven. Cover top with biscuit dough rolled to ½-inch thickness; slash center for steam to escape. Increase heat to 425° F. Bake 12 to 15 minutes.

Veal Rosalinde

½ cup dry red wine
½ teaspoon salt
⅛ teaspoon basil
⅛ teaspoon thyme
½ teaspoon monosodium
  glutamate
1 veal steak, ¾ inch thick

1½ tablespoons butter
1 can (5 ounces) water
  chestnuts, with liquid
1 can (3 ounces) sliced
  mushrooms, with liquid
2 tablespoons flour
⅛ teaspoon paprika

Combine wine, salt, basil, thyme, and monosodium glutamate. Place meat in a shallow pan; pour in wine mixture and marinate 3 hours. Drain; reserve marinade. Brown meat in butter on both sides. Add marinade; cover, simmer 35 to 40 minutes or until meat is tender. Drain water chestnuts and mushrooms and combine liquid with flour. Stir into pan. Add water chestnuts and mushrooms. Sprinkle with paprika. Heat through.

Aloha Veal Patties

1 cup ground cooked veal
2 tablespoons fine dry bread
  crumbs
2 tablespoons ketchup
2 tablespoons minced onion
¼ teaspoon salt
dash pepper

⅛ teaspoon marjoram
⅛ teaspoon rosemary
1 egg, slightly beaten
2 slices canned pineapple
1½ tablespoons butter, melted
3 tablespoons brown sugar
¼ cup pineapple syrup

Heat oven to 350° F. Combine meat, bread crumbs, ketchup, onion, seasonings, and egg; mix well. Shape into two large patties.

Place on pineapple slices in a greased shallow pan. Combine remaining ingredients and spoon over patties; cover. Bake 30 minutes. Uncover; bake 10 minutes longer, basting occasionally.

Marseilles Veal Croquettes

1 tablespoon butter
2 tablespoons flour
¼ cup milk
¼ cup light cream
1 cup ground cooked veal
1 teaspoon salt

1 tablespoon chopped onion
2 tablespoons shredded
   Cheddar cheese
¾ cup fine cracker crumbs
shortening for frying

Melt butter in a medium saucepan. Add flour and stir until blended. Add milk and cream and cook, stirring, to make a smooth, thick white sauce. Add veal, salt, onion, and cheese. Cool. Shape into 4 croquettes. Roll in cracker crumbs. Fry croquettes in hot shortening until well browned. Drain on absorbent paper. Makes 2 servings.

Veal in Wine

1½ cups cubed cooked veal
2 tablespoons butter
⅛ teaspoon marjoram
⅛ teaspoon thyme

1 small clove garlic, peeled
3 medium carrots, pared,
   diced
½ cup white wine

Brown veal in butter in a small skillet with marjoram, thyme, and garlic. Discard garlic. Add carrots. Pour wine over all. Cover; simmer 10 minutes.

Veal Italiano

An American adaptation of an Italian favorite.

4 thin slices cooked veal
½ cup cracker crumbs
½ teaspoon salt
⅛ teaspoon pepper
1 small egg, beaten

3 tablespoons shortening
1 can (8 ounces) tomato
   sauce, heated
¼ pound Mozzarella cheese,
   thinly sliced

Dip veal slices in mixture of crumbs, salt, and pepper, then in egg, and again in crumbs. Brown slices quickly on both sides in hot shortening. Place in a heatproof serving dish. Pour hot tomato sauce over them. Top with cheese. Broil 3 minutes or until cheese melts and is slightly browned.

Golden Acorn Squash

This well-known veal dish is served in many tavernas of Greece.

1 medium acorn squash	6 tablespoons light cream
¾ teaspoon salt	¾ cup finely chopped cooked
⅛ teaspoon pepper	veal
2 teaspoons butter	½ teaspoon minced parsley
2 teaspoons flour	½ cup buttered bread crumbs

Heat oven to 375° F. Cut squash crosswise; scoop out seeds and membrane. Season with half the salt and pepper. Turn upside down on a greased baking sheet; bake 30 to 35 minutes or until just tender, turning them right side up after 15 minutes. Combine butter and flour and make a smooth paste. Heat in a saucepan over medium heat, stir in cream and cook, stirring, until mixture is smooth and thickened. Season with remaining salt and pepper. Add veal and parsley. Fill cavities of squash to heaping. Cover with bread crumbs. Bake 15 minutes longer.

PORK AND HAM

Pork Chen Yuen

¼ cup chopped onion
1½ tablespoons vegetable oil
¾ cup cooked pork, cut in
  julienne strips
¾ cup chicken broth
¼ cup coarsely chopped
  celery
¼ cup thinly sliced
  mushrooms
4 water chestnuts, sliced

¼ cup canned bean sprouts,
  well drained
1 tablespoon cornstarch
⅛ teaspoon salt
⅛ teaspoon sugar
¾ tablespoon soy sauce
1 tablespoon water
1 cup Chinese noodles,
  crisped

Sauté onion in vegetable oil in a medium skillet until soft but
not brown. Add pork, chicken broth, celery, mushrooms, bean
sprouts, and water chestnuts. Cover; simmer 6 minutes. Combine
cornstarch with salt, sugar, soy sauce, and water; stir into a smooth
paste. Add to pork mixture, stirring constantly until smooth and
thickened. Serve over Chinese noodles.

Savoury Pork Pie

When you're back to two after your family has grown, this is
an ideal way to serve leftover meat.

1 package instant pie crust
  mix
1 cup coarsely chopped
  cooked pork
1 cup diced cooked potatoes
¼ cup cooked green peas
¼ cup cooked green beans
1 teaspoon minced parsley

dash ground cloves
dash nutmeg
¼ cup chopped onions,
  sautéed
1 tablespoon chopped
  mushrooms, sautéed
¼ cup water
1 teaspoon milk

Heat oven to 400° F. Prepare pie crust mix according to package directions; roll to ⅛-inch thickness. Line a 2-cup baking dish with pie crust, reserving enough for a top crust. Combine remaining ingredients, except milk. Fill baking dish with the mixture. Cover with top with crust; slash center. Pinch edges of crust together; brush top with milk. Bake 40 to 45 minutes.

Ham Casserole Parma

This is an Italian favorite which usually calls for veal, but is just as delicious made with ham.

1 cup spinach noodles
½ cup commercial sour cream
¼ cup heavy cream
¾ cup grated Swiss cheese
1 cup coarsely chopped cooked ham
½ teaspoon salt
⅛ teaspoon pepper
¼ teaspoon paprika
1½ teaspoons butter
1 tablespoon chopped parsley

Heat oven to 375° F. Cook noodles in salted boiling water 8 minutes or until just tender. Combine sour cream with heavy cream; heat in medium saucepan to just below boiling. Stir in half of the cheese and all the ham. Season with salt, pepper, and paprika. In a well-greased 1-quart baking dish alternate layers of noodles and ham mixture. Top with remaining cheese; dot with butter. Sprinkle with parsley. Bake 20 to 25 minutes or until top is lightly browned.

Amsterdam Soufflé

2 tablespoons butter
1½ tablespoons flour
½ cup milk
½ cup light cream
¼ cup grated processed American cheese
¼ cup minced celery
1 tablespoon minced pimiento
½ cup finely chopped cooked ham
½ cup thinly sliced sautéed mushrooms
½ teaspoon curry powder
pinch of mace
¾ teaspoon grated onion
2 eggs, separated
½ teaspoon salt
⅛ teaspoon pepper
½ teaspoon paprika

Heat oven to 350° F. Melt butter in a medium skillet; stir in flour and the milk and cream gradually, stirring constantly until smooth and thickened. Add cheese; stir until melted. Add celery, pimiento, ham, mushrooms, curry powder, mace and onion. Beat the egg yolks and stir them in. Season with salt, pepper, and paprika. Cool to lukewarm. Beat egg whites until stiff but not dry; carefully fold into the mixture. Turn into a well-greased 4-cup baking dish. Bake 30 to 35 minutes or until a knife inserted in the center comes out clean.

Quickie Ham Brunch

1 cup minced cooked ham	¼ teaspoon salt
1 hard-cooked egg, finely chopped	dash pepper
	1 tablespoon bacon fat
½ cup undiluted cream of mushroom soup	Parsley Rice Ring (page 183), ½ recipe

Combine ham, egg, soup, salt, and pepper. Chill 3 hours or until mixture holds its shape when formed into patties. Heat bacon fat in a skillet to sizzling point. Brown patties well on both sides. Serve at once with rice. Makes 2 servings.

Pennywise Ham Casserole

½ cup cooked macaroni	¼ teaspoon prepared mustard
½ cup finely chopped cooked ham	1 teaspoon minced onion
1 tablespoon minced celery	½ cup milk
1 tablespoon minced green pepper	¼ cup heavy cream
	1 egg, lightly beaten

Heat oven to 350° F. Turn macaroni into the bottom of a greased 1-quart baking dish. Combine ham with celery, green pepper, mustard, and onion and mix well. Spread over macaroni. Combine milk, cream, and egg. Pour over macaroni mixture. Bake 30 minutes or until firm.

Green Peppers California

2 medium green peppers	¾ cup cooked rice
1 tablespoon butter	½ teaspoon salt
1 tablespoon chopped onion	⅛ teaspoon pepper
1 tablespoon chopped celery	2 tablespoons grated
1 teaspoon flour	Parmesan cheese
¼ cup milk	2 tablespoons water
1 cup ground cooked ham	

Split peppers lengthwise; remove seeds and membrane. Parboil 3 minutes in boiling salted water. Drain peppers; carefully turn them upside down and let stand. Heat oven to 400° F. Melt butter in a medium, heavy skillet; add onion and celery and sauté until soft but not brown. Blend in flour. Gradually add milk, stirring constantly, until mixture is smooth and thickened. Stir in ham, rice, salt, and pepper. Lay pepper halves in a greased, shallow 1-quart baking dish and fill them solidly with ham mixture. Sprinkle cheese over the tops. Add water to baking dish. Bake 20 to 25 minutes.

Ham Balinese

2 medium sweet potatoes, cooked	1 tablespoon brown sugar
½ cup sliced mushrooms	dash allspice
1½ tablespoons butter	dash nutmeg
1½ tablespoons flour	¼ cup light cream
1 cup consommé	2 teaspoons Angostura bitters
1¼ cups cubed cooked ham	1 tablespoon toasted slivered
¾ cup chopped cooked cabbage	almonds

Heat oven to 350° F. Peel sweet potatoes; set aside. Sauté mushrooms in butter 3 minutes. Blend in flour. Gradually add consommé, stirring constantly, until mixture is smooth and thickened. Place ham and cabbage in a 1-quart baking dish; pour mushroom sauce over. Cover; bake 10 minutes. Mash sweet potatoes, add brown sugar, allspice, and nutmeg. Blend in cream; whip potatoes until light and fluffy. Remove baking dish from oven. Increase heat to 425° F. Stir Angostura bitters into ham mixture. Spread potatoes over the top. Sprinkle with almonds. Bake 25 minutes.

Hot Dog Special

Sherry with hot dogs? Why not—try it and you'll agree they're very compatible.

1½ teaspoons butter
1 small onion, chopped
1 tablespoon chopped green pepper
1 tablespoon chopped celery
1 teaspoon paprika
2 cooked frankfurters, cut in ½-inch pieces

1 small tomato, peeled and sliced
2 tablespoons sherry
¾ teaspoon salt
⅛ teaspoon pepper
2 eggs, well beaten

Melt butter in a heavy, medium-sized skillet; add onion, green pepper, and celery and lightly sauté until soft. Add paprika and frankfurters; sauté over very low heat 5 minutes. Add tomato and wine. Season with salt and pepper. Cover and simmer gently 12 to 15 minutes. Pour in eggs; stir gently, and cook over low heat until eggs are just set.

Lumberman's Soup

1½ teaspoons margarine
1 small onion, sliced
½ clove garlic, minced
3 tablespoons chopped green pepper
½ cup peeled, chopped tomato
1 cup consommé
2 cooked frankfurters, coarsely chopped

1 cup leftover baked beans
1 small stalk celery, cut up
½ teaspoon chopped parsley
⅛ teaspoon marjoram
⅛ teaspoon rosemary
½ teaspoon salt
⅛ teaspoon pepper
2 tablespoons sherry

Melt margarine in a small heavy pan; add onion, garlic, and pepper and sauté until tender but not brown. Add tomato, consommé, frankfurters, beans, celery, parsley, marjoram, rosemary, salt, and pepper. Bring to a boil; reduce heat and simmer 30 minutes. Stir in sherry and serve.

CHICKEN

Chicken Soufflé Nakka

In a small Swedish town called Nakka, I was served a dish similar
to this.

1 tablespoon minced onion
2 tablespoons butter
2 tablespoons flour
½ cup light cream
½ cup chicken broth
½ teaspoon salt
⅛ teaspoon pepper
1 cup finely chopped cooked
   chicken
2 tablespoons blanched,
   shredded, toasted almonds

1 tablespoon finely chopped
   mushrooms
2 tablespoons fine bread
   crumbs
1 egg yolk, slightly beaten
½ teaspoon chervil
½ teaspoon minced parsley
½ teaspoon minced celery
½ teaspoon chopped chives
2 egg whites, beaten stiff
dash nutmeg

Heat oven to 400° F. Sauté onion in butter until soft but not
brown. Stir in flour until smooth. Stir in cream and broth. Cook
over low heat, stirring constantly, until sauce is smooth and thickened.
Season with salt and pepper. Add chicken, almonds, mushrooms,
bread crumbs, egg yolk, chervil, parsley, celery, and chives. Fold
in egg whites and nutmeg. Pour into a well-greased casserole.
Bake 30 to 35 minutes or until a knife inserted in the center comes
out clean.

Chicken à la King Rogano

This is Roman style and a family specialty.

1 tablespoon butter
½ cup thinly sliced mushrooms
1 small green pepper, thinly
   sliced
¼ cup drained, sliced, canned
   pimiento
1 cup diced cooked chicken
2 tablespoons margarine
2 tablespoons flour

1 cup light cream
½ cup chicken broth
¾ teaspoon salt
¼ teaspoon white pepper
2 egg yolks
pinch of nutmeg
2 baked patty shells
2 sprigs of parsley

Heat butter in a heavy skillet; add mushrooms and green pepper and sauté until tender, about 6 minutes. Add pimiento and chicken; heat 3 minutes. Remove from heat. Combine margarine and flour in a medium saucepan and stir to a smooth paste. Slowly add cream and chicken broth and cook over low heat, stirring constantly, until mixture is smooth and thickened. Season with salt and pepper. Beat in egg yolks one at a time. Stir in nutmeg. Add chicken mixture. Reheat thoroughly. Serve in patty shells; garnish with parsley.

Chicken Omelet Marvella

Intimate and grand—for two, of course.

6 tablespoons milk
½ cup diced cooked chicken
½ can (10½ ounces)
   condensed cream of chicken
   soup
½ teaspoon Worcestershire
   sauce

dash Tabasco
¼ cup chopped black olives
4 eggs, beaten
¼ teaspoon salt
¼ teaspoon white pepper
1 tablespoon butter
1 tablespoon chopped parsley

Heat 3 tablespoons of the milk with the chicken, cream of chicken soup, Worcestershire sauce, Tabasco, and olives. Combine eggs with remaining milk, salt, and pepper. Heat butter in a medium, heavy skillet and pour in egg mixture. Cook, lifting edges with a spatula to allow uncooked egg to run under. When omelet is done, cover half with some of the hot chicken mixture; fold over and slide onto a heated platter. Top with remaining chicken mixture. Sprinkle with parsley and serve immediately.

Chicken Croquettes Maupassant

Every tourist to France should remember this.

½ cup chicken broth
1½ teaspoons butter
1 teaspoon flour
1 cup finely chopped cooked
   chicken
2 tablespoons chopped
   pistachio nuts
½ teaspoon lemon juice
½ teaspoon minced onion

1 teaspoon minced parsley
½ teaspoon minced celery
½ teaspoon chili powder
2 eggs
fine bread crumbs
shortening for frying
Mushroom Sauce (page 137),
   ½ recipe

Heat chicken broth in a saucepan. Combine butter and flour to make a paste. Add to hot broth; stir constantly until mixture is smooth and thickened. Cook 4 minutes over low heat. Stir in chicken, nuts, lemon juice, onion, parsley, celery, and chili powder. Remove from heat. Beat in 1 egg until well blended. Spread mixture on a cold platter and chill 1 hour. Beat the remaining egg in a small bowl. Mold chilled chicken mixture into four croquettes. Dip each in bread crumbs, then in beaten egg, and again in bread crumbs. Chill 3 hours. When ready to serve, fry croquettes in deep fat at 390° F. until golden brown all over. Drain on absorbent paper. Serve with Mushroom Sauce.

Kobe Chicken and Rice

1 clove garlic, cut in half
1 tablespoon butter, melted
1 tablespoon flour
½ cup chicken broth
¾ teaspoon soy sauce
½ teaspoon salt
⅛ teaspoon pepper
1 cup cooked rice
1 cup cubed cooked chicken
1 tablespoon chopped toasted
  almonds

Rub a heatproof casserole all over inside with cut garlic; discard garlic. Pour in the butter and blend in flour and chicken broth. Heat over low heat, stirring, until mixture is smooth and thick. Add soy sauce, salt, and pepper. Combine rice and chicken and add to casserole. Sprinkle almonds on top. Cover tightly; cook over very low heat 6 to 8 minutes or until just heated thoroughly.

Elegant Luncheon Salad

In Yugoslavia they prepare this salad in a special clay salad bowl.

¾ cup diced cooked chicken
½ cup small cauliflower
  flowerets
1 small tomato, peeled,
  coarsely chopped
½ cup cooked string beans,
  frenched
1 hard-cooked egg
2 tablespoons French dressing
½ teaspoon minced parsley
½ teaspoon chopped chives
1 tablespoon chopped walnuts
water cress or Bibb lettuce
  leaves

Combine chicken, cauliflower, tomato, and string beans in a salad bowl. Cut egg in two; remove yolk. Chop egg white and add to chicken mixture. Mash yolk and blend into French dressing. Toss salad lightly with dressing. Sprinkle top with parsley, chives, and walnuts. Serve on water cress or Bibb lettuce leaves.

TURKEY

Autumn Turkey Casserole

½ cup turkey gravy
2 tablespoons turkey broth
½ teaspoon tomato sauce
½ teaspoon salt
⅛ teaspoon pepper
⅛ teaspoon paprika

1 cup diced cooked turkey
½ cup cooked green peas
¼ cup sliced mushrooms,
  sautéed
1 tablespoon buttered bread
  crumbs

Heat oven to 400° F. Thin gravy with turkey broth. Add tomato sauce, salt, pepper, and paprika. Place half the turkey in a greased 1-quart baking dish. Add the peas and mushrooms to form a layer; layer remaining turkey on top. Pour the sauce over all. Sprinkle with bread crumbs. Bake 20 minutes.

Eliza's Turkey Casserole

The original recipe, which I ate with relish at an English inn, called for partridge.

1 small bunch fresh broccoli,
  cut into flowerets
1 tablespoon butter
1 tablespoon flour
½ cup milk
½ cup light cream
½ teaspoon salt
¼ teaspoon pepper

½ cup grated Parmesan cheese
1 cup cooked medium-width
  noodles
1 cup diced cooked turkey
2 tablespoons slivered toasted
  almonds
½ teaspoon paprika

Cook broccoli in salted boiling water until tender. Heat oven to 350° F. Melt butter in a medium skillet and stir in flour; cook 1 minute. Gradually add milk and cream and cook, stirring constantly, until mixture is smooth and thickened. Season with salt and pepper. Add cheese; simmer over very low heat until cheese is melted, stirring frequently. Spread noodles in the bottom of a 1½-quart baking dish. Arrange turkey over noodles; gently lay broccoli on top. Pour cream sauce over all. Sprinkle with almonds and paprika. Bake 15 minutes or until bubbly.

FISH AND SHELLFISH

Louisiana Fish Creole

2 tablespoons butter
1 tablespoon chopped onion
½ cup chopped celery
1 tablespoon chopped green
  pepper
2 tablespoons flour
1¼ cups canned tomatoes

2 tablespoons water
1 small bay leaf
½ teaspoon chopped parsley
⅛ teaspoon thyme
1 cup hot fluffy rice
1 cup cooked fish, broken in
  small pieces

Melt butter in a medium, heavy skillet; add onion, celery, and
green pepper and sauté 5 minutes or until almost tender, stirring
frequently. Blend in flour. Cook over low heat until slightly brown.
Stir in tomatoes and water. Cook, stirring constantly, until thickened.
Add remaining ingredients; blend well. Cover and simmer over
low heat 10 to 12 minutes.

Leningrad Fish

A Russian inspiration which is universally popular.

2 tablespoons minced onion
1 tablespoon butter
½ teaspoon paprika
½ cup commercial sour cream
1 egg yolk, lightly beaten
½ teaspoon salt

1 cup cooked fish, broken in
  large chunks
⅛ teaspoon pepper
1½ teaspoons lemon juice
1 cup hot fluffy rice
1 tablespoon chopped parsley

Sauté onion in butter until lightly browned. Stir in paprika. Add sour cream and heat almost to boiling, stirring constantly. Stir a little of the mixture into the egg yolk; add to remaining cream mixture. Cook over low heat, stirring gently, until slightly thickened. Add salt, fish, and pepper. Heat lemon juice and stir it into the sauce. Serve immediately over hot fluffy rice, with parsley sprinkled on top.

Codfish Jubilee

Lots of protein in this delicious dish.

¼ cup butter	1 cup milk
2 tablespoons flour	½ cup shredded Cheddar
¼ teaspoon salt	cheese
⅛ teaspoon pepper	1 cup flaked, cooked codfish
⅛ teaspoon paprika	2 tablespoons soft bread
dash Tabasco	crumbs
¼ teaspoon Worcestershire	
sauce	

Heat oven to 400° F. Melt half the butter in a medium skillet; stir in flour and seasonings, over low heat. Gradually add milk and cook, stirring, until sauce is smooth and thickened. Stir in half the cheese. Place fish in a shallow 1-quart baking dish. Pour sauce over it. Mix remaining cheese with crumbs and sprinkle over mixture. Dot with remaining butter. Bake 20 minutes. Makes 2 servings.

Springtime Salmon Ring

1 cup mashed cooked carrots	2 eggs, well beaten
1 tablespoon butter, melted	½ cup milk
¼ teaspoon salt	¾ cup leftover creamed
dash pepper	salmon
1 teaspoon minced onion	1 teaspoon chopped parsley

Heat oven to 350° F. Combine carrots, butter, salt, pepper, onion, eggs, and milk; mix well. Turn into a well-greased 2-cup ring mold. Set in a pan of hot water; bake 40 minutes or until top is firm to the touch. Let stand 3 minutes. Unmold on heated serving platter. Fill center with hot creamed salmon. Garnish with parsley.

Lobster Finesso Salad

½ cup diced cooked lobster
¼ cup diced heart of celery
¼ cup finely shredded crisp
    lettuce
1½ tablespoons mayonnaise
1½ teaspoons chili sauce
½ teaspoon ketchup
¼ teaspoon Worcestershire
    sauce

dash Tabasco
2 tablespoons peeled, finely
    chopped tomato
¼ teaspoon chopped chives
¼ teaspoon minced parsley
¼ teaspoon salt
crisp lettuce cups

Combine lobster, celery, and lettuce. Chill 30 minutes. Mix mayonnaise, chili sauce, ketchup, Worcestershire sauce, Tabasco, tomato, chives, parsley, and salt. Gently blend with lobster mixture. Heap on lettuce cups.

Chinese Soochow Lobster

A supper entrée that's perfect for a special occasion.

1 tablespoon vegetable oil
6 tablespoons finely chopped
    onion
2 tablespoons minced celery
¼ cup minced cucumber
2 tablespoons finely chopped
    mushrooms
¼ cup bean sprouts, cut up
2 water chestnuts, chopped
½ cup chicken broth

1 tablespoon butter
¾ cup finely chopped cooked
    lobster
2 tablespoons sherry
1 teaspoon flour
½ teaspoon salt
⅛ teaspoon pepper
¾ teaspoon soy sauce
1 cup hot fluffy rice

Heat oil to sizzling point; add onion, celery, cucumber, mushrooms, bean sprouts, and water chestnuts and sauté for 2 minutes, stirring constantly. Add chicken broth; reduce heat. Cover and simmer 4 minutes. Heat half the butter in a small skillet; add lobster meat and sauté 1 minute. Add sherry; simmer 2 minutes.

Combine the two mixtures; cook 3 minutes. Make a paste with the remaining butter and the flour; stir into mixture and cook, stirring, until smooth and thickened. Season with salt and pepper. Stir in soy sauce. Serve with rice.

Mariner's Coleslaw

1 cup finely shredded
  cabbage
3 tablespoons chopped,
  unpared apple
¼ cup chopped celery

½ cup flaked cooked crab meat
¼ teaspoon salt
1 tablespoon chili sauce
¼ cup mayonnaise
pinch oregano

Soak cabbage in ice water 30 minutes or until crisp. Drain well and dry on a towel. Blend cabbage with apple, celery, crabmeat, and salt. Combine chili sauce with mayonnaise and oregano. Gently stir into crab meat mixture.

Seaside Cakes

1 cup flaked cooked crab meat
½ cup soft bread crumbs
1 egg
½ teaspoon dry mustard
pinch thyme
½ teaspoon salt

⅛ teaspoon pepper
⅛ teaspoon paprika
dash Worcestershire sauce
3 tablespoons flour
shortening for frying
½ cup hot tomato sauce

Combine crab meat, bread crumbs, egg, mustard, thyme, salt, pepper, paprika, and Worcestershire sauce; blend well. Shape into four small cakes. Roll each in flour; chill 3 hours. When ready to serve, fry to golden brown on both sides in hot fat. Drain on absorbent paper. Serve with tomato sauce.

Shrimp Salad Alexandra

½ cup mayonnaise
¾ teaspoon prepared mustard
dash Worcestershire sauce
2 teaspoons minced sweet
  gherkins
1 teaspoon chopped capers
1 teaspoon minced parsley
1 teaspoon minced celery

½ teaspoon chervil
½ teaspoon tarragon
¼ teaspoon anchovy paste
½ teaspoon salt
⅛ teaspoon pepper
⅛ teaspoon paprika
1 cup cooked shrimp, halved
crisp lettuce leaves

Combine all ingredients except shrimp and lettuce leaves, beating vigorously to blend well. Add shrimp; mix well. Chill 2 hours. Serve on lettuce leaves.

Oyster Faloush

The inns in Lyons, France, often serve this dish.

½ cup heavy cream
1 tablespoon butter
1 tablespoon flour
¼ teaspoon salt

dash pepper
1 egg, slightly beaten
½ cup cooked oysters
1 teaspoon chopped parsley

Heat cream. Melt butter in a small skillet; stir in flour and cream. Cook, stirring constantly, until thickened. Season with salt and pepper. Stir in egg. Add oysters; simmer 1 minute. Serve immediately on buttered toast, patty shells, leftover hot cooked rice, or buttered noodles, or mix with cooked macaroni. Garnish with chopped parsley.

VEGETABLES

Farmer's Potato Soup

2 tablespoons coarsely
  chopped onion
1 cup mashed potatoes
1½ cups milk
1½ teaspoons butter

½ teaspoon salt
dash white pepper
1 teaspoon chopped chives
¼ teaspoon paprika

Cover onion with water in a medium saucepan; cover and simmer gently until onion is soft and water has evaporated. Stir in mashed potatoes; cook 2 minutes. Heat milk with butter almost to scalding point. Put potato mixture through a food mill or sieve; stir into hot milk. Season with salt and pepper. Heat thoroughly but do not allow to boil. Serve in soup bowls garnished with chives and paprika.

Beer Garden Potato Salad

A good, easy, and thrifty way to use leftover potatoes.

½ teaspoon sugar
¼ teaspoon salt
⅛ teaspoon dry mustard
1 tablespoon mild vinegar
½ cup commercial sour cream

¼ cup thinly sliced
  cucumber
1 tablespoon minced celery
1 cup sliced boiled potatoes
½ teaspoon paprika

Combine sugar with salt, mustard, and vinegar. Stir into sour cream and blend well. Add cucumber and celery to potatoes. Gently stir in sour cream dressing until potatoes are well coated. Sprinkle with paprika and serve at once.

Touch-Of-Spring Salad

A real pick-me-upper for wilted appetites.

¾ cup cooked lima beans,
 drained
½ teaspoon minced onion
3 tablespoons French dressing
¼ cup mayonnaise
2 hard-cooked eggs, sliced

½ cup sliced celery
½ teaspoon salt
⅛ teaspoon pepper
crisp lettuce greens
1 teaspoon chopped parsley
paprika

Moisten beans and onion with French dressing. Let stand 20 minutes, then drain. Add mayonnaise, eggs, celery, salt, and pepper. Mix lightly. Chill. Serve on lettuce greens, sprinkled with parsley and paprika.

Southern Sweet Potato Soufflé

Treat someone special to this special dish. It is easy to prepare even for only two servings.

1 cup cooked sweet potatoes
¼ cup hot milk
2 tablespoons brandy,
 heated
2 tablespoons butter, melted

dash cayenne
⅛ teaspoon nutmeg
½ teaspoon salt
½ teaspoon grated lemon rind
2 eggs, separated

Heat oven to 400° F. Beat potatoes vigorously with milk, brandy, and butter until smooth. Add seasonings. Beat egg yolks thoroughly and blend into potato mixture. Beat egg whites until stiff but not dry. Fold into potato mixture. Turn ino a well-greased 1-quart baking dish. Bake 20 minutes or until well puffed and delicately browned.

COOKING
INFORMATION

EVERYDAY LEFTOVER
COOKING HINTS

- To freshen French or Italian bread or hard rolls, sprinkle the crust with a few drops of ice water and place bread or rolls in a preheated 350° F. oven for 10 minutes.
- Save leftover sandwiches for snacks and lunches. Brush with mixture of melted butter and lemon juice. Sauté until lightly browned.
- To make cutouts for fancy sandwiches from bread slices, first freeze bread then use cookie cutters for fancy shaping.
- Save the rinds of lemons, oranges, and grapefruits. Grate them and place in tightly covered jars. Store in refrigerator until needed. Use as flavorings in frostings, sauces, and cakes.
- To use leftover ketchup, combine 3 tablespoons oil, 1 tablespoon vinegar, ⅛ teaspoon each marjoram and paprika with ¼ cup or less ketchup; shake bottle well. Makes a delicious salad dressing.
- Use leftover mashed potatoes as a frosting for cupcakes. Beat in confectioners' sugar and vanilla extract until well blended and of spreading consistency.
- Chop leftover dates and mix with apples when baking an apple pie.
- Bake leftover meat loaf or meatball mixture in greased muffin pans for attractive individual servings.
- Ground leftover salami added to ground beef will give an unusual flavor to hamburgers and meat loaf.

- Use chopped toasted almonds as a garnish for fish, or mix with string beans or peas for pleasant crunchiness.
- Use leftover sweet pickle juice instead of vinegar when making dressing for coleslaw.
- Adding a little leftover coffee to a gravy will give it a rich brown color without coffee flavor.
- Stir a little leftover oatmeal into a stew for added flavor and thickening.
- If you have a leftover frankfurter, slice it and brown in butter. Add slices to hot cream of pea soup.
- Store liquid from canned vegetables, mushrooms, etc., in freezer and use in soup stock and gravies.
- For a delicious flavor, add leftover chopped walnuts or pecans to wild rice during last ten minutes of cooking.
- To make croutons, cut stale bread in ½-inch squares and fry in butter until golden brown. Shake skillet or toss with fork. Serve in salads or atop cream soups.
- To make toast cups, cut crusts from thinly sliced stale bread and brush generously with melted butter. Press into large muffin cups. Toast in 350° F. oven 10 to 15 minutes. Fill with creamed vegetable or meat mixture.
- Cut leftover angel food cake into 2-inch square pieces. Gently mold into balls. Dip into a fluffy white frosting. Roll in moist shredded coconut and make Coconut Balls. Tint coconut, if desired.
- For Mock Angel Food—Dip stale bread slices in sweetened condensed milk, then in flaked coconut. Place on baking sheet and toast in hot oven until bread is heated through and coconut is browned.
- Cut thin slices of stale bread into fingers, rounds, or any small shape you wish. Quickly brown on one side only. These may be made ahead of time. Spread canapés topping on untoasted side just before serving.
- For any easy canapé spread mash cooked leftover crab meat, shrimp, salmon, lobster, or tuna. Moisten with mayonnaise, add a few drops lemon juice and some minced parsley.

- *To store Whole Raw Egg Yolks*
  Place yolks in jar with tight-fitting lid. Add water to cover yolks. Refrigerate, covered, until ready to use. Drain before using. Do not keep longer than 3 days.

· *To store Raw Egg Whites*
Refrigerate egg whites in jar with tight-fitting lid until ready to
use. Egg whites may be kept a week to 10 days.

· *To Cook Egg Yolks*
In small saucepan, bring 3 cups water and ½ teaspoon salt to
boiling. Gently slip an egg yolk into boiling water. Reduce heat;
simmer, uncovered, 5 minutes or until yolk is firm.

· *To Use Raw Egg Whites*
Beat one egg white with 2 tablespoons sugar until stiff. Fold
into hot cooked puddings just until combined. Or use for meringues, in frostings, cakes, etc.

· Roast meat can be cut into julienne strips and marinated in
a sharp French dressing. Use in salads or mix with vegetables.
· For an emergency supper dish, use bits and pieces of meat
combined with a cooked pasta product, commercial sour cream,
crushed bay leaf, chopped green pepper, onion, celery, and mushrooms and heated in the oven.
· Chop leftover vegetables, macaroni, spaghetti, and noodles for
mulligatawny soup.
· Make Cornish pies using leftover meat and vegetables.
· Squares of roast meats on a skewer alternated with green pepper
strips, small boiled onions, and mushrooms, and brushed with a
sharp marinade, make an emergency luncheon treat.
· Fluff and use mashed potatoes as a topping on meat loaf.
· Use leftover mashed potatoes in chocolate cake and cookies.
· Lining a casserole with mashed potatoes and filling it with a
stew gives the dish a festive appearance.
· Repeat mashed potatoes in oven with a topping of grated Cheddar
cheese and a sprinkling of chopped almonds.
· When fresh vegetables are cooked until just tender, they hold
their shape for the second time around.
· Marinate cooked vegetables in French dressing and use in salads.
· Fill omelets with cooked vegetables and baste with a hot chili
sauce.
· Add cooked carrots to pancake batter.

TABLE OF SUBSTITUTIONS

1 teaspoon *baking powder* .... 1 teaspoon cream of tartar plus 1 teaspoon baking soda

1 cup canned *beef bouillon* .... 1 beef bouillon cube or 1 envelope instant beef broth or 1 teaspoon beef extract dissolved in 1 cup boiling water

1 cup *beef stock* .... 1 cup canned beef broth

1 cup *buttermilk* .... 1 cup milk plus 1 tablespoon vinegar

1 cup canned *chicken broth* ... 1 chicken bouillon cube or 1 envelope instant chicken broth dissolved in 1 cup boiling water

1 cup *chicken stock* .... 1 cup canned chicken broth

½ cup *chili sauce* .... ½ cup tomato sauce plus 2 tablespoons sugar, 1 tablespoon vinegar, ⅛ teaspoon ground cloves

1 3-ounce can *Chinese noodles* . 2 2¼-ounce cans potato sticks

1 square (1 ounce) *chocolate* .. 3 tablespoons cocoa plus 1 tablespoon shortening

1½ cups *corn syrup* .... 1 cup sugar plus ½ cup water

1 tablespoon *cornstarch* ...... 2 tablespoons flour

1 whole *egg* .... 2 egg yolks plus 1 tablespoon water

1 cup sifted all-purpose *flour* .. 1 cup plus 2 tablespoon sifted cake flour

1½ cups diced cooked *ham* ... 1 12-ounce can pork luncheon meat, diced

⅔ cup *honey* .... 1 cup sugar plus ⅓ cup water

1 teaspoon *Italian seasoning* ... ¼ teaspoon each oregano, basil, thyme, and rosemary with dash of cayenne

½ pound fresh *mushrooms* .... 1 4-ounce can mushroom caps

1 teaspoon *oregano* .... 1 teaspoon marjoram

½ pound ground *pork* .... ½ pound sausage meat

1 teaspoon *pumpkin pie spice* .. ½ teaspoon cinnamon, ¼ teaspoon ginger, ⅛ teaspoon each ground nutmeg and cloves

½ cup seedless *raisins* .... ½ cup cut dried prunes

few drops *Tabasco* .... dash of cayenne or red pepper

½ cup *tartar sauce* .... 6 tablespoons mayonnaise plus 2 tablespoons chopped pickle relish

1 cup *tomato juice* .... ½ cup tomato sauce plus ½ cup water

1 cup canned *tomatoes* .... 1⅓ cups chopped fresh tomatoes simmered for 10 minutes

1 teaspoon *Worcestershire sauce* .... 1 teaspoon bottled steak sauce

TABLE OF EQUIVALENTS

Bread and Crackers

1 slice bread	=½ cup finely crumbled
18 small crackers	=1 cup coarsely crushed
21 small crackers	=1 cup finely crushed
9 graham cracker squares	=1 cup coarsely crumbled
12 graham cracker squares	=1 cup finely crumbled
1 cup potato chips, firmly packed	=½ cup potato chip crumbs
12 thin pretzels	=½ cup pretzel crumbs
26 vanilla wafers	=1 cup finely crumbled
9 zwieback	=1 cup finely crumbled

Cereals and Pasta

3 cups corn flakes	=1 cup crushed
1 cup corn meal	=4 cups cooked
1 cup macaroni	=2 cups cooked
1 cup noodles	=2 cups cooked
1 cup quick-cooking oats	=1¾ cups cooked
1 cup rice	=3 cups cooked
1 cup spaghetti	=2 cups cooked

Dairy Products

1 cup heavy cream	=2 cups whipped
1 pound Cheddar cheese	=4 cups shredded

Fruits

Dried:

1 pound apricots	=3½ cups	=4½ cups cooked
1 pound figs	=2¼ cups	=4½ cups cooked
1 pound peaches	=3⅔ cups	=4½ cups cooked
1 pound pears	=2⅔ cups	=5⅓ cups cooked
1 pound prunes	=2¾ cups	=4 cups cooked
1 pound raisins	=3¼ cups	=4 cups plumped
1 pound unpitted dates	=2½ cups	=1¾ cups pitted

Fresh:

1 pound apples	=3 medium	=3 cups pared, diced
1 pound cranberries	=4¾ cups	=3¼ cups sauce
1 average lemon	=⅛ cup pulp	=3 to 4 tablespoons juice
1 average orange	=¼ cup pulp	=½ cup juice
1 quart red cherries		=2 cups pitted
1 pound Tokay grapes		=2¾ cups seeded

Nuts

1 pound soft shell almonds	=2 cups shelled
1 pound hard shell almonds	=1 cup shelled
1 pound walnuts in shell	=2½ cups shelled
¼ pound walnut meats	=1 cup chopped nut meats

Vegetables
Dried:

1 cup Lima beans	=2⅓ cups cooked
1 cup red beans	=2 cups cooked
1 cup white beans	=3 cups cooked

Fresh:

1 pound beets	=4 medium	=2 cups diced
1 pound cabbage		=4 cups shredded
1 pound carrots	=8 medium	=4 cups diced
1 pound celery	=2 small bunches	=4 cups diced
12 ears corn		=3 cups cut kernels
1 pound peas in pod		=1 cup shelled
1 pound potatoes	=4 medium	=2½ cups diced

HOW TO HOME-FREEZE

In general, it can be said that most cooked foods can be frozen. It is difficult to give exact storage times in terms of maximums that should not be exceeded because so much depends upon the temperature of your freezer, the packaging materials you use, the tightness of the wrap (to exclude air) and the ingredients used in preparing the food.

Remember that the longer a food is to be stored, the more important the packaging material and the way it is wrapped becomes.

Materials for packaging frozen foods should be waterproof, moisture- and vaporproof. The best ones are saran film, polyethylene, pliofilm, heavy duty foil and laminated paper.

When packaging the food, press out as much air as possible and close the package so that it is airtight. Air which gets in through openings will dry out food.

The drugstore-wrap method is best for tight folds and snug packaging. Place the item to be wrapped in the center of the freezer wrap. The long way of the product and the wrap should be the same. Bring the opposite, long sides of the sheet together over the item and make a crease along the entire length. Make another tight fold; bring wrapper down firmly and turn it over. Fold ends toward each other. Make two snug folds on the top of the package and seal with freezer tape.

Be sure to label each item clearly with its content and the date it was frozen. Freeze in meal-sized portions so that if a member of your family is absent a certain night, you can serve proportioned food without waste.

Fill bags and containers nine-tenths full to allow room for expansion.

Many foods may go right into the oven without thawing. Plan to pack these in glass ovenproof casseroles, pie plates or aluminum foil, and simply transfer them from your freezer to the oven for preparation.

Packaging any food in a liquid such as gravy, sauce or syrup increases its keeping quality. Fish will keep longer if it is frozen in a solid piece of ice. An empty milk container filled with water and frozen around the fish will serve the purpose.

Keep a supply of packaging materials on hand for freezing. Many can be used over again if washed and dried carefully.

Most vegetables (except those eaten raw; crispness is desirable), can be frozen. Avoid freezing salad greens, cucumbers, celery, cabbage, tomatoes and radishes.

You should not add salt or other seasoning to pork, sausage or ground meats because it accelerates the development of rancidity in fat meats.

Do not refreeze thawed foods. The danger is that thawed cooked foods, particularly those containing proteins, may already have started to deteriorate.

FOODS	HOW TO FREEZE	HOW TO THAW AND SERVE
Angel, sponge, chiffon cake	Quick-freeze, unwrapped, cake quarters or serving-sized pieces with double fold of wax paper between slices. Freeze on trays, then wrap tightly to store.	Thaw at room temperature 30 minutes to one hour. Remove ice cream layered cake from freezer 15 minutes before serving.
Applesauce	Place in rigid container which is airtight.	Thaw at room temperature 20 minutes to 1 hour depending on quantity.
Bacon	Crumble the pieces, wrap in freezer packaging and store. This makes a wonderful garnish for chowders, cream soups, baked potatoes and salads.	Does not require thawing when added to hot foods.
Baked beans and chile con carne	Pack in straight-sided freezer containers. Be sure meat is covered with sauce.	Heat, unthawed, in top of double boiler or oven until bubbly.
Bread crumbs, buttered or plain	Place in rigid container or plastic bag.	Thaw at room temperature 15 to 50 minutes depending on quantity.

FOODS	HOW TO FREEZE	HOW TO THAW AND SERVE
Broth and soup stock	Pour into ice cube trays; freeze. Remove and package in bags to store.	Use cubes as desired in soups, main dishes, and gravies.
Cakes, frosted or unfrosted	Wrap and seal in foil, slip into plastic moisture-proof bag.	Thaw at room temperature 30 minutes to one hour.
Chicken, fryers	Store in freezer bags. Be sure to freeze dressings separately.	Thaw. Place in shallow pan; bake, uncovered, at 350° F. 30 to 45 minutes.
Chowder and soup	Freeze in rigid containers. For individual servings use muffin tins; when frozen, put in freezer bags to store.	Add required water or milk slowly over direct heat or in top of double boiler.
Cookies, baked, all kinds	Package in bags or rigid containers to store.	Thaw 5 to 10 minutes, then serve.
Cream, sweetened, whipped	Heap small servings on cookie sheet. Freeze, then pack in plastic bags.	Does not require thawing.
Creamed casserole dishes; meat, fish, poultry	Pack in rigid containers. Be sure meat is covered with sauce.	Heat, unthawed, in top of double boiler or in oven until bubbly.
Dessert sauces	Pack in rigid containers and freeze.	Heat in top of double boiler, or thaw and serve cold.
Doughnuts	Package in bags to store, or stack in carton and wrap in foil.	Place unthawed in 400° F. oven for 10 minutes. Use within 1 month.
Gravy and cream sauces	Pour in rigid containers. Cover.	Heat in double boiler. Stir well if gravy tends to separate.
Ham, baked	Wrap tightly with freezer wrap, or put in rigid container if broth, drippings or gravy are used.	Thaw in refrigerator 5 to 6 hours per pound.
Lemon rind	Place in small packets and put in plastic bag.	Thaw at room temperature for 5 minutes.

FOODS	HOW TO FREEZE	HOW TO THAW AND SERVE
Macaroni-and-cheese type casseroles	Spoon into rigid containers or freeze in casserole lined with foil.	Heat in top of double boiler or oven. Stir gently if sauce separates.
Meat or fish loaf	Freeze in container, then remove contents. Wrap securely.	Thaw in refrigerator 1 to 2 hours. Bake in oven. Use fish within 1 week.
Orange rind	Same as lemon rind.	
Potatoes, baked and stuffed	Place in flat freezer containers or freeze on tray then package in plastic bag.	Bake, unthawed, at 400° F. until heated through.
Sandwiches	Wrap individually. Freeze flat.	Thaw at room temperature 1 to 2 hours. Do not store longer than 1½ months.
Spaghetti sauce	Freeze in rigid wide mouthed container.	Thaw enough to remove from container by placing in pan of cold water. Heat from frozen state in top of double boiler 25 minutes.
Stew, Stroganoff, (beef, lamb, veal)	Use rigid container. Leave ½-inch headspace in carton. Or freeze in casserole lined with aluminum foil, then wrap tightly.	In rigid containers, thaw as you would spaghetti sauce. In aluminum foil, peel off foil, fit into casserole and heat in 350° F. oven, until piping hot.
Stuffed green peppers	Package in flat container, or freeze on tray and store in plastic bags.	Arrange unthawed in baking dish; bake at 375° F. 30 minutes.
Waffles	Wrap tightly or package in plastic bags.	Heat unthawed in toaster or place on cookie sheet and heat in oven.

STORAGE TIME FOR
FROZEN COOKED FOODS

Food	Storage Time
A la king dishes	3 months
Baked beans (remove pork first)	6 months
Chili con carne	1 to 1½ months
Chop Suey, Chow Mein, without pork	3 months
Gravies, thickened sauces	3 months
Hash	2 to 2½ months
Leftovers in refrigerator	4 days to 1 week
Macaroni, spaghetti, and rice dishes	2 weeks
Meat pies, except pork	3 to 4 months
Poultry pies	2 months
Newburgs, Thermidors	2 weeks
Potatoes	2 to 3 months
Sauces	1 month
Soups	2 months
Stews, without potatoes	4 to 5 months
with potatoes	1 month
Stuffings	1 month

Store under 0° F. temperature for best results.

Temperatures higher than 0° F. are satisfactory for storing frozen foods for shorter periods only.

INDEX

crab and shrimp Newburg, 214
custard
 Empress Josephine, 233
 Grandma's maple, 237
Devon shepherd's pie, 152
fish Coladone, 131
gingerbread with lemon sauce, 243
gnocchi di Brindisi, 222
Japanese chicken mousse, 98
Newburg supreme, 203
November delight, 241
Patras topping, 138
South Seas pork pie, 175
poulet en crème, 99
sauce
 hollandaise, 162
 lemon, daffodil, 238
soup
 Hong Kong egg drop, 200
 Munich, 147
sponge cake, sunshine, 238
steamboat turkey balls, 114
storing, 278
Tijuana bake, 246
using, 279
veal hash à la Drake, 177
zabaglione, 231
gravy
 beef Astoria, 9
rice
 Germain's duck soup, 117
 southern lady casserole, 98
Leg of lamb continental style, 42
Lemon
 sauce, 126
 daffodil, 238
 gingerbread with, 243
 tapioca fluff, 239
Lemony carrot squares, 243
Leningrad fish, 270
Liver sauce, turkey, 205
Lobster
 Chinese soochow, 272
 finesso salad, 272
 Romandeaux, 215
Lord Essex's roast leg of veal, 76
Louisiana
 chicken loaf, 195
 fish Creole, 270

Lumberman's soup, 262
Luncheon salad, elegant, 267
Lundi lamb casserole, 32
Luzerne potato soup, 201

Macaroni
 Frascati, 143
 savory southern, 146
Mai Kai chicken croquettes, 197
Maine ham bake, 164
Mainland meat pie, 32
Mariner's coleslaw, 273
Marseilles veal croquettes, 256
Massachusetts horseradish sauce, 3
Martha's potato candy, 232
Mashed potatoes royale, 223
Maurice's salad, 169
Meat balls
 Danish, 24
 pizza Siciliano, 146
Meat pies, see Pies, main dishes
Memphis meat casserole, 162
Meringue pie shell, 239
Meringues, dreamy, 240
Mexican
 beef and rice, 137
 chicken pie, 91
 chilis rellenos, 23
Minnesota pea soup, 50
Mock goose Trianon, 63
Monte Cristo sandwiches, 171
Mornay sauce, 222
Mousse
 ham, Bordeaux, 55
 Japanese chicken, 98
 turkey, Parisienne, 203
Mr. Chen's beef suey, 140
Munich soup, 147
Mushroom
 fresh, sauce, 195
 sauce, 137
Mushrooms
 au jambon, 158
 veal patties with, 89

Napoleon's brandy sauce, 97
Navajo corn bake, 169
Near Eastern lamb dolmas, 251
Nesselrode pie, crown, 234
New England beef, 3

salad
  pink luncheon, 219
  touch-of-spring, 276
sweet potato
  casserole delight, 221
  soufflé, southern, 276
  winter garden loaf, 217
  see also names of vegetables
Vevey chef's salad, 159
Vinaigrette, beef salad, 135
Virgin Islands fish salad, 215
Vitello tonnato, 74

Waffles, pimiento, 58

Walnut sauce, chicken thighs with, 102
Wedgewood English trifle, 244
Western-style beef, 22
Wiener Schnitzel, 74
Wild rice Limores, 120
Wine, veal in, 256
Winter garden loaf, 217
Winterland bean soup, 165
Wontons, 172

Zabaglione, 231

BEEF

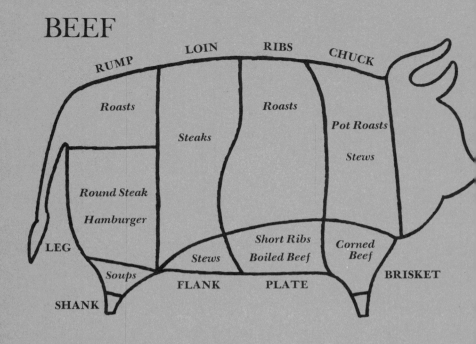

RUMP — LOIN — RIBS — CHUCK

Roasts

Steaks

Roasts

Pot Roasts

Stews

Round Steak

Hamburger

Short Ribs

Boiled Beef

Corned Beef

LEG

Stews

Soups

FLANK — PLATE — BRISKET

SHANK

VEAL

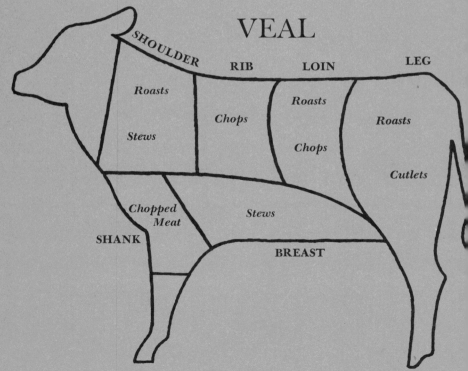

SHOULDER — RIB — LOIN — LEG

Roasts

Chops

Roasts

Roasts

Stews

Chops

Cutlets

Chopped Meat

Stews

SHANK

BREAST